D1301462

SUPER PROFITS IN CHEAP STOCKS

*The Secret World of Stocks Selling
from a Penny to $10 a Share*

FRED CARACH

Table of Contents

Who Am I?

In the stock market there is a demarcation line that is as broad and deep as the Grand Canyon. It is the dividing line between stocks selling above $10.00 a share and stocks selling below $10.00 a share. Stocks selling below $10.00 a share are generally ignored. Indeed, when they are not ignored they are treated with downright contempt. After all, why would anyone in his right mind want to buy a stock that is not a blue chip? Investors have always paid a very high price for the alleged safety and security of blue chip stocks. A safety and security that has time and again proven to be delusional. As armies of devastated ex-stock market investors can attest. By far the most ignored and detested sector in the non-blue chip universe are stocks selling for less than $10.00 a share. Indeed, most mutual funds and the vast majority of investors flatly refuse to invest in single-digit stocks on principal because they regard them as being too risky. In recent years the famous old blue chip 30 stocks of the Dow Jones Industrials have been replaced by the far more broadly based S&P 500. Any stock today that is not in the S&P 500 is by definition not a blue chip stock and is thus regarded as not being a suitable investment for most investors.

The world of sub-$10.00 stocks can be divided into three sectors. At the bottom are the notorious penny stocks which sell from a penny a share to a $1.00 a share. The next sector are stocks selling from a $1.00 a share to $5.00 a share and the last sector are stocks that sell from $5.00 a share to $10.00 a share. Within this largely ignored world the broadest and deepest demarcation line by far is the dividing line between stocks that are selling above $5.00 a share and stocks that are selling below $5.00 a share. According to SEC Regulation T any stock selling below $5.00 a share is by definition a penny stock and therefore must abide by more restrictive regulations. The specific rule is SEC Rule 3a5-1. Perhaps the most restrictive of these regulations is the margin restriction. Shares selling below $5.00 a share cannot be bought on margin. These restrictions have resulted in a perpetual cloud of suspicion and distrust hovering above these stocks. For all practical purposes, institutional investors and high net worth investors either cannot or refuse to even consider investing in these stocks on principal.

This results in a phenomenon that is seldom commented on. When these so-called small-caps (small-capitalization stocks), as they are called, for they are almost always small-caps, break above the magic $5.00 mark, they have a tendency to act as if they have been shot out of a cannon. Because a vast ocean of investors who hitherto would have never considered investing in these "dogs" will now for the first time regard them as possibly being investment worthy. Additional momentum is achieved when these stocks break above $10.00 a share. This book will introduce you to this largely ignored universe of stocks that sell from a penny a share to $10.00 a share with some profitable side excursions with stocks that are selling above the $10.00 mark that would not ordinarily be found in a work of this nature.

Think of the stock market as a vast inverted pyramid. At the bottom of this pyramid are the despised penny stocks. Perhaps only one or two percent of the entire universe of potential stock investors will ever seriously consider buying these stocks. As we move up the inverted pyramid and rise above the $1 demarcation line, the universe of potential investors probably doubles to, say, about 5% of the investing public. The next demarcation line is the big one. At $5.00 a share the historic dividing line between non-investment-grade quality stocks and possibly investment grade stocks by government edict has been breached. Perhaps 30-50% of the investing public will consider buying stocks that are selling between $5.00 and $10.00 a share; the rest will not. They will consider all single digit stocks to be too risky to invest in. At $10.00 and above the taint of the low priced stock largely vanishes and most of the investing public will consider investing in these stocks. The interesting thing about this, even if it is almost never realized by the general public, is that the controlling interests of stocks selling for less than $10.00 a share have a powerful tool at their disposal which can convert a penny stock to a $10.00 stock at will. This powerful tool is called the reverse stock split.

Let's say that a penny mining stock is selling for 75 cents a share and that the issued stock has 100 million shares outstanding. The board of directors is desperate to get the stock moving. The easiest method that exists is to simply do a 10:1 reverse stock split which will reduce the outstanding float from 100 million shares to 10 million shares and theoretically increase the price of the shares from 75 cents a share to $7.50 a share. There is an army of investors out there who will claim that the whole thing is an exercise in futility because the value of your share holdings will not change. I beg to differ. The stock price has now broken above an important demarcation line and there is now a new universe of investors who would have never bought this stock at 75 cents a share who are now potential buyers of the stock at $7.50 a share.

I recently tried to make this case at the annual meeting of the shareholders of Comstock Mines that was meeting in Virginia City, Nevada, with limited success. Comstock Mines was then selling at 17 cents a share. I will have more to say about this stock later.

But before we get started, I should introduce myself. It is a common experience for me to read a book and wish that the author had included a short biography about himself. So, let's get started. I was born and raised in Cortland, New York, a small town in upstate New York with a population of about 20,000. In my growing up years my father owned and operated the Victory Restaurant which was located on Cortland's Main Street. I knew all that I needed to know about myself and my future prospects by the time I graduated from high school. This knowledge was priceless. It prevented me from banging my head against the wall and betting everything on career success. I knew that there was an alternative that did not require others to promote me to the executive ranks. Something I regarded as being highly unlikely.

It was called the stock market. From as far back as I could remember the stock market had always fascinated me. Perhaps the original impetus for this was a local stockbroker who frequented our restaurant. He would bring in his clients while ostentatiously waving around his rolled up copy of the Wall Street Journal as if it was a status symbol. Which it was. Everyone in the restaurant would just sit there and gawk at him as he energetically waved around his status symbol. In those days every newspaper in the country sold for about five cents a copy except the Wall Street Journal which sold for 10 times that amount or more. Which was considered an outrageous price in those days. It was then said that only rich playboys and financiers bought the Wall Street Journal.

I was convinced that this could be my salvation. I knew beyond a shadow of any doubt that I was never destined to be a great career success in any organization. No one was ever going to promote me to a high-powered executive position. I knew this because there was never any danger of my being elected class president. I was always the introvert in the corner of the room that no one ever paid any attention to. If there was an election for class loser, I probably would have been a contender. Of course, it would not have been a slam dunk. There were about five other kids in our high school graduating class of 179 students that I would have been in serious competition with.

It is also safe to say that I wasn't setting the world on fire academically either.

While I was always a voracious reader and loved reading about history, economics and finance, math was always my Waterloo. I managed to flunk elementary algebra two years in a row. Largely due to my pitiful math skills I spent the first half of my senior year in a junior classroom before I managed to earn enough credits to graduate with my class. In those days after you graduated from high school there were just two options. You either went to college or you went into the service. I knew that with my report card there was no way I was going to get into college. In those days for some reason it was much harder to get into college than it is today if you had low marks. I joined the Marines as soon as I graduated at age 17. After my enlistment in the Marines I attempted to enter the local college, Cortland State College. They turned me down flat because of my less than stellar grades. Seeing absolutely no hope I enlisted again, this time in the Navy, hoping to earn a marketable skill. I learned too late that there is almost no civilian demand for radar operator. I should have attempted to become an air traffic controller, but I learned that too late. After my four years in the Navy I finally managed to get accepted at Bronx Community College. For some reason my low high school grades were no longer a problem. Later I moved to Florida and by my early 30s I had managed to get a master's degree in real estate at Florida International University. I became a state certified general real estate appraiser. This meant that I was licensed by the state of Florida to appraise everything from a chicken coop to a skyscraper.

During this entire period, I was invested up to my eyeballs in the stock market. I made my first investments at the age of 19 in 1961 and have not been out of the stock market for a single day since I was 19 years old. For all practical purposes I have been a life subscriber to three fine financial publications: Forbes, Barron's and the Northern Miner. I have always been a voracious reader of the financial press. Except for the roof over my head and a few real estate ventures on the side, every dime that I ever made was poured into the stock market.

For about six years I worked for two of the local banks in Miami as a real estate staff appraiser. In those years I thought I might have been wrong in my conviction that I would never be promoted to a high level executive position. But it didn't last. In the early 80s almost every bank in the country suddenly decided to fire their staff appraisers. They decided that it would be cheaper to hire outside fee appraisers rather than keep them on the staff. I will never forget their final words to me as I left the door. Don't worry, Fred, you are on our list of approved appraisers. We will be sure to call you when we have an assignment for you. Somehow, I wasn't reassured. I doubt that any of the bank staff appraisers who were thrown out into the streets like dogs in those years were reassured.

I spent the rest of my working career as an independent fee appraiser. Somehow, to my considerable amazement, I actually managed to earn a fairly decent living, but I never had the personality and the connections that would have enabled me to make the big bucks. This didn't surprise me. Like I said, I had it all figured out by the time I graduated from high school.

I always tell my friends that I have done only two things right in my life. The first was to join the reserves after I was discharged from the Navy and put in my 20 years and get that military pension. The second and far more important thing was my lifelong obsession with the stock market. It has made all the difference.

The message that I have for my readers is that you don't need to be a high-paid professional or a successful executive to succeed in life. You can achieve investment success just like I did on your own and what is truly important is that you don't need the approval of another human being to succeed. There is nothing more dangerous than depending on other human beings for your success. You don't have to spend your life wringing your hands and hoping that your superiors will recognize your merits and hire you or promote you to that executive position.

If you start before you are middle aged and if you have the discipline to save around 10% a year you have a real shot at financial independence by age 55 or 60. Most people can't save because they keeping hoping that by some miracle there will be something left at the end of the month to save. There never is. The secret of successful saving is to pay yourself first. That means that you set up a segregated savings account and you deposit 10% of your check into this account as soon as you are paid. Your challenge is to then learn how to live on the remaining 90%. If you establish this discipline you will find that after a few months you won't have any trouble living on 90% of your income. By financial independence I mean being able to afford pretty much anything you want in life except for a mansion, a yacht and a luxury car priced above $100,000 and you will be able to pay cash for that $100,000-plus luxury car if you are willing to put a hole in your life savings. It means being able to vacation in Europe every year like I do and being able to afford a reasonably priced second vacation home, in my case in the high desert above Reno.

By this time the alert reader will have noticed something that is very curious about me. Here is a guy who has a master's degree in real estate and was a licensed state certified general real estate appraiser and then spent most of his working career in real estate. Yet, he more or less ignores real estate as an investment. What is going on here?

I blame it all on my Uncle Paul. My Uncle Paul was a master carpenter and a big wheel in the carpenters union in the days when that really meant something in nearby Ithaca, New York, and he was very conservative. He spent years saving up before he bought his first home for cash. He bought an unimproved site and then built his dream home, most of it by himself with the assistance of his buddies in the construction industry. He built it like a bomb shelter. The family joke was that it would survive a nuclear attack. After that he branched out and purchased other properties, always with a huge down payment. I don't think he ever bought a property with less than a 50% down payment.

It is indeed strange that conversations that we hear when we are young and that appear at the time to be of no lasting consequence can cast a giant shadow over our lives and have a lifelong importance years after we heard them. I will never forget my Uncle Paul's constant refrain that "you can't lose money in real estate." Of course, the way Uncle Paul invested in real estate it is hard to see how he could lose money. Every time I heard him say you can't lose money in real estate, for some strange reason it really bothered me. Even then I was suspicious of sure things. The problem with real estate is that it is beloved by all and it is way, way too obvious as an investment. Everyone and his brother adores real estate and thinks that it is just wonderful and most of them, until the recent 2007-2012 real estate crash, would have agreed with my Uncle Paul's often-asserted refrain that you can't lose money in real estate. Even I adore real estate when I can steal it.

That adoration comes at a high price. As a category real estate always sells for top dollar. Or as an economist will tell you, real estate sells at the highest price that will clear the market. In other words, since real estate as a category is always selling for top dollar, there are only two ways that it can continue to go up. The income of the American people has to go up or the population has to increase. For almost the entire history of this country both the population and the income of the American people were increasing.

This is no longer occurring. For the first time in our country's history we are below zero population growth which is 2.1 children per average family. We are currently well below this number at 1.82 and the income growth of the median household has slowed to a crawl. In 2000 the median household income was $40,804. By 2018 it was $62,000, an annual increase of around $1,200. This is an annual percentage increase of just under 3% a year since the year 2000. This is nothing to write home about. The median household income is critical as it determines how much you can pay for a home. The old tried and true metric is that you can comfortably — the key word here being "comfortably" — afford to pay three times your annual income for a home or around $185,000 based on today's median income. It is kind of hard to see how housing prices are going to keep skyrocketing on a national basis unless these conditions change.

A critical variable that is rarely given the attention that it deserves is that where you live has a crucial impact on real estate values. Most of the counties in this country today have a population that is either stagnant or declining. In the counties where the population is still increasing, real estate is a far more attractive proposition for the obvious reason that the number of buyers keeps increasing. Real estate investing in counties with declining populations needs to be carefully considered.

I travel a lot. What continues to amaze me is the truly vast number of homes in this country that continue to be listed at well above $370,000. Or more than twice the affordable home level and a potential new real estate bubble in the making. There will always be a market for more expensive homes. The problem is not so much the price, but the sheer numbers of homes priced above $370,000. Just where is this untapped ocean of qualified mortgage borrowers going to come from? After all, you do have to qualify for the mortgage. I think that there are vast numbers of these real estate owners who are going to be in for a rude shock in the near future when they attempt to sell their $370,000-plus homes.

Of course, there will always be steal deals in real estate. When you find a steal deal in real estate you should do what I do. Jump on it. But steal deals will always be an exception and not the rule and a declining exception at that. In the old days before the internet it was very hard for outsiders to get accurate data on rentals and real estate prices. Unless, that is, you had access to the MLS (multiple listing service) books. Brokers in those days would guard these books with their lives. The only way you could get this data if you were an outsider was to pry it from the cold, dead hands of a real estate broker. Today this data that, in the old days, brokers would kill you to prevent you from having access to, is widely available for free. For an old timer like me the change is truly shocking.

I have grave doubts as to how much longer real estate brokers will be able to command the standard 6% commission now that they have lost their monopoly on real estate data which was always their power base.

This pre-internet ignorance of market rentals and market prices resulted in a happy hunting ground of steal deals. The arrival of the internet has greatly reduced the number of steal deals that are occurring through ignorance. The last remaining major source of steal deals is distress selling and this source will of course continue to exist.

In my career as an appraiser it was not unusual for the banks to call on me for a market estimate on a property that they were foreclosing on. The gimmick we used was that we might extend the mortgage on more favorable terms, depending on the results of the appraisal. This was years before the great real estate crash of 2007-2012. If it wasn't so tragic, the look of disbelief on the property owners faces when I was inspecting their property would have been comical. This is America, the faces said. How can I possibly lose money on real estate? Isn't there a law against losing money in real estate? There must be something wrong with me. I must be a loser.

Consider this. It is not uncommon to hear stock market players brag about taking a loss in the stock market. Come to think of it, even I have been known to brag about some of my stock market losses and I will introduce you to a few of my interesting stock market losses in this work. You will never, ever hear a real estate investor brag about taking a loss in real estate. Losing money in real estate is regarded as being shameful. There must be something wrong with you. After all, everybody knows you can't lose money in real estate. I just kept thinking of Uncle Paul.

I have always been a strong proponent of owning the roof over your head. What almost everyone discovers is that as a general principle, the most profitable real estate most of us will ever own is the roof over our heads. It is the most tax-favored investment that there is. It is a forced savings vehicle, and this is of critical importance. The average American couldn't save a dime if his life depended on it. Which is why the only investment that most retirees have of any consequence is their home. The only reason that they own it free and clear is that they were forced to save it. Then there is the incredible financial leverage. Often a down payment of only 3.5% is achievable on your primary residence at a fixed rate of interest for 30 years. Wall Street speculators would kill for this type of leverage. Any time you pay less than 100% down you have leveraged investment, and the smaller the down payment the greater the leverage. Contrary to popular opinion, real estate investment properties are rarely as profitable as your primary residence is. This does not mean that you should not try to own investment properties. I certainly did. I have rented out a condo for four years. I own a vacation property in the high desert near Reno. I have flipped a couple of real estate deals and bid on foreclosed property on the courthouse steps. However, I was always out-bid by people who thought that properties purchased at auction were always a bargain no matter how much they paid. I gave up after about the sixth auction because every property I was bidding on sold for more than my estimate of market value. Of course, this nonsense stopped after the real estate crash. What I discovered about real estate is that because it is so adored and loved as a category it always ends up selling for top dollar. Its profitability is thus much lower than is generally assumed and the risk is therefore greater than is generally assumed. For most of my career I never had any real job security. I never knew from month to month what I was going to earn. Purchasing substantial amounts of real estate terrified me because I was never sure that I would be able to pay the bills.

This is no idle fear. Since the 2007 real estate crash a staggering number of real estate foreclosures have occurred. Later in this work, I will give you the annual number of foreclosures that have occurred in this country each year from 2007 to 2018. It is huge. It is interesting to note that when a real estate investor is foreclosed on, he loses 100% of his investment. In the stock market losses in the 10% to 20% range are common but it is very, very rare to lose 100% of your investment.

When real estate investors are bragging about the killing they have made in real estate there are two costs that are almost never mentioned: management costs and transaction and closing costs. When I do a stock trade at Charles Schwab my transaction cost is $4.95. Charles Schwab has just announced that it is reducing its commission on stock trades to zero. The transaction and closing costs in real estate are horrific in comparison. It is common for real estate investors to have a highly profitable sale and to then observe them talking to themselves after the closing, wondering what happened to their profit after everyone and his brother got their cut. Anyone who has done real estate investing for any length of time knows exactly what I am talking about. Those transaction costs will eat you alive and they are paid both when you buy and when you sell real estate.

Management costs are another huge real estate cost that stock investors avoid. Stock investors do not have management costs although they clearly have research costs.

It is common for non-institutional real estate investors to virtually ignore many of the costs that are inherent in managing real estate, not to mention their considerable unpaid labor which they habitually place a zero value on when they are calculating their alleged profits. Consider Joe Handyman, who has just bought a fixer upper. He and his wife slave like dogs for six months fixing up the place. Six months later they sell the place at a $20,000 profit. During this time housing prices in the neighborhood haven't budged. Joe and his wife will proudly tell you that they earned their profit because they were shrewd real estate investors. The truth is that they earned their profit because they worked like dogs for six months and placed a zero value on their labor and not because they were shrewd real estate investors. If you told Joe and his wife this, rest assured that they would be outraged.

Well, that ends my biography and I hope it also explained why a licensed real estate appraiser chose the stock market over real estate. Later in this book you are going to discover that, strangely enough, I am a great fan of commercial real estate and that I firmly believe that the best way to purchase commercial real estate is in the stock market.

When asked I define myself as a conviction-contrarian. I buy small-cap and micro-cap stocks that most people have never heard of. I buy with the intention of holding my positions for at least two to five years. During this holding period I fully expect the stocks that I have purchased to have at least one decline of 10-20%. I will rarely sell a position when such a decline has occurred. On the contrary I will normally regard this decline as a buying opportunity to selectively add to my position and thus lower my average stock cost.

On Wall Street this is referred to as "adding to a losing position." The overwhelming Wall Street consensus is that adding to a losing position is an act of criminal insanity since each trade results in a loss. The smart money play according to these geniuses is to only add to a "winning position" since each trade results in a profit. This process of adding to your winning positions as they rise in value is commonly called "momentum investing." This birdbrain scheme has probably been the most popular of all investment strategies in recent decades.

Its only real virtue is its childlike simplicity. First you discover a stock that has momentum. In other words, it is going up. Then you establish an initial position. If the stock continues to go up, you add to your winning position and you keep adding to your winning position as long as the stock goes up. If the stock drops, you immediately sell the stock. Your long-term success will be determined by how quickly you can bail out. Since this strategy is so wildly popular, what happens is that momentum players are concentrated to an inordinate degree in a few dozen momentum plays. They have all been trained to invest with one foot out the door, ready to bolt at the first sign of weakness. As a result, when these stocks do decline they don't decline by 5% or 10% like normal stocks do. They can decline 20% or 30% in a single day as hysterical momentum players bail out of the stock en masse.

What adds to the brutality of your losses is that you keep adding to your position as the stock is rising so that your average cost keeps increasing. In my early years as an investor I fell for the momentum thesis hook, line and sinker. I got my head handed to me on a silver platter again and again. What I discovered is what everyone discovers. No matter how carefully you research these stocks and no matter how powerful the trend, these stocks insist on blowing up right after you buy them with a consistency that is truly remarkable. It was a painful experience. I wised up and became a contrarian.

I am a contrarian because I love buying stocks when they are being hammered into the gutter. This is another Wall Street no-no. This practice is referred to on the Street as "trying to catch a falling knife" and is regarded with great horror by the Wall Street consensus. According to these clowns you should never buy a stock unless it is going up and you should sell it at the first sign of weakness. This strategy sounds like true brilliance until you try to put it into practice. The problem is that because this strategy is so painfully obvious everyone and his brother is using it. You have no idea how hard it is on Wall Street to make money using a strategy that is childishly simple and that everyone and his brother is using, until you try it. If mindlessly buying whatever is going up and mindlessly selling whatever is going down worked, we would all be multimillionaires. This childish strategy has always been wildly popular and always will be wildly popular. It just doesn't work.

I bought my first stock when I was a 19-year-old kid more than 50 years ago and have more or less been fully invested ever since. I am a hard core speculator. If you are going to take the kind of risk that I do, then massive diversification is mandatory. An amusing story that I tell my friends occurred several years ago. My alleged investment advisor at Charles Schwab had just been assigned my account and requested that we set up a meeting. I was happy to oblige him. I wish you could have seen the poor guy. His eyes were literally rolling around in his head as he examined my stock portfolio.

"Mr. Carach, you have almost 100 positions in your account and not one of them is a blue chip." I told him that it was 105 positions. "Okay, Mr. Carach, 105 positions, how on earth can you expect to keep track of 105 positions?" I informed him that over my decades as an investor I had learned not to second-guess my stock picks. During more than 50 years as a speculator I have learned that as long as I am properly diversified, I will be right 60-80% of the time. When I take a position, it is with the intent of holding it for 2-5 years and I have found out that the longer I hold a position the better it does. He was making the mistake of staring at my stock portfolio again and his eyeballs were rolling around in his head again. "Very well, Mr. Carach, but I can't help noticing that many of your positions are penny stocks. You are a retiree. At your age don't you think you should sell these penny stocks and invest them in safer blue chips?" I answered with a single word. That word was no.

During my career as a speculator I have owned well over 1,000 positions. I have never really bothered to count them and I currently own 123 positions. Don't panic! Rest assured that I don't recommend this strategy for the typical investor who reads this book. For the typical investor dividing your investment capital into 15 or 20 positions with 5% or less in each position will do just fine. An excellent strategy that I recommend for newbies starting out would be to begin by putting your entire investment capital in a broad-based mutual fund. Vanguard's S&P 500 Stock Market Fund is my favorite and would be an excellent choice.

While this isn't strictly true as a practical matter every share of the fund that you own confers an ownership position in all of the largest listed blue chip stocks. Once this is done you will have covered for all practical purposes the entire blue chip universe. Having safely covered the blue chip universe you can now concentrate your efforts in the small-cap and micro-cap universe where you can hit some real home runs on a chump change investment. As you gradually become familiar with this ignored and often despised world where I hang out you will learn to discover what the military calls a "target of opportunity." Every time you discover one of these opportunities you could sell from 1% to 5% of the mutual fund depending on how bullish you are and invest it in the target of opportunity. Over a period of time you will be able to establish a broadly diversified portfolio of stocks. The blue chip mutual fund will confer a measure of safety and your small-cap and micro-cap stocks will provide the fireworks.

Most of my positions are less than 1% of my investment capital. Though at any one time I usually have at least 5 or 6 positions that are around 5% or more of my investment capital, because I will allow my most successful stock picks to keep growing forever as long as I continue to believe in the stocks. Under no condition whatsoever however will I invest more than 5% of my investment capital in any stock.

On the back cover of my first book, "Forty Years a Speculator," which I published in 2007, I wrote the following:

I am not a Wall Street professional. In real life I am a State Certified General Real Estate appraiser. This is the story of my transformation over more than four decades from a conservative blue chip investor into a steely eyed, riverboat gambler with nerves of steel. As the years progressed, I realized that blue chip investing wasn't the answer. It couldn't be. These Godzillas don't move. I wanted stocks that would go to the moon. Gradually, I discovered what I was looking for in the unreported and unknown world of small-cap and micro-cap investing. Allow me to introduce you into my world. The strange and wondrous world of the riverboat gambler. In a world in which most investors are happy to earn 10% a year, I shoot for the moon. Stick around and I will show you how it is done. After all, you might make the same amazing discovery that I made. You might discover that you are a riverboat gambler with nerves of steel and with ice water in your veins, but you never knew it.

Before we get to the exciting world of penny stocks and the rest of the sub-$10.00 a share world, there is a sideshow that we must visit. It is a most unique sideshow. It is a dog and pony show that mystifies millions. They call it the stock market. A better name for it would be cattle stampede central.

Wall Street Insiders often call the market "Mr. Market," a term that is used with great reverence because Mr. Market is supposed to be wiser than any stock investor, and for too many years early in my investment career I agreed with this evaluation. There are endless articles and books that scream out the superiority of the wisdom of crowds and markets over the individual, but things have gone horribly, horribly wrong with Mr. Market in recent decades. This dominant thesis is called the Efficient Market Hypothesis (EMH). In other words, the stock market is never wrong. Why is it never wrong? According to the academics and ivory tower theorists who believe in this drivel the stock market is dominated by stock market professionals in green eyeshades who carefully scrutinize every stock's finances with a magnifying glass before they invest in it. Now if the only thing you have ever owned is mutual funds it is easy to believe this drivel because you are protected from seeing individual stocks skyrocket or crash for no valid reason again and again. How anyone who has been an active investor for more than four or five years investing or speculating in individual stocks can believe this is beyond me.

Warren Buffet has correctly observed when commenting on the proponents of the EMH that because they observed that the market was frequently efficient, they went on to conclude that the market was always efficient. But the real elephant in the room is: How do you explain consistently superior or inferior performance in the stock market? If the EMH thesis were valid, the dumbest investor would be just as successful as the most knowledgeable investor. Superior knowledge would not be rewarded by superior results. No one could underperform or outperform the market because every stock would be selling at its intrinsic market value.

Warren Buffet's career would have been impossible. It is interesting to note that the strategy that made his career was to buy them when they are in the gutter. He patiently sits on a mountain of money until the stocks that he is interested in are hammered into the gutter and then he pounces. My suspicion is that these ivory tower EMH theorists have never invested in anything but mutual funds which can give you a distorted reality of what the real world is like in the blood-splattered world of the speculator. Where they drag the losers out of the blood-stained arena floor feet-first.

I have been in the Colosseum in Rome at least five times and every time I visit it, I feel a strange kinship with the gladiators of 2,000 years ago. The only real difference is that when they lost, they gushed blood and when we lose, we gush cash. But the end result is the same. Losers do not survive. They either bleed to death or are wiped out.

I have spent over half a century watching herds of investors hysterically stampeding in and out of stocks for no valid or fundamental reason whatsoever other than whether their stock is rising or falling. The cool, calculating investors with green eyeshades and a magnifying glass that the Efficient Market Hypothesis assumes is the last thing that they are. And these trend chasers are not an insignificant minority of stock investors; they are the overwhelming majority. Of course, if you ask these clowns what their investment philosophy is, they will insist that they are long-term investors.

They lie! What they mean is that they are long-term investors providing that their stock doesn't fall more than 5% or 10% which is the largest paper loss that most of these clowns can tolerate. As soon as it reaches their personal bailout point, they will hysterically sell their stock since they are convinced that the stock is heading for zero. The problem with this is that the typical stock will have a decline of 10% or more at some point during the year and will then reverse. But for vast numbers of investors that reversal will come too late and they will be blown out of their positions. The result is that they are constantly nailing down unnecessary losses by selling these stocks at a loss; if they had just held on to these stocks for another six months or a year, their paper losses would have turned into profits.

There is a competing thesis which I heartily endorse, and which is slowly gaining credibility. It is called the Random Walk Thesis. This thesis holds that in the short term, both stock prices and the movement of the stock market as a whole is essentially a random walk that cannot be predicted. You might as well toss a coin as attempt to predict market trends over the short term, but over the long term, stock prices will tend to oscillate around their intrinsic or market value. The key word here being "oscillate." How long is the long term? It is about 2-4 years. It can be shorter than this but don't plan on it. When I buy a busted stock, I expect it to take about two years before the market realizes its error and starts to really bid up the stock. I will spend a great deal of time putting both the market and today's investors under the looking glass in the first part of this book. My hope is that you will find this analysis both thought provoking and a valuable aid in your career as an investor. By the way, there is an excellent book about the Random Walk Thesis. It is written by Burton G. Malkiel. It is now in its 12th edition it is called "A Random Walk Down Wall Street."

The following is a series of articles that I wrote detailing the curious transformation of both the stock market and investor attitudes and behavior that have occurred over the course of my investment career. These articles appeared on my website or on Seeking Alpha. Regrettably there is quite a bit of repetition in these articles but that only serves to reinforce the points that I am attempting to make. I think that you will find them thought provoking and the repetition useful. Who knows? You might even agree with my radical interpretation of today's market. After you have read these articles on today's market, we will get down to the nitty gritty of investing in the small-cap universe where I hang out.

There is one last thing that I want to mention. You will notice that in this book I spend far more time analyzing and talking about my losers than I do talking about my winners. Trust me; no one survives more than five decades in this racket unless they are right at least 60% of the time. Indeed, I think it is far more important to analyze your losers than to analyze your winners and besides, I think my losers are far more interesting than my winners. By the time you finish reading this work I think you might agree with me.

The Curious Transformation of the Stock Market into a Dog and Pony Show

I have been an investor for more than five decades now, which is something that I hate to admit. During this time period, I have watched the stock market gradually transform itself from a cathedral of capitalism into a circus freak show. The curious thing about this transformation is that almost no one recognizes that it has even happened. Many ill-informed people will tell you that there never was a transformation. That the stock market was always a circus freak show or a dog and pony show. I know better. I was there when it really was a cathedral of capitalism. You could say I was there at the creation.

The decisive change that has occurred is that the stock market is becoming progressively worse in its central task of providing the public with accurate and reliable figures as to what stocks are worth. A task that is called "price discovery," a task that it performed well for generations. It is an example of the law of unintended consequences writ large. Very large.

It all started to go horribly wrong on May 1,1975, when the stock market, under pressure from the SEC, abolished fixed commissions on stock trades. At that time there was a privileged class of investors who had the exclusive right of trading stocks without paying commissions. These privileged investors were all members of the New York and American stock exchanges. The NASDAQ did not yet even exist even though there was a small and very insignificant OTC (Over The Counter) market. The OTC market comprised any stock that was not listed on the New York Stock Exchange or the smaller American Stock Exchange.

In those days being able to trade without paying a commission was a vastly more valuable benefit than it is today. In those days the commissions were so brutal that they would eat alive any day trader who was not a member of the exchanges and who had to pay the standard commissions. Indeed, it safe to say that in the pre-May Day 1975 period the brutal commissions would render day trading as it exists today a virtual impossibility.

As a result of the brutal commission structure, anyone who was not a member of the exchanges was forced to be a conviction investor. You were compelled to be a buy-and-hold investor even if you didn't want to be one. You could not afford to bail out of any trade just because it went a couple of points against you. This compelled investors to carefully research the stocks that they bought and to hold on to them even if the trade went temporarily against them. The result was that the stock market performed the way that it was supposed to. It provided the public with accurate and reliable figures of what stocks were worth.

Each decade after 1975 saw lower and lower commissions. As the commissions fell, more and more investors felt that they could ignore the cost of commissions. For the first time, they could afford to guess about the direction of stocks. They no longer were compelled to be conviction investors who carefully researched their stocks and then held on to them. The boom of the 90s coupled with the internet witnessed the full flowering of the age of the domestic day trader who for the first time could realistically trade out of his home. The age of the dog and pony show had begun.

To veteran stock investors like me the thing that hits you on the head about the new world order was that the stock market was reacting to every news event, no matter how insignificant or trivial, with a violence that had never been seen before. The stock market was becoming a perpetual over-reaction machine. Stocks and the stock market were being jerked around like a monkey on a chain by news reports that in the old days would scarcely move stocks or the market. Knowledgeable investors were noticing something else that the general public was blind to. They noticed that there was an ever-widening gap between the intrinsic value or market value of stocks and their selling price.

The rise of a new investment class of day traders and momentum trend chasers was changing the very nature of the stock market. This new class regarded stock analysis as a waste of time. They would proudly tell you that the only thing you needed to know about a stock was whether it was going up or down. You mindlessly bought whatever was going up and you mindlessly sold whatever was going down. As the conviction investor declined in numbers and influence there was no one left to mind the store. There was no one left to keep the market value of stocks from deviating more and more from their intrinsic value. This process has been greatly accelerated by the rise of index mutual funds that make no attempt whatsoever to determine the value of the stocks that they buy.

If this new class of investors regarded traditional stock analysis as a waste of time, there was something that they did not regard as a waste of time.

They were obsessed with analyzing the buying and selling actions of other investors. They could not care less about the intrinsic value of the stocks that they were buying and selling. In this new world order, stock analysis was out. Guessing which way the herd would stampede was in.

When you stop to think about it, this is very strange behavior. It is much easier to estimate what a stock is worth than to try to figure out which way the cattle are going to stampede next.

It is as if the fans in a sports stadium have decided that the best way to find out who is winning on the field is by doping out the actions of the fans in the stadium rather than following the action on the field. Welcome to the new dog and pony show. The strangest thing about this is that no one seems to have realized that it has even happened. I follow the stock market very closely and I cannot recall the subject even being brought up.

The Strange Rise of the Trend Chasers and the Death of Rational Markets

When I broke into the stock market the world of investing was radically different than it is today. The market was dominated by the individual investor and not by the institutional investors. In addition, I would strongly argue that the markets were far more rational than they are today. By rational I mean that stocks fluctuated in a rather tight band. They would oscillate in a reasonably tight range of value for a reasonable period of time and then gradually rise or fall in value based on market dynamics as investors assimilated new information and data. In other words, markets made sense. What did not exist is today's whiplash markets. Which as I stated earlier remind me of nothing so much as a monkey being violently jerked around on a chain.

There has been tremendous damage done by this change. And it has hurt our economy badly. Our markets are no longer delivering honest prices that can be trusted. These violent gyrations make it far more difficult than it used to be for investors, businesses and governments to engage in rational planning and make rational decisions.

When I look back across the decades and ask where it went wrong, two changes stand out. One change is fairly obvious and the other is hiding in plain sight.

The obvious change, of course, is the rise of the institutional investor to market dominance. In other words, fewer and much larger decision makers results in more violent price fluctuations. When you combine this fact with their undeniable tendency to engage in cattle stampede behavior, you have solved one part of the puzzle.

The stranger and perhaps the most important part of the puzzle is hiding in plain sight and no one recognizes it. And what a strange puzzle it is. It is the law of unintended consequences writ large.

As I have already mentioned in the above article, on May 1,1975, fixed commissions were outlawed on Wall Street. Stock commissions immediately dropped 40% and have been falling ever since. Prior to this time the commission to trade a stock had been so expensive that the type of in-and-out trading for small profits that is so common today would have been impossible. The commissions would have eaten you alive. The only people who could afford to be day traders or to churn their stocks for small profits were, as I have already mentioned, the professionals who owned seats on the New York and American stock exchanges and who therefore paid no stock commissions. In those days the NASDAQ scarcely existed. Its creation as the world's first electronic marketplace only occurred in 1971.

The unintended consequences of this change were amazing. Prior to this time if you were wise, you had to have a strong opinion about a stock before you invested in it. Hopefully, an opinion based on your research. You were compelled to have strong convictions because you could not afford to sell a stock just because it fell five or ten percent. You could not buy a stock for any other reason than it was trending up in the absence of a strong conviction. If you did this the commissions on your excessive trading would eat you alive. Today the commissions are so low that people can buy and sell on the weakest of whims. Changing your mind about a stock today is almost cost-free as far as the commission is concerned.

The combined impact of institutional investing and today's low, low commissions has had a devastating impact on rational markets. It has given rise to the cult of the trend chaser or momentum trader. This buffoon neither knows nor cares what the intrinsic market value is of any stock that he buys or sells. Why should he? Research and having a soundly arrived at opinion of value is now regarded by armies of investors as a dangerous waste of their valuable time. After all, having an opinion of value is dangerous. What happens if your opinion is opposed to the trend of the market? The horror of it all! Why, it would interfere with your trend chasing. And where would you be then?

In a world in which the huge majority of investors are trend chasers, sound market values are obliterated. There are fewer and fewer investors who are engaging in honest research and who are making their investment decisions based on their own estimate of market value. Yet, this is precisely what is required for markets to function correctly.

The result is today's whiplash markets, where thundering herds of mindless trend chasers stampede stocks way above and then way below any intelligent estimate of market value in oscillating cycles and with ever greater violence. The stock market has become a perpetual over-reaction machine. Markets are no longer delivering honest, reliable estimates of intrinsic value that can be trusted. Investors, businessmen and governments find it increasingly difficult to engage in rational investing, business planning or government decisions based on these highly flawed markets.

Indeed, as the number of investors who are actually attempting to ascertain market value keeps shrinking in size, the mindless herd of trend chasing cattle who have the nerve to call themselves investors keeps growing in both numbers and influence. It is calling into question how much longer we will have anything that truly resembles a market as we have historically understood the term.

Today's Irrational Stock Market and the Rise of the Propeller Heads

When I broke into the stock market in 1961 it was in my opinion a far more rational market than it is today. The type of news that will send a stock up or down four or five points today would have in the 60s and 70s only sent the stock up or down a half point. As I have already stated the stock market today resembles to an ever increasing degree a "perpetual over-reaction machine." I can't think of a better definition of what to call it. It is forever being jerked around by the transitory and usually irrelevant news of the day like a monkey on a chain.

One constantly hears alleged market authorities proudly proclaiming that the market is always looking forward six months. Not anymore! Today's market is too stupid to anticipate anything. It does not anticipate anything; it reacts in shocked surprise and with ever increasing violence to the news of the day. The question is, what has brought about this dramatic change in market behavior? The answer is that the market players and their relative strength has changed. And arguably one of the most important new factors by far has been the rise of the "propeller heads" as they are fondly called on the street. Their common name is Quants because they are engaged in quantitative analysis.

By the 80s it had become fashionable for Wall Street firms to raid college campuses for math PhDs. Then stick these certified geniuses into a room with a high-powered computer and tell them to come up with a sophisticated black-box algorithm that would enable them to beat the market. And in many cases, they succeeded. And thus, computer-generated program trading was born. These programs are usually referred to as algorithms.

The other key players in this drama were the day trader and the momentum player. Both of these players had long existed but until the 80s they were small potatoes.

In the 60s, when I started out, the stock market was dominated by the individual investor. The individual investor in those days was overwhelmingly a conviction investor. He researched stocks as best as he was able to and based on this research and his convictions (he liked the product). He bought the stock. By long-term I mean at least five to ten years. Today long-term means I might own the stock six months as long as it doesn't go down 5% or 10%. If it goes down 5% or 10%, I am out of there.

It is important to understand the distinction between a market and mob action. A market requires the prudent, informed, carefully calculated and above all else the "independent opinion" of the entire mass of the decision makers who make up this market. In the absence of these independent decision makers you don't have a market; you have a mob that is pretending to be a market. This results in ever more violent reactions to the news of the day that cannot possibly be justified when you analyze the economic realities of both stocks and the market. This assumes of course that anyone is still paying attention to tried and true fundamental analysis. After all, why waste your time with this boring stuff that may only pay off in the long term when you can participate in the excitement of the street's latest cattle stampede? Even if it is heading off a cliff. After all, we are smarter than the average herd animal, aren't we? There is no doubt that we will spot the cliff before the rest of these clowns. Did you ever see a more confused herd of sheep and goats? I don't think they could find a cliff if they tried to!

"My god how did that cliff get there? Help!!!"

Historically the stock market was soundly based on masses of independent decision makers. As time passed however, these independent decision makers were gradually replaced by the rise of the institutional investors who for all of their alleged vaunted sophistication showed a much greater tendency than the traditional individual investor to stampede with the herd. The transfer of market making power from these old-timer, buy-and-hold investors to the institutions resulted in a vast reduction in the number of independent decision makers. The growing tendency of the institutions to concentrate on short term profits and to participate in every cattle stampede went on steroids when the propeller heads arrived on the scene. Their magic black boxes based on their secret algorithms promised and more often than not delivered superior short-term returns.

Long term investment went out the window. The future was now.

As this bias took over the market the day traders and the momentum players exploded in importance. As time progressed many of the black box programs seeped down the food chain and became more readily available to all. It was found to be impossible to keep the most successful programs secret for long. As a result, everyone began to march to the same drummers. During this period the ranks of the old time conviction investor with his independent viewpoint and long-term holding pattern shrank to insignificance. And thus was born today's whiplash market.

Program trading rules the market today. What is seldom realized is that program trading for all of its alleged sophistication is all about trend chasing. These programs as often as not end up chasing the day traders and the momentum players. Strangely enough for an old school investor like myself this new world order is a gold mine. The only thing I have to do is hide in the weeds and pick off the big game as they thunder pass me in one of their mindless cattle stampedes.

Stupidity Unchained — The Curious Saga of Today's Stock Market

As I contemplate my fifty-plus years in the blood-splattered arena that we call a stock market I realize that the game has never been more favorable to the long-term, conviction investor. Charlatans and buffoons have rigged a once sane market. It is a market where stupidity has been unchained. It is a most curious saga. I saw it all. I was there at the creation. The prevailing stupidities of today's stock market are as follows:

1) Any stock that falls 10% must be sold immediately because it is going to zero.

2) All stocks are generic clones of each other and therefore all must go up together and go down together. A thesis that drives me nuts.

3) A dangerous over-reliance on macroeconomic data that is by its very nature vague and constantly being revised. As an old-time investor it is shocking to me how much reliance is placed today on vague, generalized macroeconomic data about the market and the economy rather than hard, specific data on individual companies. In fact, I would argue that macroeconomic investing has become a curse rather than a blessing.

4) The growing belief that the current stock trend is all that matters because stocks are empty boxes with no intrinsic or market value and that therefore old school fundamental stock analysis is worthless. You know, stuff like earnings per share, dividends, tangible book value, operating expense ratios, etc.

5) A dangerous over-reliance on averages and indexes that distort the truth.

When I broke into the stock market it was a much different beast than it is today. In those days, the stock market was dominated by long-term conviction investors. People understood that they were buying a business and not a lottery ticket. It would have never occurred to these investors that they were supposed to follow their stocks on a daily basis and freak out every time their stock dropped. The notion that a drop of 5% or 10% in a stock that they believed in was a cause for panic selling would have been regarded by them as a nonsense proposition. Indeed, it is quite possible that they would not even be aware that their stock had fallen by 15% or even 20%.

Remember in those days only the Wall Street Journal and the New York Times carried the stock tables and there were no TV channels or financial radio programs that followed the stock market. I doubt if most of them even looked at the stock price more than about once every six months.

Historically, great emphasis was spent upon analyzing and researching individual stocks because your success or failure depended on your ability to pick winning stocks. The prevailing notion then was that picking stocks with superior future prospects and that were selling at bargain prices was the heart and soul of successful investing. Macroeconomic factors such as guessing about the economy or guessing about whether the stock market was going up or down was regarded as a fool's game.

I am a survivor with more than fifty years in the blood-splattered arena that they call a stock market. During that period, I have owned over 1,000 stocks and almost none of them were blue chips. Guessing about what the market was going to do or what the economy was going to do or what was supposed to be happening in China or Europe has never made me any money. What has made me money was being right about individual stocks that I had researched, understood and believed in.

Consider CNBC, today everyone's default financial data source. For the most part, what you see is a bacchanalia of guessing. Guessing about the economy. Guessing about the stock market. Guessing about China and Europe. Over any sustained period, their guesses are no better than a coin toss. Except for the nifty-fifty which is the popular term for the most popular fifty blue chip stocks of the day and which are mentioned repeatedly, individual stocks that are not blue chips are almost never mentioned and when they are mentioned, the only thing you hear is vague generalities. Rarely do you hear hard, factual data on individual stocks that a serious student of the game would regard as being important.

The implication is that all stocks are clones embedded in a mass of concrete and therefore must rise and fall together. In 2010, to take just one year of the S&P 500, which is now the leading stock market benchmark that for all practical purposes has replaced the Dow Jones 30 Industrials, the S&P was up 12.8%. The top performing stock in the index that year was Cummings, which rose 105.8%. The worst performing stock in the index was Office Depot, which fell 23.4%. Is there anything more stupid than the now common belief that if the stock market is up 12.8% then that's what all investors earned? What is more important being right about the stock market or being right about individual stocks?

The whole art of stock investing used to concern itself with discovering what the intrinsic value of a stock was. This process was called "price discovery" and was regarded as one of the primary functions of the stock and commodity markets. By analyzing the stocks that investors as a group bought and sold, the market "discovered" the intrinsic value of stocks. Until about twenty years ago, nobody doubted that stocks had intrinsic value. The issue was discovering what that intrinsic value was.

Today growing armies of alleged investors believe that stocks are empty boxes with no intrinsic value. If stocks have no intrinsic value, then stock analysis is worthless. It therefore follows that what is of supreme importance is not analyzing stocks but analyzing the actions of buyers and sellers who are now regarded as "price dictators" rather than "price discoverers." In other words, stampeding with the herd is the supreme virtue.

If you gave $50,000 to a Skid Row bum today who knows nothing about the market and turned the TV on to CNBC and told him to start trading, he would be operating on a level that is equal to that of most investors today. After all what does he have to know? The short answer is nothing. He will mindlessly buy whatever the gurus are promoting and mindlessly sell whatever they are dumping. The only thing he has to do is become a trend chaser and stampede with the herd. Mindlessly buying whatever is going up and mindlessly selling whatever is going down and he will do this instinctively. There is no need for either education or training. You just find out which way the herd is stampeding and then go join it. What is totally lost in this simplistic analysis is that this strategy will always result in your stampeding behind Tom, Dick and Harry. There is a price for chasing the herd the price is that the herd is always ahead of you and you are behind the herd coughing in its dust.

The astute reader has already figured out the consequences. An ever-greater deviation between intrinsic value and stock prices as fewer and fewer investors make any attempt at all to analyze the intrinsic value or market value of stocks. At no time in the history of the stock market has there been such a dangerous over-reliance on averages and indexes to guide investment decisions. Very few investors have a clue as to just how convoluted and dubious the formulation of these averages is. I have commented about the S&P 500 index that was up 12.8% in 2010. A year in which the top stock in the index was up 105.8% and the bottom performer was down 23.4%.

Or take a gander at the famous NASDAQ 100. In 2010 this 100 stock capitalization weighted index ranked Apple as number one with a weighting of 19.7%. Google at number two has a weighting of 4.7%. The top two stocks accounted for 24.4% of the index. The bottom fifty stocks account for virtually nothing. The only reason they are in the index is to deceive the ignorant.

Averages are liars. Averages distort. A small number of usually high or low numbers in any average will throw the average off and lead you to a false conclusion. Always look for the median which is free of distortion. Once the investor realizes this, he has a powerful weapon in the unending battle for superior performance.

In such a world the elite core of investors who still analyze and invest in individual stocks are living in a golden age. It is only necessary to hide in the weeds with our high-powered investor rifles and blow away the big game animals as they stampede past us in one of their mindless cattle stampedes.

The Death of the Stock Market as I Knew It

When I broke into the stock market it was a radically different beast than it is today. It was a market overwhelmingly dominated by long-term, conviction investors who believed that they were buying or owned a real business rather than a lottery ticket. The belief then was that the stock certificate was nothing less than proof of ownership. It was not a lottery ticket. Investors then were committed owners who religiously bought the goods and services of the companies that they owned. What was important was that the stock that they purchased paid a good dividend, and in those days it usually did. It was then common for blue chip stocks to pay a dividend in the range of 4% to 6%.

It would never have dawned on investors then that they were supposed to hysterically sell their holdings if their stocks fell 10% which is now the gold standard. Today the first thing that every new day trader and momentum player is taught is that God will strike you dead with a thunderbolt if you don't hysterically sell any position that has fallen 10%. In fact, back then it was quite probable that you would not even be aware of it if your stock did drop 10% or even 20%. As I have stated elsewhere the way it worked in those days is that about every six months it dawned on you that you should break down and purchase what was then regarded as the outrageously overpriced Wall Street Journal to see what your stocks were selling for or you would call your broker and ask him what your positions were selling at. Believe it or not, in those days this was not an unusual request and it gave the broker the opportunity to sell you more stock. Then you would throw away the newspaper and not look at your holdings for another six months. It was common then to think of holding periods of five or ten years and in many cases, people expected to retire owning the stock. The dividend was going to be an important supplement to their social security. According to a recent article in the Wall Street Journal as recently as 1960 the average holding period was eight years and prior to 1960 it probably averaged around 10 years. Today it is six months and falling like a rock.

It is important to realize that in those days the overwhelming probability was that your local newspaper did not even have a financial section. When I was growing up the Cortland Standard, our local newspaper in upstate New York, did not carry the stock tables. In fact, it did not even have a financial section. And this was typical. It is probable that only the Wall Street Journal, the New York Times and a few of the nation's major newspapers even carried the stock market tables in those days.

For some reason in those days the Wall Street Journal was much more expensive relative to local newspapers than it is today. At a time when almost every newspaper in the country was selling for five cents, if I remember correctly the Wall Street Journal was selling for somewhere around a dollar. This was serious money in the 1950s when I was growing up. As I stated earlier in those days it was a common saying that only stockbrokers, rich playboys and financiers subscribed to the Wall Street Journal. Stockbrokers in those days always made a great display of consulting it and used it whenever possible as a status symbol.

When I started investing in the 60s, I refused to look at my stocks during the week. I didn't want to get caught up in the weekly cattle stampedes. I always knew that stampeding with the herd was not the answer to successful investing. I subscribed to Barron's Financial Weekly, which arrived every Saturday. I could then leisurely review my holdings over the weekend. This strategy served me well for decades. However, eventually I had to go online like everyone else. The decades of discipline however served me well. My investment strategy of long-term conviction investing remained unchanged.

Today the stock market as I knew it is dead. The long-term conviction investors who understood that they were buying a business and not a lottery ticket is now a shrinking minority group. The stock market today is dominated by the trend chasers, a category that barely existed in the 60s. It makes little difference if you call this dominant group day traders, trend chasers or momentum players. They are all united by their steely conviction that what they are buying is a lottery ticket and not a certificate of ownership in a real live company that has real assets. Regrettably, they are too stupid to realize that if you treat the stock market like a casino then the stock market will treat you like a gambler. But if you treat the stock market like an investment the stock market will treat you like an investor. Just ask Warren Buffet.

In this new world order trend chasers can be divided into two basic groups. The classic trend chasers and momentum players who simply chase after whatever stocks are showing the strongest upward momentum and a relatively new subset of the trend chasers that has risen to the status of unchallenged dominance in the trend chasing community in recent decades. This subset of the trend chasing universe are called in the trade technicians or chartists.

They have earned this title because of their iron core conviction that everything you need to know about a stock is revealed by its chart pattern. About the fundamentals of the corporations that they are following they know nothing. Indeed, they regard their ignorance as a badge of honor. They are totally clueless that there might be a real business behind the lottery tickets that they own. They are interested in only two things as they track their stocks across time on their charts, price and volume. They will be happy to inform you that the only reason to buy a stock is that it is rising in price and if it is not rising in price it is a bad investment no matter how great the fundamentals are.

All trend chasers, no matter what school they belong to, are united by their unalterable conviction that paper losses and real losses are the same thing. They have a total scorn for anyone who does not share this belief. A paper loss is a loss that would be realized if the holding was sold at its current price. Therefore, since it is their unshakable conviction that a paper loss and a real loss is the same thing their secret weapon for investment success is the stop-loss order. The stop-loss order is an order to your broker to automatically sell your stock if it falls to a predetermined price. Which is almost always set at between 5% and 10% below the current price because that is the bailout point for most investors today.

Trend chasers are adamant that all paper losses greater than 5% or 10% must be sold immediately because all such stocks are destined to go to zero. Nothing can dissuade them from this insanity. Indeed, they are quite proud of what they regard as their macho and courageous honesty of calling a spade a spade and having the courage to face the truth and turn their paper losses into real losses.

You, on the other hand, by refusing to take your losses like a man are a gutless wimp who can't handle the truth. In their world today's price trend is eternal. In my world the price trend can reverse on any given day. There isn't one of these macho investors who hasn't sold stocks at a loss that would now be solidly in the profit column if they had just held on to them. You can fill every sports stadium on planet earth with investors who have sold stocks at a loss that would have been profitable investments today if they had just held on to them for another six months. And that includes me.

Who has the better grip on reality? The investor who believes that stocks have an intrinsic value or market value and that it is his job to figure out the intrinsic value of the stocks that he buys? And who then holds on to his picks even when they go down? Or the trend chaser who believes that today's price, no matter how insane, is always intrinsic value? The brutal result is that every time the trend chasers turn around, they are being blown out of their positions by their stop-loss orders being executed. Stock declines of five to ten percent are as common as dirt in today's stock market. The trend chasers refuse to recognize this reality. This results in constant trading and in the real world the more you trade the more you lose. The impact of this constant trading is brutal on their stock portfolios.

As a conviction investor I have made a career out of turning paper losses into profits. My secret is simple: I just wait six months. You will be amazed at how often a wait of six months will turn a paper loss into a profit. If you have a good opinion on the stocks that you own and have researched them prior to purchase as you ought to be doing and just hold on most of the time the stocks will reverse their decline and your losses will turn into profits.

Very few investors who insist on turning their paper losses into real losses survive over the long term in spite of its tremendous popularity. The way it usually works is that the trend chaser is blown out of his position at or near the bottom. They then sit around in a stunned stupor as the stocks that they sold at a loss often reverse their trend in six months or less and often make back all that they have lost and more. Often much more. What is truly astonishing is that no matter how often they have seen how this movie ends, they never change their tactics. The losses keep piling up until they are so shattered by their losses that they end their investing career. Another thing that I have noticed repeatedly is a flat refusal on their part to ever again look at the price of a stock that they have sold at a loss. This refusal to face the truth does not speak well of them. How can you learn from your mistakes if you refuse to admit that you have made a mistake?

The Case Against Macroeconomic Investing

I have already commented on the subject of macroeconomics, but a fuller explanation of this critical subject is required. When I started investing the concept of macroeconomic investing was unknown. Even today, the term will cause many alleged investors to scratch their heads in wonder. The term may be unknown to them but in truth, they are slaves to an investment concept that will play havoc with their chances to be long-term successful investors.

When I broke into Wall Street, investing was a very simple concept. You concentrated like a laser on one simple concept. It was called picking winners. You did not concern yourself with what was going on in Greece, Europe or Washington because you knew that it did not matter. What mattered was picking winning stocks. Today the slaves to the concept of macroeconomic investing dominate Wall Street like a Goliath. Macroeconomic investing goes like this: First, you try to figure out the status of the current debt crisis in Greece. Then you try to figure out what is going on in Euro land.

Then you try to figure out what is going on in Washington. Then you try to figure out how the economy is doing. Then you try to figure out what is going on Wall Street. If in your analysis all systems are go, then you conclude that today is a risk-on day. This means that for today but for today only it is safe to invest in the market. After all tomorrow could very well be a risk-off day. That means you must sell everything that you own before it goes to zero. The horror of it all.

Having spent 90% of your time and effort ascertaining if it is safe to invest, you now spend the remaining 10% of your time trying to pick winning stocks. Or do you? The truth of the matter is that picking winning stocks, which in my day was the core of all successful investing, is becoming a lost art. To an ever-increasing degree, investors are uncomfortable about picking individual stocks. They are vastly more comfortable in picking an index fund or an ETF that will do the picking for them.

In my day the name of the game was beating the market. Only a loser would have been content to duplicate market performance. The problem with trying to beat the market is that you have to be willing to do research and then invest in individual stocks. For reasons that I do not pretend to understand people appear to be more and more fearful of doing this. I have never seen such a passion for stampeding with the herd. Groupthink is in.

In today's world, everyone seems more comfortable if they are stampeding with the herd. Even if the herd is stampeding off a cliff.

Not the least of the problems with macroeconomic investing is that in my humble opinion it is far harder to figure out what the market is going to do, than it is to pick winning stocks. It is truly amazing how hard it is for people to even figure out if we are in a bull or bear market. Then they compound the problem by constantly second-guessing their own opinion. Often with disastrous results. Just take a gander at the gurus on CNBC as they try to tap dance around the issue of whether we are in a bull or bear market. Have you ever seen such hemming and hawing?

Why bother? Why bother playing this stupid and ignorant game? It may amaze you to know that in my own investing I regard trying to figure out what the market is going to do as an exercise in stupidity. If I spend fifteen minutes a year trying to figure out what the market is going to do, I have just wasted ten minutes of my time. I spend even less time trying to figure out what the economy is going to do. Another exercise in futility.

The rewards go to the stock picker. Consider this, there are around 16,000 stocks that are traded in this country if you also include all the unlisted stocks . Every year there are thousands of stocks that outperform the averages. That is why they call it an average. Why not try to find these stocks that outperform the averages? After all, in a typical year somewhere around 8,000 stocks are going to outperform the averages. How difficult can it be?

Let's pick a random year; consider the Dow's 2011 performance. Though in truth I must tell you that I would not invest in a Dow stock with your money. The returns on these dinosaurs are beneath my dignity. I only invest in micro-caps, small-caps and occasionally mid-caps because that is where the performance is, but I digress.

In 2011, the Dow was up 5.6% for the year. The top two performers in the Dow in 2011 were McDonald's up 30% and IBM up 25%. The worse two performers for the year were Bank of America down 58% for the year and Alcoa down 44% for the year.

How hard do you think it would have been in 2011 to figure out that McDonald's and IBM might outperform the Dow? Not exactly mission impossible was it? You got to admit it sure beats 5.6%.

Stop playing the loser's game of macroeconomic investing and start playing the winners game of microeconomic investing. It is called picking stocks.

Missed Earnings Estimates — Betting Against the Street

In my career as a speculator I have always been a contrarian. I have always bet against the Wall Street consensus because that's where the money is. I can safely say it has never been more profitable to bet against the Wall Street consensus than it is today. Wall Street today as never before in its history is dominated by "herd behavior." Day after day, the Wall Street herd stampedes in and out of stocks based on nothing more substantial than today's headlines. Headlines that are so unsubstantial and of such transitory importance that 60 days from now no one will even remember them. Wall Street's stupidity has become one of my favorite article topics. My topic today is one of Wall Street's greatest stupidities, "missed earnings estimates."

To explain this stupidity more fully let me fabricate a tall tale. Let us imagine that five Skid Row bums decide to become stock analysts and issue estimated future earnings reports. For their first venture, they pick a stock that is currently being followed by only two analysts. Their stock pick XYZ is earning a profit, is well thought of and is rising in value. The Skid Row bums are too bullish on the stock. Their new higher consensus estimate swamps the more realistic estimate of the two old pros who have been following the stock. XYZ does well but not well enough. Its earnings are up a respectable 18 cents a share for the quarter, but the new consensus estimate was not 18 cents a share but 20 cents a share. XYZ has committed one of Wall Street's greatest crimes. It has missed an earnings estimate. The stock is brutally mauled. Therefore, the new consensus estimate for the next quarter is reduced say 1 cent a share to 19 cents. Once again, XYZ misses its earnings estimate. It reports earnings increase of only 15 cents a share and once again, the stock is hammered. The stock analysts having now been burned twice reduce their consensus earnings estimate increase for the next quarter to only 15 a share. Once again, XYZ misses the consensus earnings it reports earnings increase of only 12 cents a share.

In the eyes of Wall Street this is the kiss of death. XYZ has now missed three earnings estimates in a row. What is even worse is that the reported earnings increase has been falling for three straight quarters from 18 cents a share to 12 cents a share the stock is crushed. It is easily possible for a stock that has missed three straight earnings estimates to fall 35% or more in value. For a contrarian speculator like me this stock is now a raging buy. The overwhelming probability is that XYZ will annihilate the next quarter's earnings estimate. How do I know this? Let's take an honest look at XYZ's real performance. By any rational measure, it has performed very well indeed. In the last three quarters, it has increased its earnings by an impressive 45 cents a share and its reward for this stellar performance is that the stock has been crushed; it has fallen 35%. Why has the stock been crushed? It has been crushed because five Skid Row bums who have nothing whatsoever to do with the company they are covering fabricated over-optimistic numbers. At this point, you might inform me that stock analysts are not Skid Row bums but respected Wall Street professionals. My response to that is that when you follow these alleged pros for as long as I have it is not hard to conclude that they might as well be Skid Row bums. These guys will put you into the poor house. Welcome to the wonderful world of Wall Street where stupidity reigns supreme. There are two additional reasons to love this stock. The first reason is that the earnings of most stocks are strongly seasonally influenced. Most stocks have a historically strong quarter and a historically weak quarter each year. Think retail stores before and after the Christmas reporting season. When the Christmas numbers are reported they will report blow out numbers. The next quarter they will report the worst numbers of the year. So help me, the clowns who think these quarterly reports are a direct quote from god will base their buying and selling decisions on little else. There is nothing more common than placing an exaggerated importance on quarterly reports. Folks, it is only 90 days. You can't judge a corporation by its performance over the last 90 days. Even many good analysts fall into this trap. They do a microscopic analysis of the latest quarterly report and if it is substantially better than the previous quarterly report, they think they have discovered the next Apple. If, however, it is substantially worse, they predict doom. There are armies of trend chasers out there who are too stupid to understand this. These morons are constantly stampeding into stocks after they report their historically strong quarter of the year and then stampeding out of the same stock when it reports its historically weak quarter of the year. Let's return to XYZ. XYZ has reported three weakening quarters. Thus, there is an excellent chance that the next quarter will be its strongest quarter of the year. The most powerful reason, however, is the fact that the consensus estimate has been too bullish three times in a row. There is nothing more disastrous for stock analysts than to overestimate earnings for three quarters in a row. The investors who follow their reports are getting killed and they are not going to be happy about it. The consensus earnings estimate will now be ruthlessly cut perhaps to only 8 cents a share. The overwhelming probability is that XYZ will now report a strong quarter and will easily blow away this fear induced low-ball estimate. A return to the 18-20 cents a share range would not be out of line.

In Wall Street lingo, this is referred to as a "positive earnings surprise." XYZ has now beaten the consensus earnings estimate. There is nothing that Wall Street adores more than a positive earnings surprise and this one is big. In such a scenario, the stock could be expected to explode in value. Welcome to my world, the world of the contrarian investor.

Stopwatch Investing — Betting Against the Wall Street Consensus

I have spent five decades betting against the Wall Street consensus. In 2007 I wrote a book about it. As I look back over the decades, the most remarkable aspect of the Wall Street consensus is that it has been getting dumber and dumber. You have got to admit that this is a truly heroic achievement.

In my book and in a series of articles that I have written I have pounded away at this enigma. Let us take a look at stopwatch investing one of Wall Street's reining stupidities. There are so many of them that it is hard to know where to begin.

When I broke into the market in the 60s, people were married to their stocks. They were junior Warren Buffets. As I have already related, Buffet has famously stated on many occasions that his favorite holding period was forever.

A typical holding period back then was until retirement. After you retired, you would shift to bonds. Only crazed speculators would contemplate buying a stock that they were not willing to hold for at least five or ten years. The thinking back then was that the only sound reason to buy a stock was that you understood and believed in the stock and you wanted to be an owner of a company that had a bright future and produced what you believed was a great product or service. After all, if you did not believe this why would you want to own the stock? In other words, you were a conviction investor. You were not conditioned to bolt from your stock at the first sign of trouble. As a matter of fact, it is quite possible that your stock could fall by 15% or 20% without you even being aware of it. Back then, there was no CNBC and as I have previously stated it is probable that your newspaper did not carry the stock tables. People thought nothing of going months at a time without knowing the current sale price of the stock. After all, they knew why they owned the stock.

It was common then for stockowners to always be bragging about the stocks that they owned, and they would promote them at every opportunity. They were fiercely loyal to the companies that they owned. In those days you only bought companies that you believed in. This belief was grounded on a rock solid basis. You only bought companies whose products and services were of superior quality and you knew that they were of superior quality because you had purchased them and believed in the product.

Think about it! If you are a long-term investor, how wrong can you be if you buy only those companies who produce a good or service that you feel is of superior quality? If you owned Pepsi, you would only buy Pepsi. You would never, ever buy Coca-Cola. If you owned GM, you would only buy GM cars. This strategy has worked well for generations but has today been largely abandoned for no valid reason whatsoever. Contrast this behavior with that of a typical stockowner today. He has been taught by the gurus on CNBC and elsewhere that he who is wise is ready to bolt from his holdings at the first sign of trouble and that a 5% or 10% drop in a stock is the end of the world. After all, how many 10% drops can you survive?

What this leads to of course is stopwatch investing. If you have been in this racket for any length of time, I am sure you will agree with me that it is truly amazing how often even blue chip, high quality stocks drop 10% and even 15% for no rational reason at all. Forget about 5%.

Today's investors have been indoctrinated into believing that he who is smart always puts in a stop-loss order at 5-10% below his purchase price. This results in vast masses of stop-loss orders that are just under today's prices and appear to be triggered every time you turn around.

If the stock has not moved up in 30-60 days today's investor is ready to bail out at the first sign of trouble. They have been taught to think small and to be ready to bolt at the first sign of trouble to protect their pathetic 5% or 10% profit. With today's absurdly short holding periods it is rarely more than that. This is no way to get rich.

There remains a question that has not yet been answered. The question is, how many 10% drops can you survive?

I know the correct answer to this question. The correct answer is thousands of times and I am living proof that this is the correct answer. Or to be more specific wait six months. You will be amazed at how often just waiting six months will turn that 15% loss into a profit. This assumes of course that you are a conviction investor and researched the stock before you bought it.

If your judgment is worth a damn, you can expect to be right at least 60% of the time. Hell, chimpanzees that throw darts at stock tables are routinely right more than 50% of the time.

The fatal curse that kills stock investors is not so much that they pick bad stocks but that they keep second-guessing their stock picks. This will absolutely kill you. You will go from being right 60% of the time to being wrong most of the time.

No doubt you are wondering how I bet against the Wall Street consensus. I hope you are sitting down. Brace yourself. One of the biggest money-making strategies out there is to selectively add to your position after your stock has fallen 10%-20%.

The holding period that will maximize your profits is not 15 minutes or 60 days or god forbid 90 days but two to five years. Follow the strategies that I have outlined, and your losses will turn to profits like magic.

How I Make Money by Losing Money

I have been at this game for a very long time. I don't believe in sure things. What I do believe in is risk-reward ratios and that is the concept that I have built my life around. I think that believing in certainty in the world of investing is an exercise in delusional thinking that will destroy you. The higher the tolerance for uncertainty, the greater the rewards. At this point the "I refuse to lose my money" crowd will proudly point to the fact that they have never lost a dime in their investing because they only invest in sure things like government guaranteed savings accounts, CDs or treasury bonds.

I go nuts. The first thing I do when I hear this argument is to frantically search for a chair so that I can break it over their idiot skulls. How can anybody be stupid enough to believe that any government-guaranteed investment earns you a positive rate of return after inflation and paying taxes on your profits is beyond me. At this point doofus proudly points to the official government statistics that prove that the rate of return on government treasuries is above the rate of inflation after paying taxes.

You cannot be serious!

I am not aware of a single government on the face of the earth that does not practice what is referred to in the trade as "financial repression." This is the practice of government agencies regulating the maximum interest rates that can be paid on savings accounts and government securities to a rate that is below the rate of inflation.

There is, however, one exception to this rule. From time to time governments will embark on a "kill inflation now" crusade. During these short crusades, it is indeed possible for the true rate of interest to exceed the rate of inflation.

Except for these short-term crusades, I do not know of a single nation on the face of the earth whose government bonds will pay you a positive rate of return of more than 2% or 3% after inflation and taxes are accounted for if accurate numbers are used. I regard the 30-year government bonds as almost guaranteed certificates of confiscation to use a term that has gone out of favor. The longer the term of the bond the more certain the confiscation. What do you think the chances are that the rate of inflation will not exceed the 2.89% that is the current interest rate on 30 year treasury bonds over a holding period that long?

For the sake of argument, let us suppose that we have discovered that the ten-year bonds of Outer Mongolia will pay you a positive rate of return greater than 3% after inflation using true numbers. I am talking miracles here. When the bonds mature in ten years, you do indeed have a positive rate of return. Or do you? There is the little matter of converting the Mongolian currency into dollars. You have a positive rate of return only if the Mongolian currency is convertible into dollars at a rate that is equal to or higher than it was at the time you purchased the bonds. In other words, you could not only have a loss but you could have a very large loss on what you presumed to be a guaranteed return and this problem exists with every currency on earth.

The point that I am trying to make is that your investment in Mongolian bonds is certain only if you know with certainty what the exchange rate is going to be ten years into the future.

Recently I was pontificating at my local Starbucks about my favorite subject, the stock market. A 21-year-old kid happened to be listening and questioned me about my investing. He wanted me to recommend an investment that he could not lose money on. When I told him that I have never in a lifetime of searching found such an investment, a look of total scorn appeared on his face. He told me that only stupid people invest in things that they can lose money on. Smart people only invest in sure things. When I asked him what he regarded as a sure thing, he said a savings account and CDs. I told him that at 2% compounded it would take him 36 years to double his money and at 3% compounded it would take him 24 years to double his money. That is no way to get rich. This belief in sure things is not rare; it is as common as dirt. Nothing is more common than the belief in a sure thing. People spend their whole lives looking for it and when they think they have found it, they bet the ranch. All too often, their sure thing turns out to be a mirage and they lose everything.

I am a great admirer of Warren Buffet, who is beyond dispute one of the greatest investors of all time. Recently, however, he said something that was so far below his usual standards that it startled me. He said that the first rule of investing was to not lose money. The only trouble with this is that to follow that rule we would all have to be psychic and be able to predict the future. Fortunately, the only true psychics are safely tucked away in mental institutions, which is where they belong. It therefore follows that we cannot invest in anything because we cannot be assured in advance that we will not lose money. If you look at the cover of my first book, you will see a pair of dice on it. It is a true depiction of how I invest. It is now over 50 years that I have been an investor. Actually, it has been 57 years but who is counting? In those years I have owned more than 1,000 positions and have been successful more than 60% of the time. Anyone who tells you that his stock picks are right more than 80% of the time in this business is a liar. No one is right in this racket more than 80% of the time.

It is time to reveal the secrets. If there is a key to investment success it is above all else the willingness to lose and to put your money at risk. The willingness to take a loss overrides all other investment considerations in importance. Nothing else even comes close. It is hard to overestimate just how unwilling people are to even consider the possibility of taking a loss. Let alone taking a loss.

I am constantly astounded at how really, really, risk-averse people are. As I have made clear my typical investment in my penny stocks is less than 1% of my investment capital and only a handful of my safest investments will ever receive 5% of my investment capital. It is my iron law to never put more than 5% in any investment. I am never blind to risk, but I have never refused to buy a stock if I really believed in it no matter how great the risk. That is the reason why a standard investment in one of my penny stocks is typically 1/10 of 1% to 1/4 of 1% of my portfolio's total value. Before you snort in contempt at this understand that depending on the price of the penny stock this usually equates to a position of around 20,000 shares or more on a chump change investment. Hence the title of my book.

I am constantly talking about investing in stocks. It is my favorite subject. Almost every morning finds me at Starbucks pontificating to a crowd of regulars on my favorite small-cap stocks. It is common for people to express great interest in these unknown small-caps until I suggest that they take a small position in these stocks. The look of total horror that appears on most of their faces is remarkable to see. Folks, we are not talking about betting the ranch here. We are talking about risking chump change. A quick look at the cars in the parking lot where I hang out would assure you that the regulars are not struggling to make the rent. I have seen Rolls Royces and Ferraris parked there on more than one occasion. Suppose the worst happens. They will simply take a tax loss on it and write it off their taxes. This is not the end of the world except in their risk adverse, fear crazed little minds. I just don't get it. The only thing that has ever scarred me is betting the ranch. This truly scares me. If I had been stupid enough to bet the ranch, I probably have gone bankrupt a half a dozen times in my career. Never, ever put more than 5% of your assets in any position unless it is a mutual fund and the riskier the position the smaller your investment should be.

Not so long ago I struck up a casual relationship with another Starbucks regular. He was fascinated by the sub $5.00 and $10.00 stocks that I was always recommending. I introduced him to my current pet stock of the month so to speak which was then selling at just over $2 a share. He asked me if I thought he should take a position in this intriguing $2 stock that I was expounding on. I told him that based on the Jaguar sports car that he had in the parking lot which had cost him $110,000 it could be a splendid speculation provided he did not put more than 1% of his investment capital into the position and was willing to hold the position for at least two years.

A few months after he bought the stock it took a sudden drop to around a $1.20. My friend was not amused, to say the least, about the drop. From the way he was acting my first thought was that this moron had bet the ranch on the stock instead of the maximum 1% position that I had recommended. He then assured me that he had put only about 1/2 of 1% of his investment capital in the stock. I then informed him that in that case he had little to worry about and that I was going to add to my position in the stock because it was now a screaming bargain. I wish you could have seen the look on his face. His eyeballs were virtually rolling around in their sockets. He was staring at me as if it had just dawned on him that I was a raving lunatic. He quickly left. Several months then passed before I saw him again. By this time the stock had risen to $3.00 a share. I brought up our mutual investment in our now successful stock. His only response was a pained look on his face. I quickly dropped the subject. It was clear to me that he had probably called up his broker and had sold the stock while he was still in the parking lot after our last conversation. After all, why waste your money when you think you are following the advice of a raving lunatic?

No one likes losing money but the refusal to take any financial risks at all can have enormous consequences. There are vast numbers of people who doom themselves to a career of working at a fast food joint after they turn 65 because the miserable returns they have earned on their safe investments have never kept up with the rate of inflation let alone exceeded it. If you think you are going to get rich by getting a 2% or 3% return in a savings account or a CD be my guest. The brutal reality is If we are being honest is that it is appallingly rare for any government guaranteed investment or savings account to earn a positive rate of return after inflation and taxes have been taken into account. The ugly truth is that people who insist on investing only in sure things receive a rate of return that is so pitiful that they cripple their chances of ever getting ahead but they would rather die than admit it. For reasons that I have never been able to understand these people are quite proud of the fact that they have never taken a risk. Having dispensed with these pathetic losers, we can now consider the next category of investors.

The second class of investors are investors who are emotionally capable of accepting the fact that if they don't want to be working at a fast food joint after they turn 65 then there is no choice but to invest in investments that have risk but earn you a real return. The crisis that will determine their success or failure as investors rests largely with how they react when they have a "paper loss." It is impossible to overestimate the importance of paper losses in the minds of investors.

Paper losses is a subject that I keep coming back to again and again because it is so critical in investor success or failure. To reiterate, a paper loss is a loss that would occur on an investment that you are holding at a loss if you sold it at today's price.

It is dogma today in the trend chasing community that dominates the stock market like a Frankenstein monster that all paper losses are in fact real losses. The superior investor is that courageous investor who heroically recognizes that paper losses and real losses are the same thing and proves his heroism by immediately selling all his losing 10% positions and thereby turns his paper losses into real losses. In this community selling your losers and thus turning your paper losses into real losses is regarded as proof that you have what it takes to be a real investor.

I have spent five decades proving that these people are wrong. I have made a career out of turning paper losses into profits. It isn't hard. As I have previously stated it is the case far more often than people are willing to believe that the only thing you have to do is to wait 6-12 months. It is astounding how often waiting six months will turn that 10% or 15% loss into a profit. These geniuses will tell you that this can never happen because all stocks that fall more than 10% are destined to go to zero. Nothing can shake them from this insane belief. Including the fact that many of them have a list of stocks that they have sold at a loss that is longer than their arm. The majority of these stocks would be in the profit column today if they only had the courage of their convictions and stuck to their guns. It gets far, far worse. My ultimate crime is that I routinely increase my position in stocks that I am holding at a loss by averaging down. Another unforgivable crime according to Wall Street which insists that you must never add to a losing position. You only add to winning positions. I beg to differ. I know what these stocks are worth. I have spent decades analyzing stocks. In other words, I make money by losing money. The biggest profits I make tend to be stocks that I have increased my position in after they tanked. The trend chasers who dominate today's markets are adamant in their belief that adding to a losing position is suicidal. Then again, if you mindlessly buy stocks about which you know nothing solely because they are going up. You face a crisis when they go down. Don't you? This incidentally is the stock and trade of the trend chasing community. The ugly truth is that they do not have an opinion that is worth a dam about the true worth of the stocks that they are buying and selling. John Wayne summed it up nicely:

"Life is tough, but it is even tougher when you are stupid."

Getting Killed in Momentum Growth Stocks

If the stock market has an eternal myth it is that the way to get rich quick in the market is by buying momentum growth stocks. It all seems so plausible. Except for the curious and always denied fact that you keep getting your head handed to you on a silver platter every time you invest in these whiplash babies. Let me explain what a momentum stock is. It is a growth stock on steroids. Investors have always been dazzled by these momentum plays because their skyrocketing stock price always seems to promise quick riches.

The trend line for most momentum investors is both short and ugly. I would estimate that most momentum investors have a career that does not exceed two to four years. Those who survive learn to change their investment strategy to a more balanced approach.

The first thing that the newbie momentum stock investor quickly learns is that the corrections on the super stocks that he thinks are going to make him rich are horrific. After getting killed a few times, a wise old hand introduces him to the charms of the stop-loss order. Which I have already referred to. The newbie is ecstatic as he discovers that he can pick a price point that is, say, 5% or 10% below the current stock price for a period of up to 60 days and if the stock hits that price point his stock will automatically be sold even if he is hunting tigers in India.

I keep returning to this investment tool because it is so critical in today's investment world that there is no alternative but to fully explore its massive consequences.

The newbie is ecstatic. How long has this racket been going on? This is the answer to his prayers. The grim reality is that this is like progressing from marijuana to heroin. The stop loss-order is almost always set at one of three price points. It is set at either 5%, 7.5% or 10% below the current market price. The most common price point by a country mile is 10% below the current market price. A price point of 5% or 7.5% below the market results in your being stopped out of your trade every time you turn around. This is regarded as being intolerable by most investors. After getting blown out of your position five or six times and then watch your stock quickly recover to its former value most bag holders wise up and graduate to the standard 10% decline stock loss order.

There is a theoretical problem with the stop-loss order which most users never discover. The problem is that they become an addictive crutch and slowly destroy the judgment of the investor.

Let's now take a look at the two alternatives that the momentum stock investor has available to him. After all, why klutz around with mere growth stocks when you can get rich quicker with momentum stocks? We can quickly dismiss the now allegedly discredited buy-and-hold strategy. Or so it is now widely assumed. Now that we have the powerful stop loss-order in our toolbox. Several years ago, I took a look at the recent five-year performance of $10,000 invested in what was then some of the most highly regarded super growth stocks. During that time period the S&P 500 barely budged. While this list is somewhat dated the concept that I am trying to point out remains valid and hasn't changed.

Amazon = $24,100

Apple = $102,400

Google = $55,200

Hewlett Packard = $25,300

Oracle = $22,300

Research In Motion = $37,500

S&P 500 Index = About break even

One thing that is immediately apparent is that these super stocks delivered the goods in comparison to the break-even performance of the S&P 500 Index. Other ex-super stocks did not live up to their reputation. Such as Cisco, Intel and Dell and are not included in the above list.

Bear in mind however, that this performance was only available to the now despised buy and hold investor. The $64,000 question is, what would our shrewd, super sophisticated, trend chaser with his vaunted 10% stop-loss discipline achieve?

In the five years studied Amazon had 14 corrections of 10% or more. Six of these corrections were of 10% plus, five corrections of 20% plus, two corrections of 30% plus and one very ugly correction of greater than 40%.

Apple also had 14 corrections of 10% or more. It had 8 corrections of 10% plus, four corrections of 20% plus and three brutal corrections of 40% plus.

Google had 15 corrections of 10% or more: Eleven corrections of 10% plus, two corrections of 20% plus, one correction of 30% plus and one brutal correction of 40% plus.

Hewlett Packard is our star performer. It had only seven corrections of 10% or more: Five corrections of 10% plus and two corrections of 20% plus.

Oracle had twelve corrections of 10% or more: Nine corrections of 10% plus and three corrections of 20% plus.

Research In Motion is a busted higher flyer of particular interest. Not so long ago Fortune Magazine ranked it as number one in the magazine's top 100 list of the fastest growing stocks over the last three year period. Not just in the United States but in the world. Now it is almost totally forgotten. This proven ex-super stock had nine corrections of 10% or more: Three corrections of 10% plus and four corrections of 20% plus, one correction of 30% plus and one horrific correction of 70% plus.

How about that, pick the number one stock and get a 70% loss for your effort! Actually, it was 72%, but who is counting? Of course, this was quickly followed by a powerful snap back rally of 65%.

The S&P 500 Index did the job it was created for. It had only four corrections greater than 10% plus. Two corrections of 10% plus, one loss of 20% plus and one loss of 30% plus. I think it is safe to say that these brutal corrections on proven, high performing, super stocks are not exactly what the typical growth investor was expecting. Remember these stocks were selected because they had gone up from two to ten times in value during the five year period. Compared to break-even on the S&P 500 Index. These stocks are the holy grail of growth investing. They are proven winners.

According to growth investor stock lore, the wise investors in these stocks should have been rewarded with fabulous profits. The buy-and-hold investor who stuck it through to the end was indeed rewarded handsomely. I have grave doubts, however, about the performance of the dancing slick investor with his classic 5-10% stop-loss orders and his easy assumption that there is some rational means of timing stock swings. In more than fifty years of looking, I never found any method that outperformed a coin toss over the long run in timing stock swings. Though I grant you that there are many methods that appear to work in the short term. Until they blow up in your face.

I submit to you that the typical dancing slick, growth investor with his stop-loss orders does not get rich in momentum stocks. Slow and steady wins the race. His typical experience is to repeatedly get blown out of his positions every time his stop-loss orders are triggered. Taking a 10% loss each time. In due course his mangled body is dragged out of the arena's blood stained floor feet first. The shell-shocked victim of one too many 10% losses. After all, how many 10% losses can you take? Think about it!

At least that was the experience of my early years as an investor until I wised up and became a long term investor. The astute reader will recall that there is one strategy that does work. Buy and hold. The problem with buying and holding momentum growth stocks is that you need nerves of steel. I doubt if more than 20% of the investing public has what it takes to make this strategy work in this arena with its horrific plunges. Or as they slyly say in the trade it is too volatile. Volatile is the new, popular code word that today is much in vogue which was invented a few years ago. Volatility means that stocks or the market is declining in value. Its current popularity is due to the fact that it is being employed as a euphemism to hide this fact. After all it would not do to admit that when these super growth stocks crash the damage is horrific. The life expectancy of momentum players investing in growth stocks and super growth stocks is probably two to four years before they are wiped out because of the truly brutal corrections that are the norm in this blood splattered arena.

There is of course an alternative strategy. The strategy which I advocate. Conviction investing with a long term bias in contrarian-value plays. In more than five decades of speculating in the blood splattered battleground that they call a stock market it is the only strategy that I have ever found that works consistently. But only if you hold on for at least two years. Nothing really works consistently if your holding period is less than two years and I have the battle scars to prove it.

The essence of this strategy is that you are buying stocks that are residing in the gutter. That are current bargains based on today's price and not on tomorrow's price. When you buy growth, you are paying a premium, often a vast premium over its current intrinsic value. A premium that is based on the always-chancy assumption that the current superior growth rate will be maintained. A growth rate that in many cases must be maintained for five or ten years to justify today's extraordinary prices.

The sad truth of the matter is that trend chasers don't do nearly as well as advertised. The reason is that the market refuses to cooperate with their stop-loss orders. You see, "the boys," who are the real pros on Wall Street, have a pretty good idea of where the stop-loss orders have been placed. Their favorite game is to blow the trend chasers out of their positions by hammering the stock down 15-20%. This false decline that they have created blows all the trend chasers out of the water. As soon as they stop selling the stock returns to its old trend line this time with "the boys" on board. This tactic is called "painting the tape." The trend chasers just never wise up. It is truly remarkable how many times they can have their head handed to them on a silver platter and they can never figure it out. Then again most of them are punch drunk from all the 10% losses they are being hit with.

The Case Against Professional Money Managers — Why They Are Ruining You

Not so long ago there was a golden age of professional money managers, when giants like Sir John Templeton and Peter Lynch delivered superior performance year after year in investors' IRA's and other retirement accounts. The great Warren Buffet is in a different category because he ran his own shop and other investors were welcome to come on board as long as they followed his terms. There would be no tap dancing in and out of stocks in his world. This golden age is now over with and the question is, why?

Investors today are paying for performances that they are no longer receiving. You are essentially paying these people to duplicate the market averages. The overwhelming majority of investors today would be better off if they fired their professional money managers and invested in an S&P 500 index fund. The question that has to be answered is, what went wrong? Why are today's money managers unable to duplicate the superior market beating performance that they used to be able to produce in the past?

The short answer is that the rules have been changed. Not so long ago it was possible for superior money managers like Templeton and Lynch to march to their own drummer. They were given the freedom to make long-term bets and pick out of favor and non-index stocks. They were given the time to invest in contrarian plays that might not work out for a year or two. They could actually invest real capital in small-cap and micro-cap stocks instead of the Godzilla nifty-fifty blue-chip stocks that dominate the market today. The horror of it!

In those days the way it worked is that managers would be given X million dollars and two or three years to show what they could do. This gave superior managers the time and freedom to buy out of favor stocks that they believed in. In today's brave new world, the report card comes due every 90 days, Not in two or three years. The benchmark that your performance is always measured against is the S&P 500. Failure to duplicate or exceed that average for even a couple of quarters can end your career. The only way a manager can be certain that he will duplicate or exceed the S&P 500 is to own the iron core of that index, the nifty-fifty. These fifty blue-chip giants, IBM, Apple and Microsoft etc. that dominate the S&P 500 to an extent that is seldom understood. He then cleverly encases the nifty-fifty hard core with a careful collection of promising non-index stocks that are designed to give the impression that he is clued in and is not operating a closet index fund. The weighting, however, is such that the fund will always mimic the index. In other words, truly superior performance is highly unlikely unless the non-index stocks put in a spectacular performance.

It is important to understand why money managers do not want to be tagged with the notorious closet index fund label. By custom index fund managers earn much lower fees than active managers who are trying to outperform the market because operating an index fund is far easier and cheaper than managing an active fund.

Strangely enough it is hard to blame these frauds. You can almost say that investors today deserve to be cheated. Imagine a superior money manager today with the courage to invest in non-index stocks and to take long-term bets. Who then delivers a return 20% better than the index for four straight years and on the fifth year delivers a performance 15% worse than the index? That superior manger would be thrown out into the street like a dog. While the outfit that he worked for would be crushed as ungrateful investors hysterically stampede for the exits. While Joe-average manager who always buys index stocks and has performed in line with the index because he owns the index will never be fired.

In other words, there is a reverse Darwinism in effect. Our current system guarantees mediocrity. It is hard for people to believe this but many of Wall Street's most highly regarded old line established firms gave up trying to outperform the market years ago. They are of course very careful not to let their investors know this. They realize that careful nifty-fifty selection gives them a real shot at being in the top 20% category at least two years out of every five. A fact that they will then trumpet to the skies.

Only a small Wall Street elite today makes any real attempt to beat the averages. There was an old saying on the street during IBM's glory days that no one was ever fired for recommending IBM no matter how badly it performed. But god help you if you recommended a small-cap that bombed. They would never forget or forgive that blunder.

As for the rest of Wall Street their only concern is to make sure that no one ever figures out that they are operating a closet index fund and to guarantee that they never do worse than the averages. Which they know only too well could be a career ending experience. In other words, superior performance is only rewarded temporarily.

While inferior performance is punished permanently.

Perhaps the classic recent case of this phenomenon is the career of

Bill Miller of Legg Mason's Mutual Funds. Bill Miller's Value Trust Fund, which he ran, beat the market for 15 straight years. A winning streak that has never been beaten. Then in the bear market years of 2008 and 2009 he performed badly doing considerably worse than the S&P 500 benchmark.

This was totally to be expected. No one can outperform the indexes forever. Investors that he had made rich abandoned him like rats abandoning a sinking ship. His 15 years of superior performance meant nothing to them. I hope these ungrateful swine lost their shirts in their new investments. Bill Miller walked away from the fund. Then after the crash years he took command of Legg Mason's Opportunity Trust Fund and is now back on top with one of Wall Street's top performing funds.

It is indeed fortunate that I was never a money manager. With my contempt for nifty-fifty stocks and my passion for small-cap and micro-cap stocks my career would not have lasted very long. As my friends can attest, I am always recommending small-cap stocks and I have firsthand knowledge of the not "IBM" effect. My father was a classic example. He had total recall of every losing investment I ever got him into. Ask him about my winners and he would scratch his head. Trust me, I produced far more winners than losers for my father.

This blind spot is typical not just for my father but of all investors. I call it the rule of three. Once I recommend three losers to anyone, they suddenly develop amnesia about all the winners I produced for them. It matters not a whit how many winners I gave them. If I gave them fifty winners and three losers, they will only remember the three losers. After all, the fifty winners were because of their superior stock picking skills but the losers were all my fault. But I digress. The issue is, what is today's investor to do? The first thing you can do is to dump your "alleged" professional money manager. You can get the same performance simply by buying an S&P index fund. The Vanguard Total Stock Market Fund would be an excellent choice. The next thing to understand is that you can't get superior performance by investing in nifty-fifty dinosaurs. Their day is done. Their superior performance is in the past and contrary to popular opinion it cannot be in the future. How much bigger can a dinosaur get?

In the bear market year of 2009, I was listening to a finance program on the radio as I was driving my car. An investor called the program bemoaning the recent rotten performance of General Electric. In those years General Electric was still regarded as a blue chip. He could not understand how such a splendid company could be doing so poorly. "The answer, you fool," I screamed at the radio, "is because General Electric is the economy and the economy struggles to grow at 3% a year."

I clearly remember when GE sold in the $60s. Then for an eternity it sold in the $30s. I thought that there was an unwritten law that said that GE would always sell in the $30s. I was wrong. In January 2009 mighty GE crashed to $5.72 a share. Recently this badly tarnished blue chip was dumped from the Dow Jones Industrial average. I often wonder what the vast army of GE stockholders were thinking on that day. I am sure that many of them bought the stock when it was selling in the $30s,$40s and $50s thinking that they were giving up superior performance but that they were getting that highly touted blue chip security. It turns out that they received neither the blue chip security that they had opted for or the superior performance that they could have received by investing in the non-blue chip sector. The quest for certainty in the investment world is the ultimate sucker game. It doesn't exist. What does exist is risk-reward tradeoffs.

You could of course enter my world. The world of the small-cap and the micro-cap investor where superior performance is truly possible. A world where you can make a fortune on a chump-change investment. I wrote my first book because I wanted the average Joe to know that there is an affordable alternative to buying blue-chip stocks which then typically sold in the $40-65 a share range. Today the average S&P 500 stock sells for over $115 a share. A price that renders many blue-chip stocks unaffordable. Most Americans of moderate income cannot afford to diversify broadly enough and buy blue chip stocks in sufficient amounts to ever make them financially secure.

In my book I put in my email address so that readers could contact me. The first reader to contact me was Bill from Buffalo. Bill told me that he was forty years old and had a wife and two children. He owned a modest home and had $8,000 in life savings. He told me that he knew what his future was, and it terrified him. He was going to be working at a fast food place when he was 69 years old. That was his future. He didn't have enough time left or money to move the needle and enable him to retire at 65 if he bought blue chip stocks. Which he knew could be expected to go up 10% a year. This is a common occurrence. It is what started my career as a small-cap investor.

My way provided him with an answer. He could easily afford to buy my low priced, unknown stocks in amounts big enough to make a difference. In addition, my small-cap and micro-cap unknown stocks had better growth prospects than the old, tired blue-chip dinosaurs that everyone else is forever touting. I don't do guarantees. If you want guarantees go to the bank and see if you can get rich on the miserable 1-2% interest returns that they offer. I keep mentioning this return because it is important and bears repeating. The sad truth of the matter is that most people never earn a return greater than 3% a year in their lives. At 2% interest compounded it takes 36 years for your money to double. At 3% interest compounded it takes 24 years for your money to double and then they wonder why they can't get ahead. I would burn my money in the backyard before I would accept this return. Over a human lifetime the risk-adverse investor pays an enormous price for his refusal to accept any risk.

If you want opportunities, I am your man. I offer my readers a chance to make serious money on a chump-change investment.

The Case Against Day Trading

The life of a day trader seldom exceeds four years. Vast numbers of them depart the scene every year having been whipsawed one time too many. The strange thing is that for every departure there is a replacement and sometimes two replacements or more. The lure of easy money is strong indeed. The overwhelming majority of these rookies are going to be blown out of the water in short order.

This essay is not addressed to this soon to be roadkill. It is addressed to the old-timer day traders who remember the glory days of the 90s when they had the world by the tail with a downhill drag and who can't figure out what went wrong.

The first thing to understand is the wisdom of the old Wall Street saying. "To never confuse genius with a bull market." A bull market makes everyone look good except for the shorts. I am afraid however, that the problem goes much deeper than that. The simple truth of the matter is that there isn't much to learn about day trading. Everyone tries very hard to conceal this basic fact by using a great deal of mumbo-jumbo theories and strategies. These strategies can be broken down into two major subsets. These two strategies are technical analysis and "chasing the news" or if you are kinder than I am "trading the news." In Wall Street lingo this is called being a "Noise Trader" which if you think about it is an excellent term. Mostly it is a concoction of both fortified with the latest, hot black-box algorithm formula. Which is usually but not always technical in nature that some propeller-head is promoting.

My dark suspicion is that the brutally short-term charts that you are compelled to use in day trading are so short as to render technical analysis worthless. Almost every day some system seller comes up with a new system, which he claims has been back-tested to biblical times with great results. The back-testing that these system sellers are using is a joke. And for a very good reason. The truth is so ugly that no one wants to believe it.

All day trading systems without exception break down if you keep going back in time with your analysis. Every system in the end, no matter how well it works in the short term, is over the long term no better than a coin toss. The promoter will only back-test his hot, new system to the point where it starts to break down. He will then promote his system as having been back-tested from that point forward. He will of course remain silent about the problems that were encountered if you go back in time any farther. When this system breaks down, he will have a hot, new, improved system to sell to the same jerks who bought the original system.

After all, the prior system did work well enough in the beginning! There are promoters who make a career of selling new systems after their old systems break down. What makes all this work of course is that everyone wants desperately to believe that there are systems that work.

The real problem of course that everyone is so desperate to avoid is that the shorter the time period under consideration the more unpredictable and random market action becomes. As I have already stated I am a great believer in the Random Walk Thesis. Consider Powerhouse Industries the wonder stock of the day. It has a relative strength that will knock your eyeballs out. If your holding period is six months, the strong probability is that the stock will be up. Day traders don't care what the stock does six months from now. They need to know what the stock is going to do in the next hour or in the next five minutes.

In the time period they are forced to operate in the strongest momentum or relative strength is virtually worthless. Stock market action in periods this short is essentially random. It cannot be predicted. It is a coin toss.

There is not much to be said about chasing the news except that it seems to work less and less well all the time, as more and more idiots try to make this alleged strategy work. The strangest thing about chasing the news and being a noise trader is how anyone would be stupid enough to think that something this childish and stupid is going to make you money. Yet armies of day traders are trying to make a career out of buying every positive news report and selling every negative news report. One of the few absolute rules on Wall Street is that you can't make serious money by stampeding with the herd. How can you expect to get rich by doing what every Tom, Dick and Harry is doing? Just remember you are always stampeding behind Tom, Dick and Harry. It is pretty obvious when you stop to think about it that the herd is in front of you and not in back of you. I hope we all know that the more people that are employing a strategy the less well it works. Everyone in the world is trying to make this strategy work and therefore it cannot work.

If you expect me to reveal a day trading system that works, you are out of luck. In the 50 plus years that I have been hanging out in the blood splattered battleground that we call a stock market. I have never found a day trading system that works.

The only thing I have ever found that works is being a conviction contrarian. You must believe in your stock picks and hold on to them when they decline instead of hysterically dumping your picks at the first sign of trouble. Which is the exact opposite of what Tom, Dick and Harry instinctively want to do. I didn't say it was easy. I said it works.

A Contrarian's Viewpoint of Technical Analysis in Today's World

When I broke into the stock market in 1961 at the age of 19 if you wanted to learn technical analysis you were immediately pointed to Edwards & Magee's book, "Technical Analysis of Stock Trends" which was the bible of the industry from its first edition in 1948 until its last edition in the 1970s. Of course, technical analysis really got its formal start with the publication of the famous "Dow Theory" in a series of articles written by Charles Dow in the Wall Street Journal between 1900 and 1902.

However, until the 1970s technical analysis was frowned on by the street as being somewhat akin to astrology. It was not regarded as being respectable. Then for reasons that I don't pretend to understand it suddenly became very respectable. This respectability has come at a high cost. As a contrarian I regard today's popularity of technical analysis as a curse and not a blessing.

The founders of technical analysis regarded it as a tool for an elite minority in a world in which fundamental analysis reigned supreme. They regarded themselves as savvy predators who would hide in the weeds and knock off the big game fundamentalists as they came thundering by with their high powered technical rifles.

As many true Wall Street professionals are only too well aware of, the more popular a market indicator becomes the more useless it becomes as a profit making indicator as every Tom, Dick and Harry jumps on the hitherto successful indicator and beats it to death. To put it simply what everybody knows isn't worth knowing. It is what everybody doesn't know that is of decisive importance.

Regrettably, the current over popularity of technical analysis is not its only problem from the contrarian viewpoint. Other very ugly problems exist. The worst of these problems is today's overwhelming domination of moving average charts. This domination is very recent. The final edition of Edwards & Magee's book contained a remarkable 324 charts of which only 49 charts were moving average charts. These were stuck on at the end of the book as a sop to the ever growing power of the moving averages crowd. The earlier works contained far fewer moving average charts.

Technical analysis was regarded by the old masters as an art that had to be mastered. In those days before the triumph of moving averages swept everything before it, a technician was an expert in "pattern recognition analysis." He was someone who had a hard learned ability to analyze bullish or bearish chart patterns. Among the more common types of patterns that technicians had to be able to master were head and shoulders, tops and bottoms, W patterns, triangles, rectangles, wedges, fans and gaps.

The trouble with moving averages is that they are way too popular and even worse way too easy to analyze. Let's be honest! How much talent does it take to analyze a moving average chart? None! A drooling imbecile can glance at a moving average chart and instantly ascertain if the stock is above or below its 50 day or 200 day moving average. Which are by far the two most popular moving averages.

The triumph of technical analysis and moving averages has resulted in the worst of all worlds. A world in which everyone sees the same thing and what is truly ugly acts on it. If you are technician who uses moving averages today what is your edge? You are seeing what everyone and his brother are seeing.

The edge that the founders of technical analysis once had is now gone. Even worse there is reason to believe that technicians are now the prey of choice for a new group of predators who are hiding in the weeds and who's favorite big game animal is the technicians who are now kind enough to show the world their poker hand.

Or is it just my imagination that stocks after a breakout above their moving average are no longer advancing with the power and authority that they used to? Those long decisive runs which are the bread and butter of technical analysis seem to occur less and less often. Could the reason be unseen predators?

How difficult is it today for savvy predators with enough capital behind them to lie in wait until the final minutes of trading and then "paint the tape" with their concentrated action creating a false breakdown by driving the stock below its 50 day or 200 day moving average. Knowing full well that many technicians will fall into the trap like plump pigeons and hysterically sell their stock. After the trap is sprung of course the stock reverts back to its old mean.

Maybe you have noticed this pattern. I know I have, and it seems to be happening more and more frequently. What is to be done?

I have two answers and you are not going to like either of them.

As a contrarian I am obsessed with seeking out and finding valid metrics that are either ignored or unknown by the public. If you see what everyone else sees you have no edge. At all costs you must find an edge. You must find metrics or indicators that are valid and don't appear on everyone's radar scope.

My first suggestion is to return to the long discarded Point & Figure charts. I know what you are going to tell me. Point & Figure charts went out with the horse and buggy. They are way too simple. Why they don't even have Bollinger Bands or MACD. No serious technician would consider using something that pathetically simple in today's modern world.

Exactly! That's the whole point. I would like to remind the reader that technicians were using Point & Figure charts with some success for generations until moving averages swept away all the alternatives.

To the best of my knowledge the most recognized proponent of Point & Figure charts in recent times was Jim Dines of the highly regarded Dines Letter. Another proponent who used Point and Figure analysis on a fairly regular basis was Richard Russell's, Dow Theory Letter. This old World War II bomber veteran was the dean of investment letter writers for decades. He started writing his letter in 1958 and was still publishing it in 2015 when he died. He left behind a team that is carrying on his work. He published a book called "The Dow Theory Today" which I have never read.

If you thought my first suggestion was horrifying, you are going to love my last suggestion even less. As I am writing these words, I have a comical image of a hardcore technician blasting out of his chair in outrage and doing a triple somersault and bouncing on his head three times.

My last suggestion is that when a stock drops below its 200 day moving average it should be regarded as a bullish rather than a bearish event. There I said it.

Before going nuts I challenge the reader to pick at random a dozen 5-year, 200-day moving average charts and to see them for the very first time. What do you see? What you see is stocks endlessly oscillating above and below their 200-day moving average. Ask yourself a revolutionary question. Why isn't it better to buy a stock when its selling below its 200-day moving average rather than above its 200-day moving average. You do notice don't you, that stocks keep oscillating above and below their 200-day moving average?

I told you I was a contrarian. We are always told that we should buy low and sell high. Now is your chance.

The Case Against Stop Loss Orders

You are to be excused if you feel that I am beating the subject of stop loss orders to death, but the impact of stop loss orders is enormous and must be fully understood. Nothing is more devastating to today's investors than being "stopped out" of their stocks. Or as I fondly call it, being blown out of your position.

When I broke into the stock market only professionals used "stop loss orders." Today it has become the universal investor's crutch.

Upon learning about stop loss orders, Joe Investor is wildly enthusiastic. It sounds like the greatest thing since sliced bread. Joe is convinced that he is now running with the big boys and doing the smart, sophisticated thing. Not exactly. Quite the contrary. Joe has now put himself into the clutches of the "smart money boys," who are going to introduce Joe to Whipsaw City. Whipsaw City has many skyscrapers and the smart money is going to throw Joe and his compadres off of every one of them. The falls are brutal. In the end Joe will drag his broken, mangled body out of Whipsaw City and never be heard from again. He will have been broken by stop loss order hell.

What does the smart money know? It knows that 5-10% below the current market price of every popular "nifty-fifty" stock there is a mass of stop loss time bombs waiting to go off. The only thing they need to do to ignite this mass of stop loss time bombs is to simply drive the stock down 10-15% and all the stop loss bombs will be ignited. This eliminates the day traders and momentum players who will be automatically blown out of their positions. These are the stock market's eternal "weak sisters" whose only conviction is that all falling stocks are going to zero and they must therefore sell them at once.

This is why if you stick around for very long you will notice that stocks rarely fall just 5-10%. They almost always fall 10-15% to ensure that they have blown all the weak sisters out of their position. Having blown the weak sisters out of their position, the smart money or the boys are now ready for part two of operation whipsaw. The comeback.

I know. I know. The term sounds sexist, but it is a technical Wall Street term.

The smart money knows that the stock is now in the "strong hands" of the conviction investor. The conviction investor is the investor who actually knows why he owns the stock and can be counted on not to freak out if his stock falls 10% or 15%. Isn't that a refreshing change? The smart money knows better than to tangle with these hard cases. And why bother. They know that a strong floor now exists below the stock. The existence of a strong floor means it is now safe for the boys to buy back the stock. The smart money now begins to buy back the stock that they have previously shorted with a vengeance. Six months later the stock is selling at 30% higher than Joe's purchase price. Joe should have a 30% profit on his stock. Instead depending on his bailout point he has a loss usually in the 5-10% range and if he is a real hard case 15%. Welcome to Whipsaw City Joe.

I think that you can see that the conviction and contrarian investor has a considerable but by no means total immunity to the games that the short sellers love to play.

For this reason, the boys to the extent possible try to ignore value plays and value players. Why mess with these hard cases when easier prey is available? Their main interest is in investors whose iron conviction is that the only reason to buy a stock is that it is going up and that you should immediately sell any stock that falls 10% or more because it is going to zero. When you stop to think about it that is not a very impressive strategy is it? When choosing between shorting value plays on one side of the equation and highflyers and momentum plays on the other side of the equation the solution is obvious. Hit the momentum plays and highflyers which are the darlings of the trend chasers. The boys then ask themselves the next question. Why should we take a momentum stock down only 10-15% when we know we can take it down 50%? After all the clowns who own these stocks are day traders and momentum players who have no independent opinion whatsoever as to the true worth of their stocks. The only reason that they bought these stocks are because they were going up These eternal trend chasers are not only clueless but living in total darkness as well. As a result, once the boys break the bullish psychosis of these momentum stocks they implode. All too often it appears that there really is no bottom to these stocks once their momentum is broken as all too many trend chasers can sadly attest to.

In my early years as an investor I got nailed several times in these momentum plays, and I now refuse to have anything to do with them. I concluded that they are simply too dangerous.

There is one stop loss order however that I heartily approve of. It's called the Trailing Stop Loss Order. Let's say that you have made a killing on XYZ. It now looks expensive and you are considering selling it. In a case like this instead of trying to guess if the stock is going to go higher which is always a mistake. The best strategy is to let the market decide when you should sell. Place a 60 day trailing stop loss order about $2 or $3 below the current stock price and see what happens. If the stock falls and hits your stop loss order the stock will automatically be sold and you will have your answer. If, however, the stock rises you slowly raise the stop loss order to compensate for the rise. Every time the stock rises $3 a share you raise your stop loss order by $3 a share until you are stopped out of the stock. It is imperative that we hold our guessing to an absolute minimum. The more you guess, the more you lose. The beauty of this strategy is that you are not guessing. You are letting the market decide.

Wall Street's Strange Contempt
for High Dividend Stocks

One of Wall Street's favorite myths is that only idiots buy high dividend paying stocks. The myth goes like this. The smart money boys realize that a stock's dividend is unsustainable and will probably be cut. Being wise, they do the smart thing and start to sell the stock. As the stock falls the dividend yield that the stock pays rise inversely and the stock that is paying say a dollar a share in dividends can have its yield rise from say 3% to 6%. As the stock falls and the dividend yield that the stock is paying rises the fools rush in and buy the stock because they are too stupid to realize that the dividend is unsustainable and will be cut. In due course, the stock dividend is cut, and the suckers get crushed.

This is one of Wall Street's most cherished myths. The truth is somewhat different. If the only stocks that you will consider investing in are popular blue chip stocks like the 30 Dow stocks, the "nifty-fifty" and the S&P 500, then the myth is usually correct. As a practical matter, these are the only stocks that Wall Street cares about. The reality is that there are about 16,000 stocks in all if you count all the listed and unlisted stocks in the country. But only the 500 stocks of the S&P 500 ever appear on Wall Street's radar scope. It is in this vast ignored and unfollowed market of the small-cap universe that the real stock market opportunities are to be found.

Actually, I am being way too generous. Wall Street obsesses endlessly over the "nifty-fifty" and cares amazingly little about the remaining 450 stocks until one of them breaks into the "nifty-fifty" group. That is why you hear the pundits rhapsodizing endlessly over the same 50 stocks and rarely mention any other stock. Wall Street does not exist to serve the individual investor. It exists to serve the institutional investors. Institutional investors can only consider investing in stocks with huge capitalizations. They insist on being able to move massively in and out of stocks without influencing the price. As a practical matter, this is only possible with the top 500 or at most 1,000 stocks with the biggest capitalization. In this world, the world of the dinosaurs the myth of the dangerous high dividend paying stocks works about as advertised. If you leave this world behind and enter the unknown and unreported world of small-caps and micro-cap stocks, where I hang out, the reality changes drastically. Wall Street is blind to this reality change. When you stop to think about it the stock market is divided into two worlds. The world of big-cap blue chip stocks and everything else.

Big-cap stocks are beloved by both institutional investors and individual investors. I have already told you why they are beloved by institutional investors. The case for individual investors is somewhat different. To be perfectly blunt about it they are too stupid to even know that there is a stock universe outside of the S&P 500 stocks. Besides, they are afraid of investing in stocks that they have never heard of before. I know this from vast personal experience. I am constantly recommending small-cap stocks that no one has ever heard of. I wish you could see the look of horror on their faces at the mere thought of buying these unheard of stocks.

As a result of the concentrated buying power of both institutions and individuals, big-cap blue chips are constantly being bid up by unrelenting bidding wars. As a general principal, it can be said that small-cap and micro-cap stocks tend to sell at greater discounts to their intrinsic value than blue chips and to pay higher dividend yields than big-cap stocks of equal quality. In other words, the fact that a small-cap stock is paying a 6% dividend does not necessarily mean that the dividend is about to be cut. In fact, in the world of the small-cap it is amazing how often you can find sound high dividend stocks that pay dividends as high as the 10% to 12% range and whose dividends are more than covered by their earnings. I know because I own these stocks. These stocks all too often go begging because the instinctive reaction of investors when they see mid cap and small-cap stocks that pay dividends of 6% or higher is to automatically assume that the dividend cannot be sustained and will be cut. It is amazing how unknown these high dividend paying sectors are. The following are the sectors where reliable 6% plus dividend paying stocks can be found. REITS (Real Estate Investment Trusts), Mortgage REITS and BDCs (Business Development Companies) and some carefully selected closed-end mutual funds are also of interest.

REITS are the most commonly known. They usually specialize in owning blue chip commercial properties such as shopping centers, office buildings and residential apartment complexes. Dividends of 6% and more are common for the smaller non S&P 500 REITS but not for the large S&P 500 REITS. This is the usual big cap curse.

REITS have a less well known younger brother, the Mortgage REITS which own real estate mortgages instead of commercial real estate. Mortgage REITS and BDCs are pretty much the unchallenged kings of high dividend paying stocks.

I will have much more to say about REITS, Mortgage REITS and

BDCs later on when I discuss these high dividend kings in detail.

The most important rule in finance is the Rule of 72. This rule enables you to quickly ascertain how many years it will take your investment to double. You simply divide the dividend rate or the interest rate that you are receiving from your investment into 72 and that will tell you how many years it will take your investment to double. The thing to understand is that high dividends are not an abnormality for these nearly unknown high dividend paying sectors. They are the norm. They are legally structured so as to enable them to pay unusually high dividends. The power of compounding is a force to be reckoned with in these stocks. It is astonishing how contemptuous Wall Street is of high dividend paying stocks. Contemplate the power of compounding in the below table.

The Power of Compounding Years to Double

1% = 72 years	9% = 8 years
2% = 36 years	10% =7 years
3% = 24 years	11% = 6.5 years
4% = 18 years	12% = 6 years
5% = 14 years	13% = 5.5 years
6% = 12 years	14% = 5 years
7% =10 years	15% = 4.8 years
8% = 9 years	16% = 4.5 years

Hunting Tigers in India

In 1948 two shrewd investors purchased the same stock at the same price and for the same reason. The next day one of the investors departed for a long awaited hunting trip to India. While the great white hunter was bagging tigers in India his stock underwent a vicious 30% decline. The reason for the decline has been lost in the mists of time, but some people say it was because a stock analyst had issued a negative report on the stock.

The investor who had remained in New York panicked and sold his stock for a 30% loss. Of course, he managed to sell his stock at the exact bottom which is the typical experience for panic sellers. Meanwhile, the great white hunter in India knew nothing about this; he was having a ball blazing away at tigers. He was using a machine gun (in those days they paid you a bounty for killing tigers). The bounty on tigers was so much more profitable when you are using a machine gun.

More than three months later the great white hunter and his tiger skins returned to New York, and he discovered that his stock had by this time reversed and was now up 50%. Contemplate this well, the only distinction between these two shrewd investors is that one sold because he knew he had a loss and the other didn't sell because he didn't know that he had a loss.

The point of this fable is that selling stocks that you have researched and believe in just because they have fallen in price is a fool's game. This fable is played out countless times every day in the stock market by people who have researched and believe in their stocks. Until, that is, they decline 5% or 10%. Then they panic. They are blown out of their position and take a loss on a stock that they should have held on to.

Six months later the stock that they sold for a 10% loss is now selling for a 30% profit. They will never learn. They will keep taking losses on stocks that they were right about until they can't take the pain any longer. They will then drag their mangled bodies out of the Wall Street jungle never to be heard of again.

Wall Street is a place where you can be right and lose your shirt if you are not willing to stick to your guns. Second guessing your stock picks doesn't work any better than changing your answer in school tests did. Most investors are not willing to stick to their guns. They are losers who could be winners if they only believed in themselves.

Welcome to the New Serengeti

I hope that you have found the articles that you have just read thought provoking even if they were somewhat repetitive. My hope is that these articles will give you new insights on how markets and investors are acting today.

The largest concentration of herd animals by far that exists in the world today are the vast herds of grazing animals on the Serengeti Plains of Africa. They all employ the same proven anti-predator strategy. All members of the herd are regarded as sentries. If any member of the herd stampedes, they all stampede. It would be counterproductive for the herd members to stand around and try to discern if their first bolting herd member has made an error in judgment and there was no dangerous predator threatening the herd. This behavior results in a vast number of unnecessary, false stampedes but in Darwinian terms it is a sound strategy.

As I have tried to point out what Wall Street and today's investors have done is brought this Serengeti strategy to the stock market. At no prior time in the history of the stock market have such vast numbers of investors been so willing to dump the stocks that they own and theoretically must have believed in. For no reason other than at this moment but only at this moment the herd is stampeding out of your stock. After all, if you did not believe in the stock why would you own it?

What works for the herd animals on the Serengeti Plains does not work for investors. Every stampede out of a stock that you own and believe in is costly. It is not difficult to be right at least 60% of the time if you will take the time to research your picks carefully, are broadly diversified and you are willing to believe in your stock picks even when they go down. I repeat once you start second guessing your stock picks you are finished.

You will second guess yourself into the poor house.

The Guessathon

Today the vast mass of non-institutional investors can be broadly divided into two groups. The first group of investors are mutual fund owners who typically own their stocks in an IRA or 401(k) and rarely look at their account. In other words, they are long term investors. This is a sound basis for investing and I endorse it. I always tell newbies the they should start their investment career in a broad based mutual fund or ETF like my favorite the Vanguard S&P 500 Fund and always reinvest the dividends. As time progresses and they find what the military calls a target of opportunity they can then sell from 1% to 5% of their mutual fund and invest it in individual stocks that they like and which they believe can outperform the market. Over a period of time using this strategy they can acquire an interesting portfolio of stocks. Today the vast mass of non-institutional investors who own individual stocks rather than mutual funds in an IRA account or 401(k) want to see if they can do better than average and do a little speculating.

Obviously, I don't have a problem with this. I have been a riverboat gambler for more than 50 years. I have made a successful career out of investing in the highest risk stocks that exist, the worst of the worst, penny stocks, micro-caps and small-caps. In my world you can only continue to speculate if you are successful. They drag losers out of the blood stained arena floor where I have been hanging out for 57 years feet first. The type of stuff I own most people would not touch with a 10 foot pole. The ultimate proof that I have been successful at this is that I am writing this book instead of sleeping under a bridge. As any player can tell you if you are not winning the stock market will wipe you out. The typical momentum speculator is wiped out in about two to four years.

I have enormous problems with the assumptions and behavior of today's speculators. It simply cannot be overstated that short term buying and selling is a fool's game. Over the short term stock prices are a "random walk" which cannot be predicted but over the long term stock prices oscillate around their intrinsic value. The decisive mover of stock prices over the short term is not their intrinsic value but the news of the day and how stocks react to the news of the day and this cannot be predicted with any consistency. The vast mass of today's speculators refuse to believe this and are engaged in a perpetual guessathon in which they attempt to outguess their compadres in how the market will react to today's news. In such a guessing contest the intrinsic value of the stock counts for little. It is how the market reacts to the news that is decisive. Let me repeat, this guessa-thon is a loser's game.

The formula for successful speculating is ludicrously simple: Never put more than 5% in any position and hold your positions for at least two years and ignore price declines as long as you believe in the stock. Oh, I almost forgot. I routinely add to a great many but not all of my losing positions. The idea of adding to a losing position fills today's speculators with horror for the simple reason that they don't have any faith in their stock picks when the market contradicts them. However, it must be admitted that the typical investor today knows shockingly little about the stocks that he buys except for the price he bought the stock at and the price it is selling for today. I however am an old school conviction investor. If one of my positions falls by 10-20% I will carefully research the stock again. If I decide I was wrong about the stock I will sell it but if I feel that I was right about the stock I will hold on to it and if I feel that the stock is now greatly underpriced, I will add to my position. If my first buy was $10,000, then my second buy will be $5,000 and my third buy will be $2,500. It is not unusual for me to add to a losing position two or three times if I think I am right. Now from time to time this strategy blows up in my face but the rewards when I am right are spectacular. As I have stated nobody is right in this racket more than 80% of the time.

This is one of my pet peeves, selling stocks that you believe in just because they have declined 5% or 10%. All stocks decline. Repeat all stocks decline. If you don't believe this check out 5,000 or 10,000 stocks charts that should be enough. The popular belief of the trend chasing school which I despise is that there are two types of stocks. Stocks that are going up and therefor are destined to rise forever and stocks that are going down and are therefore destined to fall to zero. What the charts will tell you is that stocks oscillate in value and that trend reversals are as common as dirt in the real world. In the idiot world of the trend chasers trend reversals do not occur.

The guessathon boys' other stupidity is that you must follow a sell discipline. They are adamant about this. The notion that you should believe in your stock picks is an alien concept to them. I have stated elsewhere that their usual sell disciple has three must sell bail out points, 5% down, 7.5% down and the holy of holies 10% down and I am out. The glaring problem with this strategy in today's market is that over the short term the trend chasers reign supreme and their rein has consequences. Today it is common for stocks to fall 5% or 10% over nothing more substantial than a single overhyped news report that in the old days would have been totally ignored as today's trend chasers hysterically stampede out of the stock.

In such a world the trend chaser is forever locking in 5% and 10% losses on positions that if they just held on to them another six months would have been profitable. They take great pride in what they regard as their courageous behavior. They operate on a see loss, take loss quickly, quickly basis. Lock in those losses before they get away from you. Why if you waited another six months the trade might have been profitable. We can't have this happening, now can we? The typical trend chaser has a very short career.

While the trend chasers don't see it that way our hero's career while it lasted consisted of little more than locking in 5% and 10% losses until they dragged him out of the blood stained arena floor feet first. The real tragedy is that if you reviewed all of his trades, I would bet that 60-70% of his losing trades would have been profitable if he had just held on to them for another 6-12 months.

The Rules for Successful Investing

1) Never buy a stock that you haven't researched and don't believe in. If you buy stocks that you don't believe in, you will find a way to lose money on the stock even if the stock is a sound pick. I have proven this to myself on several occasions when I have lost money on stocks that were basically sound picks because I did not believe in the stocks.

2) I repeat, diversification is mandatory. Under no circumstances whatsoever is it permissible to invest more than 5% of your investment capital in any stock pick unless it is a mutual fund or ETF. No one can make sound decisions when they are betting the ranch. For stocks selling under a dollar a share the maximum acceptable position is 1% of your investment capital. My typical penny stock position is 1/10 of 1% to 1/4 of 1%. If you ever invest more than 1% of your investment capital in any penny stock, you are on your own. This is not as restrictive as it sounds. if you have a decent sized portfolio 1% or less could easily enable you to purchase 5,000 to 10,000 shares of a penny stock.

3) Long term holding periods are mandatory. No holding period of less than two years works with any consistency. The ideal holding period is two to five years. You will discover that your biggest profits will occur in the fourth and fifth year that you are holding a stock. if a stock is working for me, I will hold it forever. Forever works, ask Warren Buffet. What doesn't work is tap dancing in and out of stocks every three to six months. This is a strategy will put you in the poor house.

Under the Looking Glass

Crestmont Research is a fine firm that does excellent stock market research. Sometime after 2012 they did an excellent analysis of stock market results in the 111 years from 1901 to 2012. The results are fascinating. In this 111 year period the market was up 71 years and down only 40 years. The 40 down years can be subdivided into just four categories as follows:

One year declines occurred 17 times. Two year declines occurred 5 times. Three year declines occurred 3 times. Four year declines occurred only once.

You are probably wondering when the four year decline occurred. it occurred during the brutal depression period of 1929 to 1933. Folks, this is important information. Only four times in the 111 year period that was analyzed has a stock market decline lasted more than two years. This information is worth its weight in gold to investors. It enables us to strategically plan our buying and selling strategies during bear market periods. It means that the second year of any bear market is a terrific period for stock accumulation and that we can buy with a confidence that would otherwise be lacking.

Another report of enormous significance to investors that I rely heavily on was done by Ibbotson Associates, another fine, highly regarded research firm. They did a report titled Timeframe and Losses (1926-2008). The figures that are in their study are for the S&P 500 and include dividends and contain all possible 1,3,5 and 10 year holding periods in the 83 year period from 1926-2008. They also did a study of small-caps which closely tracked the results from the S&P 500. By year 10 in the study the small-caps loss percentage was only 3% instead of 4% for the S&P 500:

One year holding period percentages that resulted in losses was 29%.

Loss percentage in three year holding periods was 16%.

Loss percentage in five year holding periods was 14%.

Loss percentage in ten year holding periods was 4%.

Study these figures folks. They are the keys to the kingdom. By the year five there is only a 14% chance that a stock held in your portfolio will be in a loss position.

You can see how deadly today's short-term obsession with locking in Mickey Mouse profits at the first sign of a decline and the crazed insistence on turning paper losses into real losses with devastating, totally unnecessary results.

Another superb study has been done by the Boston based research firm Dalbar. In its well-regarded 2011 study it noted that in the 20 year period between December 1990 and December 2010 the market returned an average annual gain of 9.1%. But investors earned an annual return of just 3.8% during this period. A comparable study put out by J.P. Morgan that I will show you later on reports even worse results. A horrific 2.6% return. I am sure that by now this study's results are not surprising to you and you can pinpoint the reason for this stunning underperformance.

It is the mindless, hysterical selling of stocks at the first sign of weakness in a desperate attempt by investors to protect their miserable profits, if any, by an investor class that is obsessed with the price of stocks and which knows little or nothing about the intrinsic value of the stocks that they own. Indeed, many of them would deny that stocks have any intrinsic value at all other than the current market price. After all the only thing worth knowing about a stock is whether it is going up or down. Everything else is irrelevant.

The Ghost of Jesse Livermore

Jesse Livermore has almost been forgotten today except by the professional stock market community and historians. His influence on today's stock market, however, is both gigantic and unacknowledged. His ghost towers over the stock market like a colossus. Millions of investors slavishly follow his dictates without having ever heard of the man. In his heyday in the 1920s, he was the most admired and feared speculator on Wall Street. Jesse Livermore is still regarded today by many market historians as the greatest pure speculator of all time. This is a conclusion which I share. Bear in mind that Warren Buffet is an investor and not a speculator.

Jesse was born in 1877 and started his career by making a killing on every type of stock and commodity that traded. He made his first fortune in 1906 by shorting the Union Pacific railroad, which had been severely damaged by the San Francisco earthquake.

He became famous as the boy plunger of Wall Street. Despite his great talent he declared bankruptcy four times in his long career. After each bankruptcy, fellow investors confident of his superb trading skills would grub stake him for his new assaults on the market. His greatest triumph came in 1929 when his bear market raids, in the minds of many, broke the stock market and made him a fortune of $100 million, a staggering sum in those days. But, after that it was all downhill. In 1940 his once great fortune gone and facing a fifth bankruptcy, he blew his brains out in an exclusive New York nightclub.

In his suicide letter he stated that he no longer knew what worked. Since his death no momentum player or trend chaser has arrived to pick up his mantle because the short term stock trading thesis that he championed in the long run takes back from you all that it has given you and more. The buy-and-hold thesis is championed by Warren Buffett, who has famously claimed that his favorite holding period is forever and is the true basis of all lasting stock market success. This simple strategy is ignored when it is not held in scorn.

What dominates is chasing whatever is going up with your finger on the sell button. Tap dancing in and out of stocks and nailing down pitifully small profits because the stocks that they buy stop going up as soon as they buy them as if by magic. Chronic selling for miserable profits and repeatedly converting paper losses into real losses when they should have stuck to their guns is what most of today's alleged investors practice in spite of what they may claim. Above all else they are trend chasers. They don't have the guts to hold on to a stock that is falling in value. The real money has always been made by buying at the bottom and not at the top. Just try to get them to buy a stock that has fallen in value say 20%, 40% or 60% which is where the real money is made. They will stare at you as if you have lost your mind. As a small-cap and micro-cap investor I have vast personal experience in this matter. I am constantly recommending these stocks which I own to friends and acquaintances. The look of horror on their faces has to be seen to be believed.

It is common today for many investors to claim that they are long term investors. Their notion of long term investing is measured in months not in years and vanishes totally at the first sign of a decline. As they are happy to proclaim, no one ever went broke taking profits. That miserable 15% paper profit that has now fallen to 9% must be protected at all costs. The grim reality is that people go broke all the time when they settle for profits like this. Everyone in is going to have losses. If you accept Mickey Mouse profits on your winning trades, then your losing trades will bury your winning trades. This will sound very familiar to many of my readers.

Warren Buffet is in all probability the most famous investor of all time. He is an object of veneration and awe. Everyone wants Warren Buffet performance results, but no one seems to want to invest like Warren does. As I have stated Buffet has always championed long term, fundamentalist, intrinsic value investing. You are the owner of a business. The stock certificate is proof of ownership. It is not a lottery ticket. The fact that the stock temporarily declines in price is not proof that you are wrong. It is a wonderful buying opportunity to add to your position and lower the average cost of your position. Try selling that concept today! Today the average investor is renting the stock. Not owning it. Rarely does he regard himself as the owner of a business. After all, thinking of yourself as the owner of a business might interfere with your desire to make a quick killing and bail out of this sucker. Then where would you be? The average investor today holds his stock for six months. The shortest holding period in history. The average holding period going as far back as we have records for used to be measured in years and not in months.

Fundamental stock research. What for? There is only one reason to buy a stock. You buy it because it is going up. If it is not going up it doesn't matter what its fundamental value is. All this sounds very impressive until you try putting these highly popular theories into practice and then you make the painful discovery that they are not worth a damn and don't work. After all, if they worked Jesse never would have blown his brains out in that fancy New York nightclub. Jesse Livermore rules Wall Street, not Warren. Not one investor in a thousand has ever heard of him. Yet today as never before in its history the investment community follows his strategies flawlessly.

Jesse's how-to book, which I own and which outlines his strategies, is called "Reminiscences of a Stock Market Operator." It was ghost-written by Edwin Lefevre in 1923. Since that date it has sold and sold and sold. I don't think it has ever been out of print. It is among the top three investment books of all time. Jesse would feel right at home in today's market with its massive use of stop-loss orders, which he popularized, and his dictum of selling any position that fell 10%. The short-term holding periods, constantly tap dancing in and out of stocks to capture small gains. It is all pure Jesse. My major criticism with the work is that he keeps contradicting himself, but the book is well worth the read.

The other two top sellers are "How I Made Two Million Dollars in the Stock Market" and "The Intelligent Investor." Jesse's 1923 book currently ranks 1,762 on Amazon.com and has 212 customer reviews. Now unless you are an author that is not going to sound very impressive to you. Trust me it is very impressive. The royalties that book has earned since it was published must be astounding. Amazon.com tracks about six million books. As hard as this is to believe it is a triumph to rank in the top 100,000. If you rank 100,000 you are selling about 35-45 books a month. If your royalty is, say, $4.00, you are making about $1,800-$2,000 a year. If you rank 5,000 you are selling about 450 to 600 books a month or say about $24,000-$28,000 a year. At 2,000 and above you can easily afford an around the world cruise every year. My goal is to beat Jesse Livermore's sales. Up to now I haven't come close. I would estimate that today only about 20% of investors are conviction investors who actually know why they bought the stocks that they own and are willing to hang on to their position if the stocks that they own fall by more than 10%. The remaining 80% are trend chasers of various sorts. Their only conviction is that if any stock that they own falls by more than 5% or 10% that stock is history. They are primarily day traders, momentum players and technicians who in my opinion have become too powerful for their own good and for the market's long term health.

Determining Intrinsic or Market Value

We have now finished our analysis of how investors and markets work in today's world. Let's get into investing. I prefer the term intrinsic value over market value because I think that market value and market price are terms that people tend to confuse and all too often regard as the same thing. Which they are not. The term intrinsic value makes it crystal clear that it is not the same thing as the stock's current market price. The first thing I want you to do is to engage you in a cost free experiment. I want you to spend a week in your spare time making up a list of the 15 companies whose products or services you most admire. You will use no other investing criteria other than your high regard for their products or services.

No more than two of your picks can be restaurants. If I didn't put that restriction in there most readers would end up picking at least a half dozen restaurants. I might add that I gave up investing in restaurants. For some reason I have never done well in restaurants. After you have made your 15 picks carefully tape them to your bathroom mirror with their current prices and the current prices of the Dow Jones and the S&P 500 and leave them there for five years. Once a year you can take a look at how well your picks are performing. I think you will be astonished at how well your picks perform by the fourth and fifth year using no other criteria whatsoever. You will discover that buy and hold works.

The time has come to ask the $64,000 question: How do you discover a bargain and even more important how do you know that a stock that you are considering really is a bargain? Just what does a bargain look like? Let me start off by recommending my broker Charles Schwab. They have just lowered their $4.95 charge for a trade to zero. You can't beat that, and they have a superb research section. Just click on the research section and type in the stock symbol that you are researching, and you will receive a highly comprehensive page of data on the stock. Among the data presented is a stock chart going back as far as five years showing all its quarterly earnings and dividends, its PE ratio, dividend yield, shares issued, capitalization etc. etc.

But the real prize is the ratios page. This is a gold mine of data. I would never consider buying a stock without checking it out on the ratios page. Just click on the section that says ratios and the ratios page will appear and you will be presented with 50 indicators of value and for many of these indicators you will also be able to compare the stock that you are researching with the average S&P 500 stock for that value indicator. You can also select five comparable stocks and see how they measure up against your subject stock. For instance, CBL has a Price/Sales ratio of 0.81 and for the average S&P 500 stock the Price/Sales ratio is 2.20. In other words, CBL is selling for 81% of its annual sales for the year and the average S&P 500 stock is selling for 2.2 times its annual sales for the year. Let's now analyze the indicators of value that I place my primary emphasis on.

At the top of the ratios page you will see the old reliable, the Price/ Earnings ratio which has been everyone's favorite indicator of value for as long as I have been an investor. The historic average for the PE Ratio is 15. As this is being written the average PE Ratio for the S&P 500 is a dangerously high 22. We are in an extended bull market as this is being written and this ratio is way too high for my comfort. The PE Ratio should be 15 or less. PE Ratios below 10 are in bargain territory.

The next important indicator is Price/Sales Ratio. In this indicator you divide the company's market capitalization by its annual sales or revenue. It is currently 2.2 for the S&P. In other words, the current S&P 500 stock is selling at 2.2 times its annual sales. Anything below 1.5 is okay Anything below 1 is a bargain.

Next is Price/Tangible Book Value - as I have explained elsewhere this indicator has rightly largely replaced the Price/Book Value indicator which included non-tangible assets like good will. This valuation ratio expresses the price of the stock compared to its hard, tangible book value. The tangible book value is the total book value of the stock less the value of any intangible assets. The current S&P number is 3.3 which is high.

The number should be 2.0 or less. Anything below 1.5 is a bargain.

Next is Price/Cashflow - many shrewd investors today regard this indicator as being superior to the PE Ratio. Cash Flow is the after tax profit plus non-cash charges such as depreciation. In other words, it tells you how much cash is in the till. Price/Cash Flow is determined by dividing the market capitalization by the company's operating cash flow. A ratio of 8 or less is good.

Return on Equity - this indicator informs you of how many dollars of profit a company generates for each dollar of shareholder equity. This popular indicator has to be included even though I think it is overrated because it can be manipulated. Let me give you an example of what I mean. Let's say a company decides to buy back 10% of its outstanding stock. Because your equity has just been reduced by 10%, your Return on Equity receives an unjustified bump. Or let's say you have decided to buy out an intriguing corporation and to finance the purchase you increase your outstanding stock by 10%. Your Return on Equity now takes an unjustified hit in my opinion. I think Return on Assets is a more reliable figure, but it is almost never used because this figure is almost always lower than the return on equity figure would be. The current Return on Equity for the S&P 500 is +13%.

Return on Assets - this indicator informs you of how profitable your company is relative to your total assets. It is calculated by dividing the company's annual earnings by its total assets and like Return on Equity it is displayed as a percentage and this figure is almost always well below 10%

Dividend Yield - is another biggie, the current S&P 500 return is a pathetic 2% which is another reason why I currently do not own and rarely ever own any S&P 500 stocks. In my income plays I insist on a dividend yield of at least 6%.

Gross Profit Margin - we now come to the four profitability factors, Gross Profit Margin, Operating Profit Margin, Net Profit Margin and Cash Flow Margin. Of these four profit indicators, the least reliable is the Gross Profit Margin which is prone to accounting manipulation. Be especially cautious when the Gross Profit Margin is strongly positive and the other three profit indicators are negative. The classic example of this is Tesla which currently has a Gross Profit Margin of +16.13% but has an Operating Profit Margin of -15.81%, a Net Profit Margin of -15.28% and a Cash Flow Margin of -2.77%. It goes without saying that all four profitability factors should be positive. Typically, the Gross Profit number will be the highest percentage figure, the Operating Profit Margin will be a somewhat smaller figure and the Net Profit Margin figure will be the smallest percentage. The Gross Profit Margin is what is left of annual revenues after accounting for cost of goods sold. It is calculated by dividing gross profits by revenues. Anything above 15% is okay and anything above 30% is good.

Operating Profit Margin - is a measure of profitability. It calculates how much of each revenue dollar is left over after both the cost of goods sold and operating expenses are considered. Anything above 15% is okay and anything above 30% is good.

Net Profit Margin - the percentage of revenue remaining after all operating expenses, interest, taxes and preferred stock dividends but not common stock dividends have been deducted from total annual revenue.

Cash Flow Margin - is a measure of how much profit you are generating from your operations from every dollar in sales.

Current Ratio - is a liquidity ratio that measures a company's ability to pay all short term and long term debt obligations that are due in the current year. The current ratio should be at least 1.0 or the company is deficient in earnings to pay its debts due in the current year.

Quick Ratio - is also a liquidity ratio it measures how well the company can meet its short term annual debts. The Quick Ratio should be at least 1.0.

Total Debt/Capitalization - is a measure of a company's financial leverage. It is calculated by dividing the company's total debt by its total capital. Obviously the lower the percentage the better. Typically, REITS will have the highest debt to capital ratio that can be considered safe because their debt is secured by real estate. For REITS anything as high as in the 70%-80% area is okay but higher than that should be a cause for concern. But for all non REIT investments you would like it below 70% and the lower the better. Anything below 33% is good.

That ends the value indicators that I pay special attention to with one exception: The Interest Coverage Ratio on money they have borrowed. For some strange reason Charles Schwab doesn't include this figure. Historically banks required that the annual profits or earnings of the commercial enterprises that they were lending money to be at least at least 25% greater than their annual interest payments to be considered credit worthy. I follow that rule in my own investing. I like to see at least a 1.25 -1.50 ICR. As a general principal however an interest coverage ratio of 2 or greater is regarded as being secure. You can find this important figure from FINRA which is described below.

Investors that don't have access to good data can rely on FINRA (the Financial Industry Regulatory Authority), a non-profit organization authorized by Congress to protect investors from unethical stockbrokers and dealers. Just go to FINRA's market data section and type in the stock symbol and then select research and then select the key ratios section. In the key ratios section, you will find the Interest Coverage Ratio.

The annual 5 year high & low range is another important indicator when it is in the bargain range. For many years I was little more than a PE ratio investor. That was where I hung my hat. As the 90s began there was so much accounting shenanigans going on with earnings that I could no longer rely on them. I then placed primary emphasis on the P/S,P/CF and the P/B indicators because they were not being tampered with. The annual five year high and low for a stock are hugely important. You can almost earn a living in the stock market by doing nothing more than buying stocks when they are approaching their five year low and selling them when they approach their five year high.

Investors have always placed great importance in the operating income ratio and the net profit margin indicators. It is beyond dispute that they are important and should be positive. Almost all highflyers have exceptionally high operating income ratios and net profit margins just before they crash. Beware of exceptional high operating income ratios and net profit margins in highflyers. They cannot be sustained over the long term.

An important point to realize is that what will have the worst operating income ratios and net profit margins you ever saw are the gutter stocks that will make you serious money. Stocks that have been crushed and pulverized so badly that you will need a ladder to take you to the bottom of the crater where they reside. If these stocks have cratered badly watch closely for the operating income ratio and net profit margin to turn positive. Even a small increase as long as it is a plus figure in both these indicators can be decisive.

Now in the world of below $10.00 stocks it will be common for some of the above indicators not to be applicable because the stocks will not be earning a profit or in the case of penny stocks, they may have neither revenues nor profits. When we enter the world of penny mining stocks it is not unusual at all for there to be no recurring annual revenue at all except for the issuance of new stock every few years but the stocks may have enormous untapped wealth in their mining claims.

Dealing With Losses

This is as good a place as any to discuss the important matter of how you should deal with your losses. I have already commented on these factors before, but I am going to deal with these factors more fully here. You will find that most of your stock market losses will be caused by the four factors listed below.

Missed Earnings Estimates - Analysts' Downgrades - Dividend Cuts - Macroeconomic Factors

The first three factors - missed earnings estimates, dividend cuts and analysts' downgrades - all operate in the same manner. These three factors follow the same formula. At the end of the trading day after the market closes the missed earnings estimates, dividend cuts and analysts' down grades are reported to the press. Panic! Fear! Hysterics! Sell that dog before it goes to zero. Excuse me! You bought that dog, didn't you? Maybe you should do something truly remarkable. Maybe instead of hysterically selling the stock you should have faith in your own judgment and stick to your guns. I am of course assuming that you followed the rules. You researched the stock before you bought it and not after you bought it and that your position in the stock does not exceed 5% of your investment capital and that the riskier the stock is the less of your capital you have invested in it.

Now here is how it works. The bad news is typically reported to the press after trading closes usually between 4:00 PM and 6:00 PM. The day traders and momentum players on hearing the news go berserk. They all hysterically place orders to sell this dog at the market as soon as trading opens the next day. They are all united in their idiotic belief that they are pulling a fast one by selling their stock at the opening and that they are beating the stupids to the punch. They could not be more wrong. They are the stupids. Every imbecile on the planet who owns the stock and who has decided to sell the stock based on the news report has made the same decision. They all think they are pulling a fast one and will be beating everyone else to the punch by selling at the market as soon as trading begins. When trading begins the next morning, an avalanche of sell orders hits the stock. All of these sell-at-the-market orders were placed in the same basket that night and are sold at the opening bell in one hideous mass. The low for the day is almost always established in the first two frenzied hours of trading. During the first two trading hours it would not be at all unusual for the stock to fall by 15% to 30% below yesterday's close and horrific falls of more than 30% are becoming more and more common as the dominance of the trend chasers grows. As I have commented elsewhere in this work the trend chasers always invest with one foot out the door. They are ready to bolt out of any stock they own any time a negative news report hits the wires. By noon the selling pressure has usually started to exhaust itself and the jerks have taken a brutal and unnecessary loss. At around 3:30 in the afternoon in the last half hour of trading the smart money boys show up to cash in on the stupidity of the hysterical sellers and pick up the bargains. The post panic rally period often begins at 3:30 that day. No matter how bad the news has been the typical stock can expect to rally for one or two weeks off of the panic low. It is not unusual for the stock to recover between 50%-75% off of the panic lows in this period. If you are a wise investor who happens to own the stock and you have decided that your stock must be sold, then for god's sake do not put in an order to sell the stock the next morning. Wait for the post recovery rally to kick in. The best time to sell is in the first or second week after the bad news has been reported. Don't ever sell your stock before 3:30 in the afternoon on the date that the bad news was reported.

You have just seen the stupid money in action. Now let's see how the smart money operates. The smart money reads the reports that night and decides whether the stock is worth a play. If they decide that the stock is worth a play here is how they will play it. XYZ closed last night at say $30. They know that in the first two frenzied hours of trading the stock could easily fall 15% to 30% or more. Let's say that they decide that a price that is 35% below yesterday's close meets their requirements. They then place not a market order but a limit order to purchase the stock if it falls to $19.50. If the stock does not fall to $19.50 by the end of the trading day, they can just kill the order. If the stock does fall to $19.50 the order will be executed and they will have picked up a screaming bargain at $19.50. Indeed, if the hysteria is great enough, they might even pick up the stock at below $19.50. Let's say that the stupids have totally lost it and the market is engulfed in a tidal wave of selling. The opening trade in that case could be at $18.00 a share and your order would then be executed not at $19.50 a share but at $18.00 a share

Remember the critical distinction between a market order and a limit order. A market order will be executed at whatever the market price is when the order hits the market. A limit order is only executed if the price of the stock falls to the price you have specified in your order. If you are buying and selling using market orders stop this insanity at once. You are killing yourself. Stop using market orders and start using stop loss orders and limit orders. I use stop loss orders and limit orders on 99% of my transactions.

One of my favorite investing techniques is to use 60 day limit orders to steal the stock.

In fact, as I have just stated 99% of all my buy orders are 60 day limit orders. When I find a stock that I wish to purchase I try to steal the stock. First, I check out its trading pattern and based on its trading pattern I will place my buy order 5-15% below the current price or even lower if it is being hammered. If a stock starts running away from me, I will make adjustments. It is not unusual for me to roll over my 60 day orders two or three times before it is executed. Using this strategy, it is not unusual for me to have purchased a stock that I like at the lowest price it has sold for in the last in the last 3,6 or 9 months. It is called stealing the stock. Make this your practice and you will not regret it. I typically have about 10 or 15, 60 day limit orders in effect on stocks that I am trying to steal. Now occasionally the stock will run away from you and you will end up paying more for the stock than if you had put in an order to buy at the market. Get over it! As I have already stated in the stock market nothing works more than 80% of the time.

The third great cause of stock market losses is due to macroeconomic factors that affect the market as a whole or a sector of the market rather than a specific stock and the action has a waterfall effect that may continue for months. The two greatest macroeconomic factors are recessions and rising interest rates. I don't think I have to explain to my readers why recessions have a dire effect on the stock market. But the number two factor, interest rates, have a much greater impact than the typical investor realizes. Rising interest rates have a brutal impact on both the stock market and the bond market because they raise the cost of capital for both markets. While both markets are hammered by rising interest rates the bond market is hurt worse by rising rates than the stock market. I really don't have any useful advice to give on these broad based macroeconomic factors. Macroeconomic factors based on a subset of the market or a stock market sector are another story. In recent years it has become more and more common to buy and sell sectors of the stock market rather than individual stocks as the indexing craze has grown more and more popular. Sector ETF's based on the 10 S&P 500 market sectors which has recently been raise to 11 sectors with the long delayed inclusion of the REIT sector enjoys great popularity today as a convenient method of buying out of favor sectors. Today's popular notion that all stocks within a designated sector are clones of one another is a concept that I have zero tolerance for. In every sector there is the good, the bad and the ugly and arbitrarily dumping them all in the same basket as is commonly done today and pretending that because you have dumped them all in the same basket makes them all clones is both stupid and wrong. A great example of this in which I am personally involved in and have commented about elsewhere in this book are the Mall REITS or real estate investment trusts. For several years now the stock market has decided that real estate malls are all dinosaurs that are doomed to become extinct because of the rising power of Amazon and the internet. It has therefore dumped all the Mall REITS in the same basket and has been relentlessly selling all of them without any regard for their true value. I think we can all agree that this country is over-malled and that many malls in this country face rough sledding but to proclaim that they are all doomed and all clones of each other is nonsense. Of course, today's market no longer seems capable of making these distinctions. Distinctions that hitherto to the present day it never had any difficulty in making. This of course a classic macroeconomic play. I will have more to say about Mall REITS later on.

The Importance of Capitalization

Capitalization is of enormous importance in the small-cap world. Capitalization is computed by multiplying the number of shares that have been issued times the share price. For instance, if XYZ has 5,000,000 share issued and the shares are selling at $5.00 a share you then multiply the 5,000,000 shares times $5.00 a share and the capitalization of the company is $25 million. In other words, you can buy the whole company lock, stock and barrel for $25 million.

The smaller the capitalization the easier it is for the company's stock to double. This reality seldom dawns on the average investor whose analysis of a small-cap stock seldom encompasses the stock's capitalization and the outstanding shares issued.

As an example, imagine that on the same day five investors each decided to purchase 20,000 shares in XYZ a small-cap with a stock float of only 10 million shares, and they were stupid enough to put in market orders instead of limit orders. The stock would explode. Indeed, if a sizable percentage of the stock was closely held by insiders which is typically the case for corporations of this size their buying power alone could cause the stock to double. It is not unusual for micro-caps in this category to have days in which the entire number of shares traded is 20,000 shares or less.

As I have stated I am a great believer in placing 60 day limit orders in for the stocks that I am trying to steal. I mean buy. When the limit order expires, I simply renew it for another 60 days. In all categories I currently have 15 limit orders which is typical. Why buy a stock when you can steal it?

The key criteria you should look at when you are analyzing small-cap capitalization is the number of shares issued since this is the only component of capitalization that is fixed. The other component, the share price, fluctuates every day. Below is an analysis of the desirability of different categories of stock issuance in the small-cap and micro-cap universe for stocks selling below $5.00 a share:

> 0 - 25 million shares issued - Outstanding
> 25 - 50 million shares issued - Excellent
> 50 - 150 million shares issued - OK
> 150 - 300 million shares issued - Mediocre
> Above 300 million shares - Not good

Now I hope it is self-evident that the larger a firm's operations are the larger the acceptable stock float. It is common for large corporations to have hundreds of millions of shares issued. Remember the above figures are for small-cap and micro-cap stocks selling for under $5.00 a share.

Now from time to time you are going to discover a small-cap stock that has great prospects but has a stock float that exceeds these guidelines. I happen to own such stocks and from time to time they will come through for me but in all honesty, I would be better off if I stuck to the above guidelines.

When you own a micro-cap with more than 300 million shares issued there is a very high probability that you will be introduced to reverse stock split hell. Small-caps with a stock float this big have enormous problems. The stock will react poorly even to persistent good news and it will react very badly to even modestly unfavorable news. The stock float is simply too big for the corporation. The solution to this vexing problem is a reverse stock split. The typical reverse stock split is either 5:1 or 10:1 if the stock is selling below $1.00 share. In other words, a 1,000 share holding will be reduced to either 200 shares or 100 shares. As I have explained earlier, I am a great fan of reverse stock splits in cases such as this. Mathematically speaking after the reverse stock split every shareholder owns the same percentage of the corporation as he did before the reverse stock split. Regrettably investors don't see it that way. They feel that they have been robbed. Yesterday they owned 1,000 of XYZ. Today they own 100 or 200 shares. Where is the sell button on my computer? The result is that after the announcement of every reverse stock split the stock typically gets hammered for two or three weeks until these disgruntled investors depart the scene. Once they depart the situation changes radically. As I have already stressed earlier reverse stock splits are always a long term plus. On a 5:1 reverse stock split an intolerable 300 million stock float is reduced to a comfortable 60 million shares. On a 10:1 reverse stock split the float is reduced to only 30 million shares. XYZ is back in business.

From the Big Board to the Pink Sheets

Before we go any further in our analysis of the explosive world of small-cap stocks, we have to know who the players are. Historically stock trading in America was divided into three categories. At the top was the New York Stock Exchange (NYSE) founded in 1792. It is the world's largest stock exchange and is often referred to as the big board. Historically the NYSE specialized in large, well established blue chip corporations.

More junior, small-cap corporations that could not meet the big board requirements were listed on the American Stock Exchange (AMEX) which had existed in the 19th century but was only formalized in 1908. It was originally called the Curb because initially trading was done outdoors on the curb. In 1921 it finally moved into its own building. In 2008 it merged with the NYSE. Post-merger the junior stocks that used to be listed on the Amex are now listed on the NYSE American Market.

Nasdaq (over-the-counter market)- has historically been the stock market's bottom of the barrel catch all category of stocks that could not meet the listing requirements of either the NYSE or the more junior AMEX. Historically it meant that OTC stocks were not traded on any organized exchange or centralized trading location. They traded as their initials imply over-the-counter between broker-dealers who chose to become a market maker in certain OTC stocks that they selected.

The historic relationship between the NYSE, AMEX and the OTC changed forever on January 1971 when the OTC gave birth to the NASDAQ. The world's first electronic stock exchange. The creation of the NASDAQ called into question the need for centralized exchanges like the NYSE and the AMEX. Since its birth it has evolved into the world's second largest stock exchange.

In 1985 the OTC Markets Group, the umbrella agency for the OTC complex, created the NASDAQ 100. This creation of the 100 largest capitalization NASDAQ stocks enabled the old OTC now rebranded as the NASDAQ to compete head to head with the NYSE for the first time in history. It was now engaged for the first time across the entire panorama of the stock market, from blue chips to pink sheets.

Let's now take a look at how the different operating segments of the rebranded roughly 10,000 stocks in the OTC universe operates in today's world. OTC Markets Group - is the umbrella headquarters group for the entire OTC complex except for the OTCBB which is a broker- dealer operation.

OTCQX - This tier consists of multinational stocks and higher quality domestic stocks. Stocks in this tier are not required to register or report to the SEC but are required to report financial data to the umbrella OTC Markets Group. The stocks in this group must be operating companies, not shells and cannot be in bankruptcy. Additional oversight is provided by the requirement for all stocks in this tier to be sponsored by approved third party investment banks or law firms.

OTCQB - corporations in this tier must be registered and reporting to the SEC. There are no other reporting or minimum standards to be met.

OTCBB - or the OTC Bulletin Board as it is usually called has requirements that are almost identical to the OTCQB, but it does not come under the auspices of the OTC Markets Group. It operates under the auspices of broker-dealer market makers. Stocks in this category must fully report to and meet all the requirements of the SEC but have no other minimum requirements to meet such as a minimum share price. It is often the case that stocks in this category are dually listed on both the OTCBB and on the OTCQB.

OTC PINK SHEETS - is an open marketplace. Corporations in this tier are not registered with the SEC and do not report to the SEC or to the OTC umbrella Market Group. At their discretion corporations in this tier may have limited or no public disclosure. The first pink sheets were published in 1913. They were called pink sheets because they were originally printed on pink paper. Pink sheets are correctly regarded as being the riskiest type of stock investment.

The pink sheets have a well-deserved reputation for being the land of "pump and dump schemes." The words pump and dump are pretty descriptive of the process. The way it usually works is that a shell corporation is created which possesses no real assets. An expensive promotion campaign is launched of mailings and on the internet. This is the pump. This is where you appear on the scene.

The way it usually works is that you receive an unsolicited and very professional looking report in the mail from a stock analyst who you have never heard of before promoting a pink sheet penny stock that neither you or anyone else has ever heard of because it was just created. This is truly your lucky day you can get in on the ground floor and make a killing on this undiscovered jewel. I don't have to tell you how it ends. The dump occurs when the promoters feel they have corralled the maximum number of victims feasible. We all know how this ends. They then dump their holdings and vanish. Leaving you holding the empty bag.

From this point onward on our pump and dump victim regards all stocks that are selling in the below $5.00 a share region as being worthless pump and dump schemes and nothing will convince him otherwise. After all he is now an expert.

I share the well-founded distrust of pink sheets and with one glaring exception which I will detail in this work have never invested in them. Very early on in my investment career as I have related elsewhere, I discovered by accident an alternative universe of penny stocks that are virtually free of the pump and dump shenanigans that so scar the pink sheets. It lies hiding in plain sight north of the border in Canada's two stock exchanges. The TSX or Toronto Stock Exchange and the TSX Venture Exchange. Unlike the pink sheets these are enterprises that command respect.

TMX Group is the umbrella group for Canada's two largest stock exchanges. TSX is the senior exchange and is the largest stock exchange in Canada and is the third largest stock exchange in North America. It ranks seventh in the world by market capitalization and is the world leader in mining and oil & gas companies. More mining and oil & gas companies are listed on the TSX and its junior arm the Venture Exchange than on any other exchange in the world. It currently has over 1500 listings.

TSX Venture - is the junior subsidiary of the TSX. the Venture Exchange trades junior stocks that do not qualify for a listing on the senior exchange. It currently has over 2,300 listings.

It is important here to note that numbers of stock listed on all exchanges can fluctuate by a considerable number every year as new stocks are listed on the exchanges or are merged out of existence or delisted. Many junior companies that are listed on the TSX and the junior TSX Venture Exchange will also have a secondary listing on the NYSE American Market which is as you now know the successor to the old American Stock Exchange but usually trades under a different symbol. This creates endless confusion with investors. The all-important take home from this is that as long as the stock is listed on a Canadian exchange it doesn't matter where you purchase it or what the symbol is. You are protected by the comprehensive listing requirements of the exchanges and the Canadian stock regulators who for my money do a far better job of protecting investors than the SEC does. In other words, the Canadian exchanges with their thousands of stocks selling for under $5.00 a share are the perfect alternative to pink sheet hell. While the exchanges are not perfect in protecting investors, it is very rare for a con artist or pump and dump scheme to get by them. It is truly amazing how few Americans ever consider investing in Canadian stocks.

It is time to give you some insight on how I discovered the world of penny mining stocks. The Northern Miner has been publishing its weekly newspaper since 1915 and is generally regarded as the Wall Street Journal of the global mining industry. It graciously consented to publish my review of my first book "Forty Years A Speculator." Here is my article as it appeared in the Northern Miner.

Forty Years a Speculator—
Northern Miner Book Review

Picture this; the year is 1968, the place is the USS Little Rock, the flagship of the mighty U.S. sixth fleet. We were sailing in the Mediterranean Sea off the west coast of Italy somewhere between Rome and Naples. I was waiting to go on watch in the CIC (the Combat Information Center) or as we fondly called it: the center of intense confusion. I was reading a magazine article; I think it was Saga magazine or some other men's magazine that had my undivided attention. The article was written by someone who had just made a killing speculating in penny mining stocks. I have always been fascinated with the concept of making big bucks on a chump change investment and this was right up my alley. The most important part of this article was that the writer informed the reader that if you were going to speculate in penny mining stocks, you had to subscribe to the Northern Miner, and what is even more important, he gave the address. I sent off a letter requesting a subscription. I remain a subscriber to this day.

Now I know what you are thinking. You are thinking; why penny mining stocks? Why not penny stocks in general? What is so great about penny mining stocks?

I thought you would never ask. First, it needs to be understood that I only invest in mining stocks that are listed on the Toronto Stock Exchange or its related junior stock exchange the TSE Venture Exchange, with a few minor exceptions. Contrary to popular belief, our northern friends do an excellent job of policing and regulating their mining industry so long as perfection isn't expected. And they provide an excellent filter by mandating minimum requirements that the companies must adhere to. How many penny stocks do you know of that are listed on an exchange and have to meet minimum requirements that aren't mining related? The correct answer is almost none. Another advantage is that only a tiny percentage of these stocks are producers. The vast majority of these stocks have no operating income at all. I regard this as a plus because then they can be analyzed strictly as an asset play; and they are asset plays with a vengeance. There is no other investment on earth that routinely has such colossal asset values in relation to their stock prices. Then there is their astounding ability which no other type of stock possesses to go into hibernation for years, if necessary for decades, and maintain their listing. All other stocks perish if they can't maintain operations. Lastly, I am of the belief that we are entering a golden age of natural resources that should last for at least another decade.

Let's take a look at Porcupine Mines, its successor is currently called Moneta Porcupine Mines. It was incorporated in 1910, and I believe it has been listed on the TSE since 1926. It was a gold producer from 1938-1943, but since then it has produced nothing. It owns ten gold properties on which there are a total of 26 past producing mines. It has 1679 mining claims. In the United States the typical mining claim is 20 acres in size. In Canada the typical mining claim is 40 acres in size. Moneta owns a total of 67,160 acres. The stock currently sells for about 16 cents a share. At that price the entire market capitalization is about $11,860,000. That is for the whole company, lock, stock, and barrel; not to mention the 67,160 acres! At that price the market is placing a value of $176.59 for every acre that Moneta owns. Of course, Moneta hasn't earned a penny in operating income since 1943, but somehow it doesn't seem to matter. In the last five years the price has fluctuated between 6 cents a share and 22 cents a share. Where else are you going to find asset values like this for under a dollar?

Let me tell you about another penny stock that will illustrate some points that I want to make. This was back in the early days. There was this jewel called Arctic Gold and Silver Mines. When I bought it, I remember thinking that the name alone was worth the 46 cents a share I was paying. I was wrong. The company was delisted, and I wrote off the investment. But it wasn't a total loss. I had this rather attractive stock certificate that they had mailed me. In those days they still mailed you the stock certificate. I was going to frame it on the wall. It would make a wonderful conversation piece, but it wasn't to be. I never got around to framing it because about a year later Arctic Gold and Silver Mines rose from the dead. In Canada, mining companies can reconstitute themselves. If they pay their back taxes and fees, they can reclaim their charter, mining claims, and listing. Provided no one has acquired their claims in the interim. This happens more often than you would think. Arctic Gold and Silver Mines was back in action, but I was no longer a believer. When the stock had struggled back to about 25% of what I had paid for it, I took the money and ran. The stock was delisted again, this time forever. I now regret sending back the stock certificate; it would look wonderful on the wall. The amount I received for the stock was trivial. In those days my standard investment was 500 shares.

At this point you are probably wondering how it is possible for penny mining stocks to survive for years and indeed decades without any operating income. It is tied up with the ability of penny mining stocks and penny mining stocks alone of all other investment categories to hibernate or go into suspended animation. It isn't unusual for a penny mining stock to have only three employees, the president, the secretary, and the geologist who usually doubles as the vice president. Until recent years it was possible for a determined president to operate a bare-bones operation like this for as little as $250,000 a year or less. Today it can be done for $500,000 a year or less. Only the fact that penny mining stocks are the purest asset plays on earth allows this type of set up to be feasible.

Since they typically earn no income, the normal means of funding by a broker-promoted secondary offering doesn't work for mining stocks once they have been around for a few years and their stock is still selling for pennies. One of the most popular methods by which penny mining stocks raise capital is by way of what is called a private placement. In this model the president solicits money directly from private investors whenever it is needed. Under ideal circumstances it can work like this. The president invites say four to six serious, heavyweight investors out to investigate the mining site. If he is smart, he will provide each investor with one of those cute geologist's hammers and a jeweler's loupe with a chain so that they can wear their new status symbol around their necks. A jeweler's loupe is a small ten-power magnifying glass that is the status symbol of three professions; jewelers, coin collectors, and geologists. Each profession loves these status symbols and never misses an opportunity to employ them with great ostentation.

I made it a point to buy a jeweler's loupe years ago. At the mine site the investors will be invited to chip off rock samples with their cute little hammers and examine them under their jeweler's loupe. For lunch they go down to the lake and have a picnic. If they are lucky, they can watch soaring eagles capturing fish while they lunch. How do I know that there is a lake? There are hundreds of thousands of lakes in Canada; I kid you not. Nearly every mine I have ever owned has been within sight of a lake and two of them were located on islands in the middle of a lake. It is a common tradition in Canada to name mines and mining regions after the name of the nearest available lake. In the afternoon, time will be set aside for some fishing, and late in the afternoon or evening there will be fried fish over an enormous fire. If the weather is good, getting the investors to write a check is like shooting fish in a barrel. A determined president can keep his company solvent for years using this technique.

Let's now take a look at the type of profits that penny mining stocks can generate by looking at three of my recent successes.

Exall Resources was a stock that was an old favorite of mine. I had sold it twice before at a profit. This time I purchased it at 18 cents a share. Exall was now under new management and the new management had decided that it would re-deploy its assets into the oil and gas sector and place all its gold assets into a new gold company that would be called Gold Eagle Mines and then spin Gold Eagle Mines off to Exall's owners. This was fine with me. I am a big energy fan. Now Gold Eagle's Mine was located in the fabulous Red Lake mining camp. This is Canada's most prolific gold mining area. At this time a new drilling program was underway at Gold Eagle. The stock was rising nicely, but nothing out of the ordinary. When suddenly the stock jumped overnight from about 30 cents a share to $1.20 a share. For an old salt like myself it wasn't too difficult to figure out what had happened. The arrival of the Northern Miner provided the answer. The drill program was a success and reported high-grade gold intercepts, much higher than anybody had expected. The president hastily informed the owners that the program to spin off Gold Eagle had been canceled, a wise decision. At this point my normal procedure would be to take the money and run. Normally after a report like this the stock blows off and then declines. A decline back to the 60 cents to 80 cents a share range would be normal. But this was the Red Lake mining camp and the core samples were very rich. Against my better judgment I held on. To my considerable surprise the stock didn't decline as I expected; it continued to rise. There were now three drills on site instead of one. This was highly unusual action for a penny mining stock, which must hoard their limited resources. And they were reporting bonanza grades. It looked like Gold Eagle was a mine in the making. I was holding on. As this is being written, Exall Resources is selling for $2.00 a share. Not bad for an 18-cents-a-share investment and this move may not be over. Exall Resources 2005 annual report was a joy to read. It began like this.

Our company has not seen a year like 2005 in its entire 71-year history. With a major discovery at the Gold Eagle property, the very property that formed the foundation of Exall's incorporation as a company on February 13, 1934, we have come full circle, coincident with a very exciting time in the gold business.

But the part I liked best in the annual report was the part that said that Exall's stock had climbed 1,100% during the second half of 2005 based on positive drill results.

Another favorite that I am very keen on is Canadian Zinc. The saga of Canadian Zinc, and it truly is a saga, begins with the famous Hunt brothers and their attempt to corner the silver market in 1980. In the process the price of silver was driven to $50 an ounce. As this was going on the Hunt brothers were building what is today's Prairie Creek mine in Canada's Northwest Territories. The Hunt brothers sank $50,000,000 into building the mining infrastructure, which was 90% complete when the Hunt brothers declared bankruptcy and lost the mine. Over the years a total $100,000,000 has been spent to build the infrastructure that is now virtually complete. The ore body is extraordinary, 11.8 million tons of lead, zinc, and silver. If silver were a base metal the deposit would probably rank as the richest base metal deposit in the North American Continent that wasn't in production. The deposit contains 70 million ounces of silver, 3 billion pounds of zinc and 2.2 billion pounds of lead.

I know what you are thinking: "Fred, how much did you have to pay to buy into this treasure trove?" I made my initial buy in 2002 for nine cents a share, but my average cost is now 20 cents a share. As this is being written, silver is selling for about $17 an ounce, zinc is selling for $1.02 a pound, and lead is selling for 53 cents a pound. Now if my figures are right you come up with a total ore body value of about $4.86 billion rounded. Currently Canadian Zinc has about 93.4 million shares issued. Therefore, each share represents about $52 in ore value. As this is being written, Canadian Zinc is selling for about 80 cents a share. The best is yet to come. Now the astute reader is going to point out that what is really important isn't the value of the ore body, but whether it can be extracted at a profit. And this is of course true, but when you own 60-70 penny mining stocks and each position is considerably less than 1% of your investment capital, you need a quick and useful indicator of value, and this is one of the best. For years I struggled with this problem. There are many mining claims for which no reliable ore estimates exist. How do you estimate value? For a real estate appraiser this was a serious matter that I couldn't resolve.

One day as I was reading the Northern Miner, I was trying to make sense out of the core drilling samples that had just been reported to the press by a company that I was following, but of course I wasn't having any luck. The only thing I know about geology I learned in a college course. As I agonized over the data, the second great revelation of my stock market career occurred. In a flash I realized that penny mining companies weren't mining companies at all unless they were producers; and this is very rare.

They are in reality real-estate companies in drag. They are "location plays." And I had always been too stupid to figure it out.

In real estate the classic location play is raw acreage. You find out in what direction the city is growing and you drive out in that direction until you reach the point where the land is sold by the acre rather than by the lot, then you just buy and wait for the city's growth to reach you. Penny mining stocks' only asset is their mining claim, which is real estate. And the value of that mining claim is overwhelmingly determined by its location in a mining camp or proven mineral trend. When a mining camp reports a rich strike, all the mining stocks go up in value and the cheapest stocks go up the most. Armed with this rather obvious knowledge I was able to take bigger positions and bet with more confidence than had ever been possible before.

There is one last penny market play that I have to tell you about. The reason why is that it is one of the greatest profit makers I have ever had on a percentage basis. It started out in an unusual manner.

In the year 2001 I bought a little jewel called Pioneer Metals for 12 cents a share. I liked the stock because it had a nice package of properties and it was being run by the highly regarded mining promoter Stephen Sorensen. A year later in 2002 the owners of Pioneer Metals received a most intriguing letter. We were informed that the company had decided to spin off its uranium properties into a new corporation to be called UEX. I was only vaguely aware that it even had uranium properties. I had purchased the stock because it had an interesting stable of gold properties. But what blew me away was their brilliant analysis of the coming boom in uranium. Until that time uranium didn't even appear on my radarscope. By the time I finished reading the report, I was a raging bull on uranium. At that time uranium was selling for about $18 a pound, today it is selling for $45.50 a pound. The shortage is so acute that $60 a pound should be in the bag in the next two years; at its birth in 2002 UEX was blessed with about 247,000 very strategic acres in Canada's Athabasca basin in northern Saskatchewan. The Athabasca basin is the richest, but not the largest, uranium camp in the world and produces about 30% of the world's uranium. I was so impressed with UEX's potential that after the spinoff, I increased my position by an additional 25%. Because the value of Pioneer Mines was worth more after the spin off than when I purchased it, I decided that for accounting purposes I would regard the cost of the spin off shares as zero. Currently Pioneer Metals is selling for about 57 cents a share. When I consolidated the free spin off shares with my purchased shares of UEX the average cost of my position was seven cents a share.

I wasn't the only one who was impressed with the potential of this new creation. From the moment it went public, its rise was relentless. UEX at that time sold for $4.25 a share. My investment had increased in value about 60 times and the sky is still the limit. As I have stated before, it is possible for an investment to be too good to be true if people are unaware of its existence. The penny mining stock universe is the secret citadel of stocks that the investing public would regard as being too good to be true if they knew it existed. Where else can you routinely make micro-bets or chump change investments and get returns like this? I rest my case.

Regrettably time has not dealt lightly with the stocks I mentioned in the Norther Miner book review.

The Gold Standard of Penny Stocks

By now it should not come as any shock to the reader that the gold standard of penny stocks are the mining and oil & gas stocks listed on the Canadian exchanges. First, we can eliminate the NYSE and the NASDAQ. Both the NYSE and the NASDAQ have remarkably similar rules. Any stock that trades below a dollar a share for 30 consecutive days faces delisting. The corporation is required to immediately inform their exchange how they are going to ensure that the stock will trade above a dollar or it will be delisted. The solution is almost always a reverse split. A 5 or 10 to one reverse split will almost always get the job done.

Canada is the unchallenged king of natural resource stocks. According to the authoritative Norther Miner, in 2017 Canada produced an impressive $44 billion in 60 different minerals. Its financial capital is located on Bay Street in Toronto. Half of the world's mining and exploration stocks are listed on the Canadian exchange.

Toronto has two stock exchanges; the TSX or the Toronto Stock Exchange is where their more seasoned senior stocks are listed. The more junior stocks are listed on the TSXV or the Toronto Venture Exchange. Currently 23% of all the listed stocks are in the mining sector and an additional 18 % are in the oil and gas sector. There are 1,561 stocks listed on the TSX and there are 2,424 stocks listed on the TSXV for a total 3,985 listed stocks.

It is impossible to overestimate the importance of being a listed penny stock on a Canadian exchange. First of all, the Canadian exchanges and Canadian regulators do a fantastic job of keeping the system honest. The annual report that all listed companies must issue is critical. The knowledge that they must issue an audited annual report keeps everyone on the straight and narrow and reading the annual report enables you to make intelligent decisions.

Then there is the Northern Miner, the Wall Street Journal of mining published weekly since 1915. I have been a subscriber for decades. This is an additional gold mine of valuable investment information and a must have tool in your investment toolbox. The advantages of investing in Canadian listed penny stocks is overwhelming when compared to the pathetic smoke and mirrors world of the OTC Pink Sheets which is the only place in the United States where penny stocks are listed and is a national disgrace. Penny Mining Stocks are hard asset plays. It is far, far easier to make an intelligent decision about a penny mining stock that owns hundreds of acres in mining claims and usually thousands of acres in mining claims often with a dormant mill that might have cost millions and in some cases more than $10 million to build. The market in its infinite wisdom will usually place a value of nearly zero on this infrastructure because it is not producing any revenue. This is where I hang out.

But wait there are more advantages. To be perfectly frank about it, blue chip mining corporations are rarely a good investment. Junior producing mining corporations and penny mining stocks are far better investments. The reason for this is the unrelenting force of depletion. The backbone of every blue chip miner is their major producing mines which year after year are depleting away and which typically report declining ore grades as the years progress. As a result, they are forced to pay top dollar to junior producers and non-producing penny mining stocks with proven ore bodies to restore their relentlessly declining ore bodies. Need I say that this is a huge benefit that does not exist in the world of branded products where no depletion occurs.

There is one last advantage that I have incredible difficulty getting across to people. Every time I try to explain this to people, they just sit there and drool at me. Natural resource stocks are commodities and not brands. Let's see what the means. As I am writing this retail stocks are getting crushed. In the fullness of time retail will recover but will all the brands recover? Will deeply wounded Sears and J.C. Penney and other badly wounded retail stocks recover? Who knows? In another words while retail will recover the badly wounded brands may not. In the world of natural resources this is not a concern. There are no brands only commodities. Consider copper. When the copper cycle recovers all the copper stocks that own proven ore bodies can be relied upon to recover after due allowances are made for things like the size and richness of the ore body. No exceptions. In other words when you buy natural resources at the bottom of their cycle you have an assurance that you can never have when you buy branded products at the bottom of their cycle because they are selling commodities and not unique brands. Thus, when the commodity goes up, they all go up because they are selling the same commodity and not a brand. What this means is that picking winners at the bottom of a cycle is much easier in the world of commodities than picking winners at the bottom of a cycle in the world of brands.

The Cornucopian World View

We live in a world in which the prevailing viewpoint is cornucopian. That is the belief that for all practical purposes natural resources are inexhaustible. Yes, yes, some day hundreds of years in the future natural resource scarcity might be a problem but not in our lifetimes. How convenient! How very convenient! There are sound reasons for believing that the world of natural resource abundance is gradually coming to an end.

Mankind has been mining the wealth of the earth since the dawn of recorded history but until the industrial revolution started in the 1790s his efforts didn't amount to much. The industrial revolution and global population growth since the 1790s have resulted in an ever increasing spiral of demand on natural resources. In 1800 the global population was only 800 million. Today the global population is 7 billion and rising. As more and more people acquire first world status and rising living standards their consumption of commodities skyrockets.

In the world of natural resources, you always exploit the richest and the most readily available ore bodies first. As time progresses the richest and most readily accessible ore bodies are depleted, and it is necessary to exploit ore bodies with ever lower grades at ever more remote and inaccessible locations.

Today mining and energy companies are operating in politically hostile and dangerous regions that they would have never considered operating in even 20 years ago. They are operating there for only one reason. Because they have no choice.

The ore grades for every metal keep dropping relentlessly. When I first began investing in gold and silver miners in the 1960s a rich gold mine would have an ore grade of between a half troy ounce and one troy ounce of gold for each ton of ore. Precious metals are weighed in troy ounces. A troy ounce is 10% heavier than a standard ounce and weighs 31 grams. Today the average ore grade of a producing gold mine gold is a shockingly low 1 gram a ton. Gold mines with ore bodies of 3 grams a ton or higher are now regarded as being rich mines.

Today there are less than five gold mines on earth which have ore grades above a half ounce per ton.

As late as the 1960s rich silver mines had ore bodies that averaged about 12-16 troy ounces a ton. Today the ore body in the average silver mine is about 3 troy ounces a ton. You can count the silver mines that have ore grades of 9 ounces a ton or higher on one hand and have one or two fingers left over.

One hundred years ago a typical copper mine had an ore grade of 4% copper, today a typical copper mine has an ore grade of 1% or less. You can quote similar statistics for every natural resource.

There are four precious metals, gold, silver, platinum and palladium. Precious metals are always priced in troy ounces. All other metals are regarded as being base metals and are priced in either pounds or tons. The same relentless process is also occurring in the world's base metal mines as well.

This brings up the critical point of just what is a mine. Historically a mine was a hole in the ground that enabled you to access a rich vein of ore. The 20th and now the 21st century has given rise to the age of the open pit mine. The old timers would deny that these open pit bodies are mines at all, and they would have a point. The principal point here that the old timers would have no trouble in grasping is that in reality an open pit mine is an earth moving operation that is pretending to be a mine. The ore grades of these mines are shockingly low by historical standards.

The old timers would take one look at the alleged ore in these open pit operations and proclaim them worthless rock and they would not be too far wrong. It is only the brute power of the diesel engine and the humongous ore transporting trucks that the diesel engine makes possible that enables these low grade, open pit mines to exist. The diesel oil consumption of these mines is staggering. The great danger here is that any substantial increase in the price of oil would spell the doom of many of these open pit operations.

Lastly, there is the environmental movement that casts its giant shadow over the world of natural resources. Make no mistake. It is truly a giant shadow. The common belief throughout the world is that the environmental movement only opposes a few egregious projects that are so damaging to the environment that they should never be allowed to go into production. I wish that were true, but it isn't close to being true. The truth of the matter is that the environmental movement opposes a shockingly high percentage of all new energy and mining proposals and its batting average is sensational.

I would conservatively estimate that the environmentalist movement wins at least 80% of all the battles it chooses to fight.

Consider the alleged mighty oil and gas industry. I am hard pressed to think of a major victory that the industry has won over the environmental movement in the last 20 years. The classic example of course is the vast oil and gas reserves that are estimated to exist along the thousands of miles of US coastline from Maine to Washington state. How many people know that the only coastal area where oil exploration and production is allowed is in the western Gulf of Mexico in a band stretching from Texas to the coast of Alabama? It is forbidden everywhere else. Or how about ANWAR on the Arctic Circle? This Arctic swamp, or marsh if you prefer, in the summertime is a godforsaken hellhole infested with unbearable clouds of mosquitoes and in the winter it is frozen wasteland. The highest and best use for ANWAR is probably as a nuclear test site. Yet for decades the environmental movement has easily crushed every attempt by the presumed mighty oil and gas industry to put ANWAR into production.

Or take a gander at the now notorious Keystone XL Pipeline. The North American oil industry has struggled for years to build this pipeline and has until recently been stopped dead in its tracks by the environmental movement. However, the need for this pipeline is so overwhelming that I think the oil industry has about a 35% chance of winning this one. Rather than their usual 10% chance.

Even in the third world where one would think that natural resource firms would have an easy time of it this is not the case. Here is what happens. Well-meaning environmentalists who are willing to work for little or nothing and are convinced that they are saving the world descend on these hot spots and convince the peasants that the energy or mining firm is poisoning the peasants water supply. It works like a charm. The peasants go berserk and the project is stopped dead in its tracks.

At this point the reader may be wondering why on earth I am so keen on natural resource investing. The answer is simple. Historically mining with good reason has been regarded as a low profit enterprise. There was always too much competition. The rise of the environmental movement and the relentless depletion of our natural resource base has gone a long way to eliminating that problem. It has insured that for those companies that can actually prove up an ore body or oil field and overcome the environmental roadblocks will be capable of earning spectacular profits. In other words, if you can achieve production the green movement is your greatest ally. After all it has obligingly eliminated much of the competition. In the years to come I think that the investment community will be shocked at just how profitable the world of natural resources is going to be.

There is an additional powerful reason for investing in the world of natural resources. In a world ravaged by inflation, natural resources, the wealth of the earth, is the ultimate inflation hedge. Any time the printing press gets into a war with natural resources the printing press is going to lose.

For those requiring mathematical proof there is an outstanding 18 page report put out by the highly regarded Jeremy Grantham of the GMO organization at www.gmo.com. It is their quarterly letter of April 2011 which I strongly recommend if it is still available. When you read Jeremy's letters it quickly becomes clear that he is in the wrong profession; he should have been a math professor. The high point of the letter for me was the following statement. "Rapid growth is not ours by divine right; it is not even mathematically possible over a sustained period."

Battleground Stocks

A battleground stock is a stock in which the bulls and the bears have a violent disagreement about the intrinsic value of the stock. This violent disagreement always shows itself in the stock's short position, which is enormous, usually 20 % or higher. The overwhelming majority of stocks have a short interest in the 5% range or less. Recently I held positions in two of these battleground stocks and was blown out of both of my positions. In my career as a speculator I have held over a thousand positions. Rather than pretending that all my plays are winning plays as many writers do, I thought you would find my experiences in these two battleground plays to be of interest. As I have previously stated no one is right in this business more than 80% of the time.

CBL & Associates - A Screaming Bargain???

My first battleground stock is CBL & Assoc. (CBL). What follows is my analysis of the stock before I was blown out of my position:

CBL is a Mall REIT which in my opinion is a screaming bargain. Of course, this is a minority opinion. The opinion of the majority is that a "Retail Apocalypse" is under way that will bankrupt every mall in the country. I beg to differ. There is no doubt that this country is over-malled and indeed has way too much retail space in general. This retail surplus is being cured in the old-fashioned way by mass bankruptcies. The excess will be purged but many will survive and prosper, and I was convinced that CBL would be one of the survivors.

Of course, if you took a gander at the stock trend the only conclusion you could draw is that it is going bankrupt. In the last four years the stock has fallen from $21.36 a share to a low of $4.30 a share. The first thing you probably want to know is how much has this dog been losing? The answer is it had been solidly profitable for the last five years. I think the odds still favor it surviving. The critics will be happy to inform you that it is just a question of time until Sears and J. C. Penney go bankrupt and when they do every mall in the country will fail.

Guess again! While it is beyond dispute that Sears and J.C. Penny are two very sick puppies their failure will have a very limited impact on CBL. In its latest annual report CBL listed all its top renters and the percentage of total annual rentals that each tenant accounts for. J.C. Penney accounts for only 0.99% of

CBL's annual rentals and Sears accounts for 0.96% of its annual rentals. Each tenant therefore accounts for less than 1% of total annual rental income.

CBL's properties are located in 26 states. They own 68 malls, 23 associated centers, 9 community centers and 5 office buildings for a total of 105 properties. Until the last six months except for its stock price which has been devastated CBL somehow or another has managed to escape the "Retail Apocalypse" we keep hearing about. Its properties are currently 93% leased. This is a very impressive figure. The rule of thumb that has held true for decades is that commercial properties that are at least 90% leased can be expected to be profitable.

Aw, but what about the skyrocketing debt that will sink every mall in the country? Since 2013 CBL has reduced, not increased, its total debt by an impressive $740 million dollars and the interest rate on its remaining debt has declined from 4.87% to 4.65%. Folks, these are not the type of figures you see for a corporation that is facing bankruptcy. Let's continue. At its current $4.30 price CBL is paying an annual dividend of 80 cents a share for a shocking dividend yield of 18.78%. The current average stock dividend in the blue chip S&P 500 is a pathetic 1.90% which is another reason why I don't own blue chips.

According to the rule of 72 if you reinvested the dividends into purchasing more shares of CBL which you should always do for all of your dividend paying stocks, at the prevailing dividend yield of 18.78% you will double your money in a stunning 3.8 years. As hard as it is to believe the numbers, it gets even better. Not only is the dividend fully covered but it is covered a stunning two times over. At this point it is very important to understand that what determines a REITS' ability to pay dividends is not the EPS (earnings per share) which is what millions of misguided investors believe but FFO (Funds From Operations). I can't begin to tell you how often I have recommended a REIT to someone and have doofus call me back to tell me that the stock is a bad investment because the EPS doesn't cover the dividend. I have news for you, doofus, the dividend is covered. I sincerely hope that my fellow investors continue to believe this so that I can continue to cash in on their stupidity.

According to accounting standards, which every corporation must follow, physical assets must be depreciated every year and subtracted from annual profits according to the depreciation schedule. In commercial real estate the depreciation is enormous. Let me give you an example. Say a REIT has received $15,000,000 in rental profits this year. It cannot report $15,000,000 in profits. it has to subtract depreciation from its profits. Let's say that the depreciation was $5,000,000 an amount that would not be out of line. It would then report earnings not of $15,0000,0000 but $10,000,000. It is important to understand that this is a paper accounting deduction and not a real deduction. The cash is still in the till and available to pay dividends continues to be $15,000,000 and not $10,000,000. To get the true income that the REIT has earned you then add back the depreciation the result of course will be $15,000,000 and this figure is referred to as funds from operations or FFO. In other words, the annual rentals received. Let's take a look at what doofus sees when he analyses CBL. CBL is currently paying an annual dividend of 80 cents a share but its reported earnings per share, or EPS, is only 26 cents a share. Therefore, the dividend is not covered. Case closed. Wrong! In its current annual report CBL reported an FFO of $2.08 a share in other words the current dividend of 80 cents a share is covered more than twice over.

Let's take a look at another shocking number for CBL, its short interest; it is a mind blowing 26%. The typical stock has a short interest of around 5% or less. A short interest of 26% is an attention grabber when you understand what this is costing the shorts. Being short is not cost free. Especially in this case. When you are short your broker will require you to pay margin interest which is usually around 6%. You are also required to pay the dividend. That's right folks for the privilege of being short you are paying about 24% in interest and in dividends. It gets worse, it becomes even more insane if that is possible.

If the stock was at say $20.00 and you were convinced that it was going bankrupt, you could see where you would earn a handsome profit by being short but your maximum profit in this case is only $4.30. What are the shorts thinking of? These shorts have to possess an iron core conviction that CBL is toast. The only thing that worries me about this stock is the short position. Could I be wrong? Back to the drawing boards. Now it is beyond dispute that the earnings for all mall owners has been falling for the last couple of years but in CBL's case the horrific decline from $21.36 a share wipes out the decline in earnings several times over. Let's take another hard look at profitability. Have we been missing something?

There are four profitability factors and CBL is solidly profitable in all four factors. Its Gross Profit Margin is 71%, the Operating Profit Margin is 24%,the Net Profit Margin 13% and the Cash Flow Margin is an amazing 45%. All right, what about Tangible Book Value, which has rightly, virtually replaced the inferior and outdated concept of traditional book value which includes highly dubious distorting factors like good will? It is $5.71 a share. In other words, theoretically if they liquidated the company and paid off all the debts and then sold off all the assets the shareholders would receive $5.71 a share. All right what about indebtedness? Here the shorts are on to something: The Total Debt to Capital Ratio is 76% which is higher than I would like to see but this is not out of line for a REIT. The Interest Coverage Ratio is a reasonably healthy 1.41. It is important when considering this ratio to understand that commercial banks traditionally will lend to businesses on a margin as low as + 25%. In other words, as long as the annual profits of a business exceeds its annual debt payments by at least 25% it will broadly speaking be considered credit worthy. CBL was not going bankrupt.

There is one more stunning figure, the Price/Sales ratio. In the typical blue chip, the P/S is typically in the range of 2.5 to 4 times sales. In CBL it is a stunning 0.81. In other words folks, the market was valuing the entire market value of CBL or its capitalization at only 81% of its annual sales. Every time I look at the stats for CBL I end up rubbing my eyes in disbelief. This ends my bullish analysis of CBL.

Well what went wrong? The short answer is that shorts had superior insider information. Right from the beginning the only thing that worried me about this play was the iron core conviction of the shorts and their refusal to cover their positions when the stock fell. This was truly astonishing behavior for anyone who understands how the shorts operate. The game ended when CBL reported two disastrous quarters and cut its annual dividend from 80 cents a share to 30 cents a share and the stock crashed to $1.25 a share. Its current price is $1.35. At that price it pays a dividend of 22%. But what really got my attention was the action of the shorts. Instead of closing their short positions and locking in their hefty profits to my total amazement they increased their short position from a stunning 26% to an even more stunning 29%. I could not believe my eyes. There could be just one explanation, insider data. The shorts don't think CBL is going bankrupt they know it is going bankrupt. I threw in the towel and sold my position at $2.50 a share.

I still follow CBL carefully. For me to get back into the stock Two things must happen. The short interest must drop below 15 % and the stock has to be paying a fully covered dividend above 10% or it isn't worth the risk.

There is an important lesson to be learned here. Be very concerned anytime the short position in a stock is greater than 20% and be very, very concerned anytime the shorts refuse to cover their positions by selling their short positions when the stock sustains a big drop.

Being short a stock is far more dangerous than being long the stock. I regard it as being far too dangerous for me. If I want to short a stock, I will buy put options on the stock which is a far safer strategy if you want to short the stock because you can never lose more than the option price. If you are short the stock your potential loss cannot be calculated because it is infinity. The higher the stock price rises the greater your loss becomes. Because of these risks the shorts are notorious for how quickly they will bolt out of a position at the first sign of trouble. When they refuse to close a position that they have huge profits on it is a cause for extreme caution.

Tesla the Cult Stock

In my Tesla play I took the opposite position I ran with the bears instead of the bulls. Here is what I wrote:

Elon Musk's, Tesla Corporation is beyond a doubt today's leading cult stock. Fundamentals and numbers mean nothing. As long as the dear leader and his merry crew are running the company nothing can possibly go wrong. After all his fan boys are convinced that the dear leader can walk on water. Before this is over with Elon Musk, will have to walk on water to save his company. It is hard to believe that a company with numbers this bad can sell for $308 a share. In the last 12 months the company has lost an incredible $9.65 a share. Fortune Magazine in its 2017 annual review ranked Tesla at position 260 in its annual sales ranking. In that year it lost $1.96 billion. It is currently losing a staggering $1 billion a quarter. However, it is also interesting to note that in 2017, 53 of the Fortune 500 lost money. This is a company that has reported losses every year since its founding in 2003 and can no longer be characterized as a startup. Let's look at the numbers.

The first number under consideration is high but not totally outrageous. Price/Sales is 4.23, the average for the S&P 500 is 2.2. The Price/Tangible Book Value however is a disaster. The stock is selling at a stunning 13.06 times Tangible Book Value for a Tangible book value of $23.82 per share. The typical number for an S&P 500 stock today is 3.3 times Tangible Book.

It is not unusual for a Tesla fan boy to claim that if things get bad a high tech company like Google will step in and save the company. As soon as you look at Tesla's 13 times Book Value number you know that this is never going to happen. You have to understand what 13 times Tangible Book Value means. A potential purchaser could reproduce every asset Tesla has, its real estate, manufacturing plants and equipment 13 times over at Tesla's current stock price. No corporation in its right mind would pay such a horrific premium.

One of the repeated claims that is made to justify Tesla's stratospheric stock price is to claim that it is not really a car company but a high tech Silicon Valley type company masquerading as a car company. If Tesla made its own electric batteries, there would be some truth to this claim. But it does not and never has. Panasonic has always been Tesla's exclusive battery provider for all of its car models including the Model 3. Panasonic has also provided $1.6 billion of the $5 billion needed to build the Gigafactory. Panasonic and Tesla jointly operate the Gigafactory. It is also interesting to note that Panasonic and not Tesla owns and operates all the battery producing equipment.

I can vividly recall when the fan boys were crowing that while the traditional auto makers were producing the highly complicated internal combustion engines, Tesla would cruise to victory because it was producing the much simpler to produce electric vehicles. Oh, and by the way the traditional manufactures were only producing "compliance" electric vehicles which of course would always be inferior to Tesla's. This stupid argument died when every auto manufacturer announced that it would be producing a line of electric vehicles.

In the world of the EV the battery is the ballgame. The EV is so simple to build compared to an internal combustion engine that an intelligent orangutan could build an EV in his garage if you provided him with the electric batteries.

Let's take a look at another horrific number, Tesla is selling for a staggering 447 times its Price/Cashflow, the average S&P 500 number is 13 times Cashflow. While I am not a fan of Return on Equity the Tesla number is an ugly -34%, the typical S&P number is + 13%. Let's now take a look at the four profitability stats. The Gross Profit Margin is unusual in that it is actually a positive +16.13%. How the hell did that happen? the Operating Profit Margin is -15.81%, the Net Profit Margin is -15.28 and the Cashflow Margin is -2.77%. Just try comparing these profitability numbers with CBL which is supposed to be going bankrupt. Their Current Ratio is 0.74 and the Quick Ratio is 0.44. Anything below 1 is regarded as substandard. Return on Invested Capital is -10.89%, Return on Assets is -7.28%, Return on Investment is -34.29% all these figures are horrible and should be positive.

As this is being written a great hue and cry is occurring about when Tesla auto production will finally exit the "production hell" that the dear leader is always talking about and reach the magic 5,000 cars a week number. I regard this as being totally irrelevant. The issue is whether he will ever be able to sell his cars at a profit. Something he has never been able to do. Investors have got to stop pretending the Tesla is still a startup. Tesla is no longer a startup; it is 15 years old and it is still trapped in "production hell" according to Elon. This is a serious blot on the company. Can you think of any manufacturer that is 15 years old and still can't figure out how to operate its assembly line? The overwhelming majority of all the cars Tesla has sold have been priced at around $110,000. How do you sell 200,000 cars at an average price of $110,000 and manage to lose money at it? This is truly a heroic achievement.

For EV manufacturers 200,000 cars is the magic number. The purchaser of an electric car receives a $7,500 subsidy until the manufacturer who built it produces 200,000 cars after which the subsidy is greatly reduced and soon vanishes. I think it is impossible to overestimate how important that $7,500 subsidy is to the average electric car buyer. As this is being written Tesla has just announced that it has produced its 200,000th vehicle. This is very bad news. Its competitors will have this valuable subsidy which Tesla will have lost forever and which they can utilize for at least several years until they reach 200,000 in EV sales.

Another potential Tesla killer is the dangerously generous battery warranty on its Model 3 which is far more generous than the warranties on its previous models S and X. It has cleverly increased the warranty while reducing the cobalt in the Model 3 batteries and cobalt is critical for maintaining the life expectancy of the battery. No one knows for sure how long these batteries are going to last and if a substantial number of batteries fail during the warranty period this alone could sink the company.

Another cause for concern is Tesla's skyrocketing debt. As recently as 2014 it was only $3 billion. Today it is $10 billion. If Tesla was breaking even Elon's fan boys would support the company forever, but Tesla is not breaking even. It is generating an ocean of red ink every year. It is intriguing to notice that incredibly CBL has a higher short interest a 27% than Tesla has at 20%.

The way I am playing this is that I have purchased a basket of long term put options and as the options expire, I am rolling them over. Being short is way too dangerous. When you are short you can lose an amount that exceeds the value of your short investment. But when you are long put option contracts you can never lose an amount that exceeds your investment. That ended my bearish analysis.

Well what happened? In October 2018 Tesla reported a quarterly profit of $1.25 a share and the stock skyrocketed from $260 a share to over $350 a share and I was blown out of my position. I am still a careful observer of this stock. What will it take to get me back in? The stock has to fall below $240 a share at that price the technical analysis boys will turn against it because the stock will have fallen below its 50 day and 200 day moving averages. Which is always a huge negative for the technical analysis boys. Also, at below $240 a share vast numbers of Elon's fan boys will have severe losses for the first time, and this may snap them out of their cult worship.

My Pink Sheet Gamble

As you know I am not a fan of pink sheets. The investor who wants to invest in penny stocks or micro-cap plays is far better served by investing in the penny stocks and micro-caps listed on the Canadian exchanges which do a fantastic job of protecting investors and their listed stocks are required to issue an annual report every year. Something that I regard as vital so that investors can research the status of their investments. It is impossible to make intelligent decisions about a stock unless you are receiving annual reports.

It all began in 2007. In that year I discovered that a conference, for the want of a better word, called the Silver Summit would be held in Spokane, Washington, in which silver miners, jewelers, and coin and bullion dealers would give lectures and promote their wares. This was like catnip to a lifelong gold and silver bug like me. I attended all the lectures that I felt would be interesting and then went on the bus tour to nearby Wallace, Idaho, the capital of Shoshone County which is located in the Idaho panhandle and is in the heart of the Coeur d'Alene silver region. This region has been the top silver producing region in the United States since the 1880s. We had an excellent meal in downtown Wallace which like all the mining boomtowns of the west seems frozen in time with the usual 19th century Victorian architecture.

After the meal we visited the New Jersey Mining mill. New Jersey Mining has a rather unusual operation. They have what is usually called a custom mill or refinery. Any miner in the region could ship their ore to the mill and they would process the ore for a fee. They also had a collection of dormant mining plays that had some potential. I was impressed by the tour; this was obviously a fully functional mill that was processing ore as we were touring the mill.

Before I left the conference, I purchased David Bond's book, "The Silver Pennies," which of course was a book about the silver plays in the Coeur d'Alene Valley which the locals call the Silver Valley. David Bond was also the promotor of the Silver Summit and was a local big wheel in the Wallace area and a recognized national authority on mining in the region.

On the flight back home, I carefully read David Bond's book. From the book I selected the below 10 plays, all of which were selling for under 10 cents a share, for further investigation.

Highland Surprise Consolidated (HSCM)
Hunter Creek Mining (HTRC)
Inspiration Lead (ILDIA)
Lucky Friday Extension Mining (LFEX)
Mascot Silver & Lead (MSLM)
National Silver & Lead (NSLM)
New Jersey Mining (NJMC)
Shoshone Silver Mining (SHSH)
Silver Buckle Mines (SBUM)
Silverore Mines (SVMN)

There were several things that I discovered when I read David Bond's book which got my immediate attention. The first thing I noticed was that the incorporation date for these beauties were decades old. Many of them going back to the early 20th century. This is highly unusual in the world of penny stocks. The average life expectancy of a penny stock unless it lucks out and makes a major discovery is 10 or 15 years. Even a penny stock has annual expenses which must be paid the most important of which is the taxes on the mining claims. Within this 10 or 15 year period the penny stock must either manage to go into production, prove up its claims and sell out to a major miner or be merged out of existence.

The second thing that really got my attention was the amazingly small stock float. The typical stock float today for a penny stock is around 50-75 million issued shares and stock floats of 300 million and higher are not unknown. The issued shares of all the corporations I was considering were much smaller than that; most of them were under 8 million shares. This really got my attention. Below is the pertinent data on my 8 beauties.

There are two outliers in the group Shoshone Silver which is now bankrupt and New Jersey Mining Which I now realize is the only legitimate play in the entire group. One last thing with the exception of New Jersey Mining any stock transaction above 6 cents a share in these beauties must be regarded with great suspicion. In Wall Street lingo these stocks trade by appointment only. Weeks and in some cases, months pass without a trade. In cases such as this manipulating the price would be a piece of cake. The overwhelming majority of these transactions occur in the 2 cents to 6 cents a share range. Quite frankly if you put in a 60 day limit order for 50,000 shares in the 2-5 cents a share range there is an excellent probability that the order will be executed. Keep that in mind when you are analyzing the annual price spread for these stocks.

I am using 2 cents a share in my analysis to value the stock of each of these companies because with the exception of New Jersey Mining they are all pink sheets that trade by appointment only. It is not unusual for several weeks to pass without a single trade. In such a scenario the purchaser who put in a 60 day limit order for a large block of stock at 2 cents a share would have an excellent chance of it being executed. Which is what I do. I have rounded the below figures where appropriate.

Highland Surprise Consolidated (HSCM) was incorporated in 1912. It has 2,479,000 shares issued and the recent annual share price ranged from 2 cents to 10 cents a share. At 2 cents a share the total capitalization is $50,000. That's right folks you can buy the whole company for just $50,000. Wait until you get a gander at the price per acre. It has 197 acres of patented claims with 500 registered shareholders. When we divide $50,000 by 197 acres the price per acre is a stunningly low $254 an acre. Can anyone say value play?

Hunter Creek Mining (HTRC) was incorporated in 1945 and has 3,488,000 shares issued and the recent annual share price ranged from 2 cents to 4 cents a share. At 2 cents a share the total capitalization is $70,000. It owns 90 net acres. Divide $70,000 by 90 acres and the price per acre is just $777. In addition, its location is adjacent to the Lucky Friday Mine which is one of the region's major producing mines.

Inspiration Lead (ILDIA) has 6,803,000 shares issued and the recent annual share price ranged from 1-6 cents a share. At 2 cents a share the total capitalization is $136,000. Divide this amount by the 180 acres of land that it owns and the resulting value $755 an acre.

Lucky Friday Extension Mining (LFEX) has 11,500,000 shares issued and the recent annual share price ranged from 1 cent to 3 cents a share. At 2 cents a share the total capitalization $230,000. Divide this amount by the 260 acres of land that it owns, and the resulting value is $884 an acre. Its acreage also adjoins the Lucky Friday Mine. Hence its name.

Mascot Silver & Lead Mines (MSLM) is currently a grey market stock without an active market. At the time I bought it the stock had an annual range from 2-6 cents a share. Mascot was incorporated in 1950 and has 7,793,000 shares issued. At 2 cents a share it has a total stock market capitalization of $155,000. Divide this amount by the 203 acres that it owns, and the resulting value is $763 an acre. It also includes the Pittsburgh Mine, an ex-producer which was in production from 1941-1953. This is always a big plus for me.

National Silver & lead (NSLM) was incorporated in 1906 and has 10,000,000 shares issued and owns 140 acres. Nothing further needs to be said about this stock. I got lucky and sold this stock for a quick $4,000 profit two months after I bought it. Ordinarily I would have never settled for such a small profit, but I have a very low confidence in these stocks because with the exception of New Jersey Mining they don't issue annual reports.

Without annual reports it is impossible to make intelligent decisions about a stock.

New Jersey Mining (NJMC) has 122,500,000 shares issued and is an outlier that is an operating company. Therefor no calculation is being made for this stock. I still own it and it is the jewel of the bunch. I have a double in the stock.

Shoshone Silver (SHSH) was incorporated in 1969 and has 60,000,000 shares issued and is the villain of the group. It had great assets when I bought it and then like magic the assets vanished, the office was closed and its website, email and telephone were disconnected without any explanation to the shareholders. The stock is now worthless. It had 1,635 shareholders of record who were thrown to the wolves. I and the others mailed letters of complaint to everyone and his brother including the SEC and the governor and attorney general of Idaho since it was an Idaho licensed corporation. No one would do a thing.

Silver Buckle Mines (SBUM) was incorporated in 1963. It has 11,998,0000 shares issued and the annual stock price ranged from 2 cents a share to 7 cents a share. At 2 cents a share the total capitalization is $240,000. Divide this amount by the 1,884 acres it owns, and the resulting figure is a stunning $127 an acre.

Silverore Mines (SVMN) was incorporated in 1946 and has 3,692,000 shares listed and the annual stock price ranged from 2 cents a share to 3 cents a share. At 2 cents a share the total capitalization is $74,000. Divide the capitalization by the 374 acres that the corporation owns, and the resulting figure is $197 an acre.

I am sure that you will agree with me that these are extraordinary numbers. I would estimate that at least 80% of all the acreage sales in the country sell for at least $10,000 an acre. There was no way I was going to pass up bargains like this. After establishing a position in each of the plays I wrote a letter to the president of each of the plays with the exception of the outliers Shoshone Silver and New Jersey Mining and informed them that the time had come to terminate the corporation and cash in on the real estate values. None of them even bothered to respond to my letter. Which didn't surprise me all that much. I had chump change invested in these plays and I knew these were going to be long term investments.

I had two strategies in mind. The first strategy was to just wait until they announced to their shareholders that they were going to do the right thing and terminate the corporation. At that point I would do two things. First, I would place a limit order to purchase a large block of the stock at a suitable price. The second thing would be to fly to Idaho to bid on the real estate. Being the generous type if I liked what I saw I was prepared to bid up to $3,000 an acre. The beauty of this strategy was that a percentage of my winning bids would be returned to me by an increase in the stock's liquidation value.

The second strategy was to take a controlling interest in these beauties. Based on the prices that I have already shown you this was well within my means. The next year when I attended David Bond's Silver Summit, I paid a visit to Mascot Silver's office which was located on the second floor of Wallace's main street.

The president's desk faced the entrance, the back of the chair that he was sitting on faced a large second floor window. After introducing myself I informed him that I wanted to purchase the controlling interest in Mascot Silver. His reaction was extraordinary. He pushed his chair violently back against the window, threw back his arms in horror and shouted no. I remember thinking that if he had pushed back the chair a little harder he and the chair would have fallen out of the large second story window to the street below. This was for a stock which had last sold at 3 cents a share and hadn't traded in the prior two weeks. You would have thought that I had told him that I had come to steal his first born child. I left him my business card and told him to contact me if he changed his mind. Of course, he never did.

After that I decided to place a colored half page ad in the local newspaper. I needed to know if there were any local sellers out there. The ad said: Florida speculator will pay $10,000 for the controlling interest in any of the below local penny stocks. Interested parties contact Fred Carach. It then listed the stocks. I did not get a single response. I then decided to mail a copy of the ad to the offices of each of my beauties to see what the reaction would be. I got the usual no response.

In a last attempt I sent a letter to each of my beauties asking them if the controlling interest was for sale without mentioning any price at all. To my amazement I got one response from Burton Onstine who was the president of Hunter Creek, Inspiration Lead and Silverore Mines. Neither he nor the Board of Directors, he informed me had any interest in selling the controlling interest of their corporations and that's where the matter now lies. I intend to hold on to my beauties. I have chump-change invested in them and I want to see how this game ends. After that the annual Silver Summit was moved to San Francisco. There is just one thing left to tell you about and that is local boy David Bond's last letter which I have included below. After all he was the prime mover as far as I was concerned.

Why I Am Quitting Writing About Mining

First and foremost, I have lost interest. I find tube hi-fi much more interesting. Second, I have been connived and fooled by the best in the business and passed this tomfoolery off to my readers.

Justin Rice and the Russell brothers took me and many friends into near bankruptcy on the Azteca gold project up Two Mile just northeast of Wallace. I republished many of their lies and I am ashamed of it. I trusted them. Their lies seemed true at the time. Secondly, I am being hauled into federal court involving a lawsuit between shareholders and Bob Genovese over a mine I wrote about, the Liberty Silver Trinity, silver property near Lovelock, Nevada. I still think it is a good prospect, discovered by US Borax and heavily and positivity reviewed by a respected mining evaluator, SRK, but after my writing a positive article, the stock tanked and the longs lost well their shorts and have dragged me into their filth. I never owned a share of Liberty. I did lose $7,000 on Justin's gambit, long after I wrote about it and I could probably sue Justin for his lies, but really, why sue because I am stupid and gullible. Maybe Ralph Nader could knock some sense into me.

Whatever happened to, you pays your money and you take your chances? Ain't that the American way? Capitalism is by nature creative and destructive. What do we taxpayers owe the buggy whip makers for going out of business because of the automobile, which did not require horses? Precisely nothing. But then in steps the modern federal government, to sue Henry Ford for buggy whip damages. This latter mindset prevails today and it is why your kids can't read. But that is another rant.

I am not abandoning in spirt the hard rock miners for what they do, which if you think about it is magnificent. But having been conned twice and having passed along bad advice, it is time to move on. And I have some very precious vacuum tubes I need to sell.

—David Bond

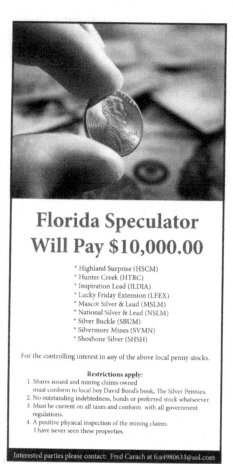

Florida Speculator
Will Pay $10,000.00

* Highland Surprise (HSCM)
* Hunter Creek (HTRC)
* Inspiration Lead (ILDIA)
* Lucky Friday Extension (LFEX)
* Mascot Silver & Lead (MSLM)
* National Silver & Lead (NSLM)
* Silver Buckle (SBUM)
* Silvermore Mines (SVMN)
* Shoshone Silver (SHSH)

For the controlling interest in any of the above local penny stocks.

Restrictions apply:
1. Shares issued and mining claims owned
   must conform to local boy David Bond's book, The Silver Pennies.
2. No outstanding indebtedness, bonds or preferred stock whatsoever.
3. Must be current on all taxes and conform with all government regulations.
4. A positive physical inspection of the mining claims.
   I have never seen these properties.

Interested parties please contact: Fred Carach at fca4980633@aol.com

My High Tech Commodity Plays

We have now completed all the background sections and we are now ready to take a look at the cheap stocks that have been my happy hunting ground for decades. I own and like all these stocks. I don't recommend stocks that I don't own but only you can decide if they are suitable for you. We will start out with the high tech commodity plays that are essential if the electric vehicle is to ever achieve its promise. The three essential commodities are lithium, cobalt and surprisingly enough graphite. The electric vehicle is going nowhere without these three commodities. It is very important to understand that typically in an EV (electric vehicle) the batteries account for about 50% of the total car cost and that the raw materials in the battery, cobalt, lithium and graphite account for about 70% of the battery's cost. I dismiss nickel and magnesium in my analysis because the annual production of both is so great that the amount consumed in EV batteries is not significant in relation to the total annual production of these metals.

Graphite is the surprise here. The only thing people know about graphite is that it is used in pencils and therefore they assume that it is as common as dirt. It is the most common of the three essential commodities, but it is not nearly as common as people seem to think.

Let's take a look at the gold standard for the electric car battery. It is called the Lithium-ion NCM battery. The battery is divided into four components. The negative electrode which is made out of graphite. The positive electrode is where the battery gets its name. It is one-third nickel, one third cobalt and one third magnesium. Then there is the separator which is essential but which we can ignore and lastly the electrolyte which is made out of lithium. That is all there is to the lithium battery.

The most expensive component in the battery is cobalt which is a rare and expensive metal. Since cobalt is a rare and expensive metal why pray tell was it included in the battery? It was included in the battery because it has the highest energy density of any know material and was regarded as essential in maintaining the life expectancy of the battery and to keep the battery from heating up and bursting into flames. This is no idle fear.

Lithium is the lightest metal known. If you toss a one-pound ingot of lithium into the water, it will float. If you put a match to it, the lithium will burst into flames as it is floating in the water. Water will not put out a lithium fire.

Ever since Tesla introduced his latest car the Model 3, Elon Musk and the boys have been crowing about their latest genius play. Because of their towering genius they have discovered that cobalt is really a stupid extravagance and that the amount of cobalt in the battery can be greatly reduced by increasing the nickel component in the battery and by reducing the cobalt component. What genius! You are probably wondering how they made this breakthrough discovery. Their breakthrough discovery came when they realized that cobalt was selling at $30 a pound and that nickel costs $6.00 a pound.

The inventors of the Lithium-ion NCM battery were obviously drooling imbeciles. Imagine being so stupid as to include this costly and largely unnecessary metal to the battery. Thank god for the dear one. How far this will all go is unknown but at this time they have reduced the cobalt in their batteries from 11kg in their Model S to 4.5 kg in their newest car the Model 3 and Elon thinks they can reduce the cobalt component in the future as he put it to almost nothing. How convenient! How very convenient!

It is not hard to figure out why Elon and his merry crew are so eager to ditch cobalt. The more you look at the cobalt supply line the more you realize that cobalt has the entire EV market by the throat unless the annual supply of cobalt can be dramatically increased. This increase in production can happen and will happen but only if the price of cobalt skyrockets.

Most of the world's cobalt today is produced as a byproduct of copper and nickel mines. Historically the major demand for cobalt was as an alloy in jet engines. Today 50% of all cobalt consumption is for EV batteries and this amount is increasing relentlessly every year. In the latest year a stunning 2/3 of the world's cobalt was produced in the war torn Democratic Republic of the Congo as a byproduct from its copper mines. This is not what Elon and his merry crew want to hear.

Reducing the cobalt component in the battery is a highly dangerous exercise to put it mildly. As you will recall as you reduce the amount of cobalt in the battery and increase the amount of nickel to compensate for the reduction, the battery cells tend to overheat which increases the chances that the batteries will burst into flames. Reducing the cobalt also increases the risk that the life cycle of the battery cell will be reduced. This is also highly dangerous for the car producer. The standard EV today has a battery warranty of 8 years or 50,000 miles whichever comes first at 70% of the original battery's capacity. If the batteries fail the car producer is on the hook and must replace the batteries. Recall that about 50 % of the EV's cost is the batteries. It is Tesla's new Model 3 that is at the greatest risk. They have reduced the cobalt in the batteries while they have increased

the warranty to 100,000 miles at 70% of capacity. No one will really have a good idea until at least four or five years from now if the batteries will outlast their warranty. But Tesla is taking a huge gamble with what may be an insanely generous warranty. You know if you stop to think about it there are more ways that Tesla can blow up than you can shake a stick at. Elon and the boys are playing Russian Roulette.

I remain a committed cobalt bull. It is my strong belief that the inventors of the Lithium-Ion NCM battery were not stupid and that cobalt is a necessary and critical component in the EV battery and while it may be reduced somewhat it cannot be eliminated and in the case off the Model 3 it may have been reduced to the point where it may be dangerous.

We need to say something about lithium, after all it is the lithium-ion battery. About 54% of the world's lithium reserves are located in South America's aptly named Lithium Triangle. The Lithium Triangle is located in the Atacama Desert area where Chile, Argentina and Bolivia meet. Historically for generations Chile has produced almost all of the world's lithium, Bolivia and Argentina virtually nothing. Now that Argentina has its first business friendly government in god only knows how long corporations are starting to invest in Argentina's section of the Lithium Triangle.

Chile's lithium production is controlled by just two producers. It's state owned SQM Corporation and Albemarle. The world's big three lithium producers are SQM, Albemarle (ALB) and FMC (FMC). Albemarle and FMC are listed on the NYSE. Albemarle currently sells at around $90 a share and FMC sells at around $80 a share. Albemarle manufactures polymers, chemicals and related products and has a lithium division. FMC is an old line agricultural chemical producer that was established in 1883 and has a lithium division.

I have a perpetual lifetime bias against stocks that are selling much above $20 a share. I am a great believer in financial leverage. If there are two stocks that I like and one stock sells at a dollar a share and the other stock sells at $100 a share and they both rise in value by $1 a share my profit in the $1 a share stock has doubled and in the $100 a share stock it has risen by a princely 1%. Guess which stock I am going to buy? I have a small position in Albemarle. The way I have handled it and the strategy that I usually use to handle my investments in high priced stocks is this. I buy long term 2 year call options on the stock and this gives me the low cost option that I require along with a hefty amount of leverage.

Bolivia is lost in a perpetual stupor under the violent anti-business and anti-foreigner regime of Evo Morales or is that "Evil Morales," sorry just joking. Evo has been Bolivia's president since 2006 and is an avowed socialist who is convinced that all the foreigners who invest in Bolivia have come to rob and plunder the Bolivian people. But he is wise to their treachery. As a result, lithium production has been virtually nil as Bolivia tries to become a lithium producer based solely on its sadly lacking professional mining skills as it relates to brine production. Bolivia has a history of hard rock mining, but this is of little use when extracting lithium from brine deposits.

Australia is the fast rising number two in lithium production. It is important to understand that there are two sources of lithium. The first and historically almost the only source was to extract the lithium from the lithium rich brine pools or lakes located in desert regions such as South America's lithium triangle which they call salares. Nevada and some other desert areas possess these brine lakes. The other source is what is called hard rock mining of lithium from the ore called spodumene. All of Australia's rapidly rising production comes from Western Australia's spodumene deposits located primarily in the so-called Pilgangoora region. Two of my picks Altura Mining and Pilbara Minerals are located in this region and are scheduled to go into production in 2019.

While historically the brine producers were always the lowest cost lithium producers brine production has a problem. The way the lithium brine is processed is that it is scattered for the want of a better word over hundreds of acres of the desert floor and left to evaporate and bleach in the sun for months at a time until the evaporation process slowly increases the lithium grade to the point where it has economic value and then it is gathered up and sold. Spodumene lithium production is hard rock mining and is processed in the standard way. The rock is finely ground in the mill and then processed.

In the last few years the price of lithium and cobalt has oscillated wildly in value. Lithium went on a dramatic rise that took it to $20,000 a ton and it has now fallen below $15,000 a ton. Cobalt has taken an even more dramatic plunge from $30 a pound to $15 a pound. The question is why these two valuable commodities have suddenly gotten hammered when you would think the reverse would be true. The answer is the stupidity of the market gurus. As these two critical metals skyrocketed in value the gurus called up the producers and a host of newly formed alleged lithium and cobalt miners who no one had ever heard of and who had never produced a pound of lithium and cobalt. These alleged soon to be producers told tall tales about how they would all be in production in a year or two and would be producing astonishing amounts of cobalt and lithium. Naturally the gurus lapped up every word of this nonsense and compiled a list of future production estimates that would crush the lithium and cobalt markets like a bug. Folks the vast majority of this production will never occur in the years and in the amounts predicted. It is an impossibility.

When I broke into the market in the 60s it was perfectly possible for a new proposed mine to go from announcement into production in a year's time. Today it takes 10 to 20 years. When you tell people that they think that you are out of your mind. Let's take a look at what has changed since the 60s and the barriers that a new proposed mine faces today before it can go into production. Let's call it the three hells:

Regulation Hell
Green Hell
The Suits Hell

Regulation Hell is the hellish government regulations that the miners must comply with before a new mine can go into production. Complying with these regulations in today's world can easily take five to ten years.

Next comes Green Hell during the regulation hell period the greens have been hiding in the weeds while cheering on the government regulators and demanding the toughest regulatory compliance possible and now they pounce. They hit the miners with a lawsuit and drag the lawsuit out for as many years as possible. Then they hit them with another lawsuit and drag that out for as many years as possible and then they hit them with another lawsuit. This process can easily take from five years to eternity.

Having successfully gone through Regulation Hell and Green Hell the new mining prospect now has to deal with the suits. The simple truth of the matter is that 95% of the mining firms on this planet cannot finance a new mine of any consequence without raising new capital that only the suits on Bay Street, which is Canada's financial capital, and Wall Street can provide. Raising this capital is never a walk in the park and can easily consume more years. Without the approval of the suits almost no new mine gets built. Then and only then can a new mine go into production. This is the brutal gauntlet that all proposed new mines face in today's world.

In a recent article the authoritative Northern Miner newspaper claimed that in North America it can now take up to twenty years to go from announcement to production. Trust me this is not a myth it is a fact. The guru generated reports of a coming tidal wave of new lithium and cobalt production has resulted in a severe decline in the prices of these commodities and in the stock prices of the miners that are attempting to produce them. Rendering their coming tidal wave scenario even more impossible and implausible. If they can't raise the capital they can't go into production. Let's now take a look at some of the lithium plays that I own and like but first a word of warning:

Many of you are going to be shocked! Shocked! at some of the prices of the stocks that I am willing to buy are selling for.

"What! What! You paid 20 cents a share for a stock? I would never buy a stock that is selling for 20 cents a share".

You are going to be equally shocked when I show you my income portfolio which is packed with stocks that are paying dividends of 6%, 8%, 10%, 12%, 14% and in a couple of cases 15%.

"You must be stupid. Don't you know that stocks that pay dividends above 4% or 5% are sucker plays and that the only reason that they are paying dividends at this level is that the dividend cannot be maintained and will soon be cut?"

Folks, I have been doing this for 57 years. In the blood-stained gladiator's arena where I choose to hang out, they drag losers out of its blood stained sands feet first. They call it the stock market. If you don't know what you are doing the stock market will wipe you out real quick like. The highest risk and the most unforgiving part of this blood stained arena is obviously not in the blue chip market. It is in the small-cap, micro-cap and penny stock arena. If I wasn't making money at this, I wouldn't be writing this book. I would be bankrupt and sleeping under a bridge.

Altura Mining (ALTAF) is currently selling at 10 cents a share. Its 52 week range is from 8 - 37 cents a share and its mine is located in Western Australia's Pilgangoora region. It is not currently profitable and has just started lithium production in October 2018.

Lithium Americas (LAC) is currently selling at $4.35 a share. Its 52 week range is from $2.75- $6.86. It is not currently profitable. It has two big lithium projects. Its 100% owned Thacker Pass project located in Nevada is expected to go on stream in the near future. It has a 50% owned partnership with China's Gangfeng in the Cauchari-Olaroz project located in Argentina which is scheduled to go into production in 2020.

Orocobre Ltd (OROCF) is currently selling for $2.35 a share. Its 52 week range is from $1.99 - $4.84. It is currently profitable and has a PE Ratio of 36. It has a portfolio of potash, boron and lithium assets. It has recently commenced operations of a brine-based lithium operation in Argentina's Lithium Triangle.

Pilbara Minerals (PILBF) is currently selling for 50 cents a share. Its 52 week range is from 35 cents - 82 cents a share. It is not currently profitable. Its lithium mine is located in the same area as Altura Mining in Western Australia's Pilgangoora region. It has just started production.

Pure Energy Minerals (PEMIF) - this stock is almost too risky even for me. I came very close to deciding not to include this stock in this book. This is an option play. If they can pull it off and come up with the capital needed to exercise their options, they can make a killing. If they can't come up with the capital needed to exercise their options, then the stock is worth very little. The stock is currently selling for 6 cents a share and has a 52 week price range of 3 - 24 cents a share. It is not profitable and has just made a $300,000 option payment on its Clayton Valley Brine Project in Nevada by issuing more shares. Its 26,000 acre Clayton Valley project is strategically located adjacent to Albemarle's lithium project which is the only producing lithium mine in North America. It has just announced the completion of a pilot plant in the Clayton Valley. It also has the Terra Cotta lithium brine project in Argentina's Lithium Triangle.

My cobalt plays begin in Canada. Its cobalt plays have an interesting story. They are almost all located in the area around the town of Cobalt, Ontario, which is a mining town with a current population of around 1,000. In 1908 it was a mining boom town and was the largest silver producer in the world. The town was called Cobalt because the rich silver ore bodies in the area had a heavy concentration of cobalt in the silver ore, hence the name Cobalt. The cobalt ore at that time was probably regarded by the miners as almost a nuisance ore. Canada Cobalt Works (CCWOF) is currently selling for 28 cents a share. Its 52 week range is from 14 cents - 67 cents a share. It is not profitable. Its assets of course are located in Canada's cobalt region. The most interesting asset is the ex-producer Castle Silver mine which was in production from 1917-1989 and produced 22 million ounces of silver and 300,000 pounds of cobalt. It also owns two other ex-silver producers, the Beaver and Violet mines, which of course are also located in the Cobalt region. As I have already stated I am a big fan of ex-producers. The old timers had it right, the best place to find gold is where it has already been discovered.

Cobalt 27 Capital (CBLLF) is currently selling for $2.91 with a 52 week range of $2.45- $10.30. It is not currently profitable. This is probably the blue chip in the group with a fascinating strategy. It acquires and holds physical cobalt. It also invests in royalty streams. I am a big believer in royalty streams and in certain cases it holds minority positions in cobalt properties. The company currently holds an amazing 2,905 tons of cobalt in its warehouses. It is interesting to note that cobalt has not been mined in the US since 1971 and that the government stockpile of cobalt is just 301 tons.

Its biggest royalty stream is the recent purchase for $300 million of 32.6% of all the cobalt produced from Vale's world class Voisey Bay mine in Canada which is to be settled by physical delivery for the life of the mine.

Ecobalt Solutions (ECSIF) is currently selling for 27 cents a share with a 52 week range of 18 cents - $1.30. It is not currently profitable. The company's flagship project is the Idaho Cobalt Project which is located in the historic Idaho Cobalt Belt. The Idaho Cobalt Belt produced 2 million tons of cobalt from the early to the mid-1900s. This property covers an area of 4,080 acres and consist of the mine, mill and concentrator. It is currently the only environmentally permitted primary cobalt project in the United States. The company is currently debt free.

First Cobalt Corporation (FTSSF) is currently selling for 13 cents a share with a 52 week range of 10 cents - 87 cents a share. It is not currently profitable. Its flagship property is the Iron Creek Cobalt project located in the Idaho Cobalt Belt in Lehmi County, Idaho with an area of 1,700 acres. The company other assets include 10,000 hectares with more than 50 past-producing silver/cobalt mines in Canada's Cobalt Camp. A hectare is 2.47 acres. It currently has the only fully permitted cobalt mill in Canada.

Leading Edge Materials (LEMIF) is my only graphite play. it is currently selling at 12 cents a share and has a 52 week range from 10 cents to 61 cents a share. It is not currently profitable. This is a Canadian listed company whose principal assets are located in Sweden. it has an operation ready graphite mill complex located in Woxna, Sweden, which is on a care and maintenance basis and they also have a 100 % ownership interest in their Bergby lithium project also located in Sweden which is currently undergoing exploratory drilling.

The Death of the Dollar and Gold

As these words are being written the United States is enjoying a strong economy courtesy of the corporate tax cut that went into effect in 2018 and cut corporate taxes from 35% to 21%. It is almost impossible to overestimate the importance of this tax cut. It is huge. As hard as it is to believe our alleged capitalist nation had a corporate tax rate of 35%, the fourth highest corporate tax rate in the world. According to a recent article in Fortune Magazine the average corporate tax rate in the EU is 21.68%. But is it enough to offset the frightening manufacturing decline that this nation has been experiencing since the 1970s? I don't think it is. What is shocking to me is how little understanding and commentary there has been on this truly horrific decline.

No other nation on earth would have allowed its manufacturing base to be systematically destroyed as we have. There will be consequences. Of this I am sure. The vast majority of our population is totally unconcerned with this industrial devastation and regards it as a matter of little concern.

If you ask the average citizen whether manufacturing is important to our prosperity, they will say no. That manufacturing is so 20th century. I beg to differ. A word of caution about this chapter. It is long and involved and, on the surface, appears to have little to do with this book's title. Stick with me on this chapter and by the end of the chapter it will all make sense. Container ships the size of aircraft carriers now enter our ports filled with manufactured goods and they depart our ports empty because we have nothing to sell to the rest of the world. If you ask the typical American how we will pay for this tidal wave of manufactured goods he will shrug his shoulders in total unconcern and say through our service industries. Just what services pray tell do we export to the rest of the world that can compensate for the tidal wave of foreign manufactured goods that are swamping our shores? The correct answer is none.

For generations America had a positive foreign trade balance. We routinely exported more than we imported. Then in the middle 1970s it vanished forever, never to return. This country has not witnessed a positive foreign trade balance since 1974. The world has never seen anything like it. When you look at our foreign trade figures, they are so bad that you can't believe that they are real. We have a positive balance of trade with almost nobody. We can't compete with first world countries. We can't compete with second world countries. We can't even compete with third world countries. We must be a fourth world country because we can compete with no one.

I was born into an America that had the highest standard of living on earth and proudly proclaimed that it had wiped out poverty. I was born into an America in which everyone was middle class. Until the day I die I will remember my third grade teacher telling us that America was a great country because it had wiped out poverty. In the years between 1945-1955 it was common to hear commentators bragging that America had wiped out poverty. No one makes that claim today. Today America has the highest number of people living in poverty than at any time since the Great Depression of the 1930s. A shocking 40.6 million live in poverty. This is roughly about 15% of the population This would have been inconceivable in the America in which I was born. In recent years the poverty rate in America has oscillated between 13%-15% of the population. Today America has the highest rate of poverty in the developed first world. What a disgrace!

I was born into an America that was the industrial powerhouse of the world.

I was born into an America in which everything you bought said "Made in the USA." I now live in an America where almost nothing you buy says "Made in the USA." I was born into an America in which there were no gated communities because when everyone is middle class you don't need gated communities. I was born into an America that in any international ranking would rank in the top three and it would usually be number one. Now in any international ranking we are lucky to rank in the top 15.

We are becoming a parasite nation that manufactures almost nothing and consumes the wealth of the world. When curious foreigners visit this country and stray outside the typical tourist sites, they cannot believe their eyes. They think they have arrived in Calcutta instead of the United States and they are not far wrong because our cities are turning into Calcuttas. The average American is blind to the fact that today's prosperity is a fake prosperity built on America's past achievements and not on our current achievements. Let me be clear: You manufacture or you die, and we are dying. In 1970 manufacturing was 23% of the US economy. Today it is 12% of the economy.

No doubt you have heard of the Rust Belt. Well I have news for you; the Rust Belt is not a belt; it covers most of the nation. The prosperous regions of America are the Boston-Washington corridor which extends from Boston to Washington, D.C.; the states of Florida, Texas and California and the Seattle, Washington region. With a few other exceptions like Denver and Atlanta the rest of the nation is either stagnant or declining. Let me give you an example, upstate New York where I was born and raised. As you know I was born in Cortland, N.Y with a population of 20,000. It was an industrial powerhouse. It had Brockway Trucks. That's right it produced trucks. It had Wickwire Brothers that produced wire in its factory for various purposes. It had Smith-Corona Marchant that produced typewriters and office products. It had the Crescent Factory that manufactured women's undergarments. It had Cortland Fishline where my grandfather worked for decades. This was in a town of only 20,000 people. Each one of these firms employed hundreds of workers and today they are all gone. The only survivor is Cortland Fishline which has been reduced to a pathetic 30 employees. Do you know what Cortland produces today? According to my classmate who never left Cortland, it produces drug addicts. When she told me this I couldn't believe it. In the Cortland that I grew up in, crime and drug addiction were unknown. Forget about leaving the front door unlocked. You could have left the front door wide open and gone on vacation for two weeks in total safety.

Take a look at the once industrial powerhouses of Syracuse, Buffalo and Rochester in upstate New York. These powerhouses made New York State the Empire State. Today all three of them are wrecked shadows of their former selves. With population declines of up to 50%% and poverty rates of 30%. Folks, in the America that I grew up in a poverty rate of 10% would have been inconceivable.

The population of Buffalo has declined a stunning 50% since 1950 and it has a poverty rate of 30.5%. Rochester has lost 34% of its population and has a poverty rate of 32%. Syracuse has lost 33% of its population and has a poverty rate of 32%. Detroit, once the auto manufacturing heartland ranks the highest in the country with a poverty rate of 35%. Since 1950 its population has fallen a stunning 61%. What appears to happen is that every time the poverty rate approaches the 30% area you have a mass out migration of people as they pack their bags and leave seeking a more prosperous place to live. Most people wisely decide that they are not interested in living in a city with a poverty rate of 30%. In every case the cause of the catastrophic decline was the same. The factories were the economic base of these communities and when they were closed the economy collapsed.

We now come to the $64,000 question, how have we been able to get away with this scam? Why do other nations continue to export their goods to us if we manufacture almost nothing that they want in return for their valuable exports? According to the classical economists in a free trade world over any prolonged period exports and imports should balance out. So that your exports should pay for your imports. Our trade figures over decades prove conclusively that this has not been happening. So why do foreign countries continue to export their products to us when we have almost nothing to sell them in return that any of them want?

The answer is that the dollar is the world's reserve currency. Many commentators and economists who should know better think that being the world's reserve is a tremendous economic plus. It is not; it is a curse. In the history of the world there have been only two reserve currencies. First the British pound and now the US dollar. Being the world's reserve currency destroyed what was then called Great Britain and now it is destroying us. Before then for 26 centuries gold and silver alone were the world's reserve currency.

When you are the world's reserve currency it means that your currency is perpetually over valued which has a devastating impact on your export industries and means that your domestic industries must compete with a tidal wave of cheap imports because your currency is overpriced.

Why is the reserve currency perpetually overpriced? Because the world's foreign trade and international finance is conducted in the reserve currency. Here's an example of what I mean. Say India wants to buy a tanker shipment of oil from Saudi Arabia. There is no way that Saudi Arabia is going to accept Indian rupees as payment for its valuable oil. It is going to demand payment in US dollars, the world's reserve currency. India will then have to go into the international market and purchase dollars to pay for its oil imports. The foreign trade of the world is huge and almost all of it is paid for in dollars.

Another example is in international finance that has to be conducted in dollars. This example occurs when third world nations need to borrow money from abroad for national purposes. They are forced to issue dollar bonds when they borrow from abroad. They cannot borrow in their third world domestic currency because international finance is conducted in dollars and third world currencies are death in global finance.

So how does America pay for its tidal wave of imports? Not through its hopelessly inadequate exports I can assure you of that. Nope, we just go to our printing press and print the dollars to pay for our imports. How sweet it is! They send us their cars, televisions and other valuable goodies and we just print the money to pay for it. Such a deal. We are operating the greatest counterfeiting scheme in the history of the world. But it can't last forever.

There is one more prop to the dollar that must be mentioned, the interest rate on our government debt. One of the alleged benefits of being the world's reserve currency is that your government should be capable of borrowing money at a cheaper rate than anyone else. But our crafty central banker, The Federal Reserve Board has put a stop to that nonsense. We are paying just about the highest interest rates on our long term government bonds of any first world nation. This is one more reason why we can't compete with the rest of the world. Our overpriced dollar is destroying our economy.

As this is being written on our long term government bonds, we are currently paying an interest rate of 2.89%. Let's compare this rate with the current rates being paid on long term debt by six nations with high credit ratings. The United Kingdom currently pays 1.5%, Germany pays 1.25%, Japan pays .70%, Canada pays 2.2%, France pays .70%, the Netherlands pays .50%. Why can they borrow money for so much less than we do? Because they are not stupid and we are stupid, that's why!

Let's now take a look at what some countries with credit ratings considerably worse than ours are currently paying on their long term debt. South Korea pays 2.54%, Spain pays 1.37%, Portugal pays 1.78% and Poland pays 2.84%. You will observe that the good, the bad and the ugly all pay rates that are below ours. Why can all these counties pay rates below ours? Let me repeat the answer, the answer is because they are not stupid and we are stupid.

Here is the way intelligent first world countries handle this problem. They decide that based on their status they should be able to borrow money at 1.5% and they issue their bonds at 1.5% on a take it or leave it basis. They are not in the least concerned as to whether the market can absorb all the bonds that they issue at 1.5%. You see they have a secret weapon. Their central banks have a printing press in the basement. And their central banks unlike our central bank are ready, able and willing to print all the money required to purchase all the bonds that the market cannot absorb at the 1.5% rate.

Meanwhile our alleged leaders are running around in a tizzy proclaiming that we are too broke to fix our roads and bridges and that therefore we must let them rot away as we continue our insane march to third world status. Nobody ever asks the real important question. Why are we paying three times as much and more in interest than other countries? The correct answer is that our leaders are so stupid that they don't even know that we are paying three times and more in interest rates than other nations.

This game is destined to end, and it will end badly. It will end when the torrents of dollars that we spend abroad to pay for our imports exceeds the amount that is required to finance international trade and finance. When that day happens, the dollar will start a relentless decline as countries that export to America start to ask themselves why are they selling their valuable products in exchange for dollars that are declining relentlessly in value and that are a drug on the market.

The depression of the 1930s was caused by the stock market crash. America's next depression will be caused by the collapse of the dollar. But it will be a golden period for world commodities because they are all priced in dollars. When the dollar crashes commodity prices will all explode in value. Gold and silver will go to the moon. Historically gold and silver have been the alternative to the world's reserve currency. Silver is often referred to as the poor man's gold with considerable justification. Gold could easily sell for $5,000 an ounce in a dollar collapse. Now you may think that I am nuts. Let's see if I can prove my case.

The History of the Dollar and Gold

When we were in high school studying American history, we were told about America's first dollar, the Continental dollar. It had ended up as a failure because it had been drastically over printed in a desperate attempt to finance the Revolutionary War. In those days when something was totally worthless it was proclaimed that "it ain't worth a Continental" because it was the most worthless thing that anybody could think of.

When the founding fathers wrote the Constitution of the United States in 1788 they were determined that this would never occur again. Section 10 of the Constitution states that only gold and silver coins can be money. They fixed the price of gold at $20 for an ounce of gold and the price of silver at $1.29 an ounce. Have you seen any gold or silver coins lately in your money supply?

This relationship of $20 for an ounce of gold held true until January 1934 when President Franklin D. Roosevelt devalued the dollar by over 40% from $20 an ounce to $35 an ounce. The dollar remained fixed at $35 an ounce until President Nixon in August 1971 took the dollar off of the Gold Exchange Standard thus ending the dollar's convertibility to gold forever and a great bull market in gold began.

In 2011 gold finally peaked at $1,920 an increase of nearly 55 times over the $35 an ounce figure. By 2015 it had crashed to a low of $1,046 an ounce and as this is being written it has risen to around $1,300 an ounce. To get to $5,000 an ounce from today's price would only require an increase in value of only four times. Not an impossibility.

It is common for me to hear Americans say that they don't understand gold. Okay let me explain it for you. The unstated assumption here is that back in the day a group of men secretly gathered in a smoke filled room and arbitrarily and for no good reason at all picked gold and silver, the poor man's gold, to be the money supply. The assumption here is that they could have just as arbitrarily have picked lead, copper, iron, wampum or beaver pelts all of which have historically served as money. The truth is that men were indeed gathering in smoke filled rooms before tobacco was even discovered and arbitrarily choosing lead, copper, iron, wampum, beaver skins, silk and dozens of other commodities as money but it never stuck. Only gold and silver stuck. The first gold coins were minted in Turkey in 600 B.C. They were made out of electrum a natural alloy of gold and silver found in the region. In a Darwinian struggle encompassing 26 centuries of history gold and silver triumphed over all other contenders. Gold and silver triumphed not because they were arbitrarily picked in a smoke filled room but because they were rare, beautiful, desirable and cannot be debased by government action.

When archeologists dig into grave sites that are more than 4,000 years old, they find treasured gold and silver objects. When they dig into grave sites that are 3,000 years old, they find treasured gold and silver objects. When they dig into grave sites that are 2,000 years old, they find treasured gold and silver objects. When they dig into grave sites that are 1,000 years old, they find treasured gold and silver objects. It also does not matter whether the grave sites are discovered in the high Andes or in Mexico, China, India, Scandinavia, Egypt or the Persian Gulf.

Let me refine that. They find gold and silver in the grave sites of the kings, the nobility, the high priests and the war lords. In the graves of the middle class they find silver but no gold. In the graves of peasants they find no gold and no silver. Throughout history, gold and silver have conferred status.

They are history's ultimate status symbols. Get the picture?

When archaeologists discover the tomb of any pharaoh in Egypt that has not been looted, they always find gold and silver. When the conquistadors conquered the Aztecs and the Incas in Mexico and Peru, they found their temples covered with gold and silver just like pharaohs' tombs in Egypt. Their kings or emperors and high priests adorned themselves with gold and silver just like the Egyptian high priests did thousands of years before they were born. Yet, the Incas and the Aztecs not only had never heard of each other but were separated from the pharaohs of Egypt by thousands of miles in distance and thousands of years in time.

The key words here are adornment and status. Gold and silver were always prized as adornment in the form of jewelry and for the status that they provided. That is what gave them their value. Consider the bride showing off her gold wedding ring. That gold wedding ring confirms that she has status. It confirms that someone thinks she is important as nothing else could. When someone with a ghetto background becomes successful, the first thing they do is to cover themselves with "bling," as they refer to gold and silver jewelry. No one tells them to do this; they do it automatically. Gold and silver have been conferring status since civilization began 5,000 years ago.

From there it was an easy step for gold and silver to become money. Even today most of the world's annual gold production is turned into jewelry. What is the first thing that comes to mind if you need quick cash for a week or two? It is the pawn shop. They will be eager to take your gold and silver because they know that gold and silver can easily be converted into cash.

A popular refrain from the "Gold is a barbarous relic" crowd is that gold has no practical value and therefore is not a good investment. What is the Mona Lisa worth? What is the practical value of the global art market? What is the practical value of the global music industry? What is the practical value of the entertainment industry? What is the practical value of a Hollywood film studio? According to this logic casinos should be a bad investment because gambling is not practical.

When the females of the world agree that they would rather have their wedding ring made out of copper rather than gold because copper is a practical metal unlike gold give me a call.

Having said that, gold has more practical uses than is generally realized. The mix of global gold consumption changes every year but in the period between 1981 to 2005 jewelry demand alone accounted for an amazing 78% of annual gold production. What happens is that as investment demand for gold increases it crowds out jewelry demand which cannot compete with investment demand. These figures always surprise people who assume that almost all demand for gold is investment demand.

The last argument of the anti-gold forces is that gold is a bad investment because it pays no interest. To hear them rant and rave about the subject the wise investor will become rich, rich just by opening a savings account and collecting those big, big interest payments.

Obviously, these clowns haven't opened a savings account in recent years. Recently I read an article in the Wall Street Journal that did a survey of what the typical savings interest rate being paid to savers is today. Brace yourself, it is 1%. Earlier in this work I introduced you to the rule of 72. As you will recall you divide the interest rate being paid into 72 and that will tell you how many years it will take for the power of compounding to double your money. At 8% money doubles in 9 years. At 6% it doubles in 12 years etc. At 1% it doubles in 72 years at 2% it doubles in 36 years. Folks, this could be a human lifetime! But wait, we have to pay taxes on that big, big interest that we are earning, don't we? How many years will it take for your savings account to double after you subtract the annual taxes from your savings account? Folks, you are not going to live long enough to see a double.

Not to worry. Being the crafty interest rate investor that you are you have been following government bonds. In the world of bonds, the longer the maturity date the higher the interest rate paid. For example, as these words are being written the two year treasury bond is currently paying an interest rate of 2.4% and the longest dated treasury bond, the 30 year bond, is paying about 2.9%. Stupid people think you can't lose money on long term government bonds. Guess again. While it is true that there is no default risk on long term government bonds there is interest rate risk. That is why 30 year bonds pay a higher rate of interest than 2 year bonds.

It is important to understand that in the world of bonds interest rates and bond prices are inversely correlated. In other words, as interest rates go up bond prices fall in value and as interest decline bond prices rise in value. But you have your priorities straight. You are going for that big, big interest payment. After all there is no default risk in government bonds. You have just heard that the government is issuing new 30 year bonds that are going to pay 3% interest. Being the financial genius that you are you close your savings account where you were earning that big, big 1% interest rate and rush to buy that 30 year bond that is paying a whopping 3% interest rate to lock in the rate for 30 years. You know that according the rule of 72 at 3% your money doubles in 24 years. You will be rich, rich. That sure beats 36 years. Now as long as interest rates remain at 3% everything is going to be fine. Every year for the next 30 years you will receive that big, big interest payment of $30 on your $1,000 30 year bond. At the end of 30 years the bond will mature, and the government will pay you back your $1,000.

But what happens if the interest rate that the government pays on 30 year bonds shifts? Now things are going to get very, very interesting for all 30 year bond holders. Remember that bonds and interest rates are inversely correlated. Let's say that the rate of interest on newly issued 30 year government bonds has fallen from 3% to 1.5% for some obscure reason. You sly dog. You are now a financial genius. All the 30 year bonds that were issued at 3% will now skyrocket in value. Let's take a look at why.

You are receiving $30 a year in interest payments on your 30 year bond but the new 30 year bonds that are being issued pay only $15 a year. What will happen is that all the 30 year bonds that were issued to you at $1,000 will now skyrocket in price until they reach $2,000 at which point they will be paying the same interest rate in dollars received as the new 30 year bond which is paying a 1.5% rate.

Now let's take a look at what happens if the interest rate on new 30 year bonds rises instead of falling and rises to 6%. Things are going to get very ugly. Investors on newly issued 30 year bonds are now receiving not the $30 a year in interest payments that you are receiving but $60 a year. The value of your bond must now fall to $500 for investors to receive the going rate of a 6% return on their investment. In other words, while there is no default risk in government bonds there is interest rate risk and the longer the maturity of the bond the greater the interest rate risk.

Then there is the little matter of the taxes you have to pay on those big, big interest rates.

I am a coin collector and have held gold and silver coins in my collection for many years. I purchased my first gold coin, a gorgeous $20 gold piece, which is more than 100 years old and contains nearly one ounce of gold, years ago at $250. Today it is worth somewhere around $1,800-$2,000. Guess what! I have never paid a dime in taxes on that profit. You see, folks, gold pays no interest. I think that you can tell that I am broken-hearted that my gold coins don't pay any interest. Furthermore, I will never have to pay any taxes whatsoever on my capital gains until the collection is sold.

Since I have brought up the subject let me tell you my story about my investment career in gold and silver. I think you may find it interesting.

I became a coin collector in the late 1960's. Even then I had my priorities straight. I limited my collection almost exclusively to silver dollars and gold coins. The smallest coin I would collect was the half dollar coin. In those days the dime, quarter and half dollar were all 90% silver. The government had decreed that the price of silver would never rise above $1.29 an ounce because above that price it would become profitable to melt down the coins for their silver content. Naturally I believed that the price of silver would never rise above $1.29 an ounce. Boy was I stupid.

For the coin collector the greatest prestige coin is the gorgeous $20 gold piece. The nation's largest gold coin. The satisfying heft and feel of a $20 gold piece is something you will never forget once you have held it in your hand. You will then know beyond the shadow of any doubt that you are holding something of true worth and the passion that has caused every gold rush in history becomes clear. The $20 gold piece contains about 9/10th of an ounce of gold. I really wanted to add the $20 gold piece to my collection, but I was stopped dead in my tracks by the fact that the government had decreed that the price of gold would be forever fixed at $35 an ounce. Naturally I believed that the price of gold would never rise above $35 an ounce. How could the all wise, all powerful U.S. government be wrong. At that time the ads in Coin World were offering to sell the $20 gold piece for $70. The problem was that the $20 gold piece only had a gold content of about $35. At that time, I didn't have much money and $70 was worth a lot more than it is today. I just could not talk myself into paying $70 for a gold coin that I was convinced would never have a gold value of more than $35. In addition to that there were rumors that the U.S. might stop buying gold at $35 an ounce. Economists were lined up three times around the block in those days predicting that if the government stopped supporting the price of gold at $35 an ounce it would fall to its true value of $20 an ounce.

My faith in economists has never recovered in spite of the fact that I majored in economics in college. In 1971 the government stopped supporting the price of gold at $35 an ounce and instead of falling to $20 an ounce as these brilliant economists had predicted gold began its relentless rise. The economists who had predicted that the price of gold would fall to $20 an ounce vanished and were never heard from again. When the price of the $20 gold piece reached $250, I suddenly was able to talk myself into buying it. I still have those $20 gold pieces in my collection.

One day I woke up and discovered that I had $28,000 in gold and silver coins in my collection at home where anyone could walk in and steal it. The next day I rented the biggest safety deposit box that the Bank of America offers and I stuffed my coin collection and my 10 ounce silver bars in it. Once or twice a year I go to the bank and visit my collection. That's my story.

The 2018 global gold demand figures are typical of what has been happening in recent years with demand. Jewelry was about 65% of global demand, industrial/dental was 14%, and coins & bars was only 15%. Other uses came in at 6%. The figure of 15% for gold bars and coins is far lower than the common perception which assumes that almost all gold demand is investment demand in gold bars and coins.

The experts are unable to agree on the total amount of gold produced since gold mining began but the consensus estimates are between 155,000 metric tons to 174,000 metric tons or around 5.6 billion troy ounces. Nearly all of which is still in existence since gold is rarely consumed. What the experts can agree on is that the gold stock since 1900 has grown only about 1% or 2% a year.

If you wanted to give every human being on earth a one ounce gold ring you could not do it because the global population exceeds all the gold that has ever been mined. The world's population is 7.7 billion people and there is only about 5.6 billion ounces of gold in existence. A gold ring weighing about three-quarters of an ounce of gold would consume all the gold produced in history. That is when the true rarity of gold sinks in. It is interesting to note that today about 19% of the world's gold supply is still held by central banks and what is more remarkable in recent years the central bank holdings of the barbarous relic has actually been increasing after a long period of decline.

If you stop and think about it, it isn't hard to figure out why. Since the great recession of 2007-2009 central banks all over the world have dropped their interest rates to nearly zero and are engaged in a bacchanalia of currency debasements to support their domestic industries. Many central banks for the first time in history are proudly paying negative interest rates to their suckers. I mean bond holders. Somehow, I don't think that negative interest rates were what the gold bashers had in mind when they were ranting and raving that gold was a bad investment because it didn't pay interest. Now let's take a look at where gold is produced.

From 1905 to 2007 South Africa was the world's largest producer of gold. It has been estimated that 50% of all the gold ever produced came from South Africa. In 2007 China replaced South Africa as the world's top gold producer.

Experts believe that 80% of the gold ever mined has been mined since 1900 when 393 tons was produced. By 2017 the figure was 3,150 tons the highest figure in history. It is interesting to note that today about 25% of all the gold produced comes from so-called artisanal production. This refers to small mom and pop operators who are often regarded as being semi-legal producers since they often don't own the land they are extracting the ore from. Below are two charts of the 2018 top gold producing and consuming nations.

2018 Top Gold Producing Nations

China = 426 tons

Australia = 295 tons

Russia = 270 tons

United States = 230 tons

Canada = 175 tons

Peru = 162 tons
Indonesia = 154 tons
South Africa = 139 tons

2018 Top Gold Consuming Nations
China = 984 tons
India = 849 tons
USA = 193 tons
Germany = 124 tons
Thailand = 90 tons
Saudi Arabia = 85 tons
United Arab Emirates = 58 tons
Turkey = 72 tons

The above charts reveal some interesting facts about the world of gold. The most astonishing fact about the gold producing nations is the amazing rise of China from nowhere to become the world's top producer and the collapse of South Africa as a gold producer. For more than 100 years it was the world's top gold producer. This collapse has been abetted by the militant South African mine unions who seem to have a death wish. They can't seem to wrap their minds around the concept that the South African mining industry is in deep, deep trouble. The industry is compelled to dig deeper and deeper and the ore grades keep declining. This is a fatal combination. If they keep on striking, they will strike themselves into oblivion.

The second intriguing fact about the producers is that the United States produces more gold than Canada does largely from its open pit, low grade mines. This is in spite of the fact that Canada's top producers have a much higher grade ore.

When we look at the top gold consuming nations what sticks out is the overwhelming dominance of India and China. Another point of interest is the enormous gold consumption of Saudi Arabia and the United Arab Emirates given their small populations. Together they consume almost as much gold as the U.S. Lastly of the top eight consuming nations all are Asian except for the USA and Germany.

Apparently, the populace of the western nations of the world can't figure out for the life of them why anyone would want to own gold. After all, didn't Keynes say gold was a barbarous relic? In the 19th century the United States had no problem understanding gold; it was the most gold mad country on earth. It began with the California Gold Rush of 1849 and for the rest of the 19th century Americans stampeded from one gold and silver strike in the west to the next. It finally ended with the Yukon gold rush of 1898. Today the average American sits around scratching his head in wonder as he tries to figure out what the scoop is about gold and silver. It has been estimated that only about 5% of Americans own any gold or silver coins or bars.

The next chapter in the history of gold and silver will be written in Asia where it is adored and not in the west where it is scorned and regarded as a barbaric relic.

Who among us has not noticed that every time you pass a pawn shop it has signs saying, "We buy gold"? They never have signs saying, "Hey sucker, we want to sell you this worthless gold and it doesn't matter how high or how low the price of gold is." The pawn shops are always buying. The reason for this is because they have what in the marketplace is called a "permanent bid." The permanent bidder is Asia. After the pawn shops acquire the gold and silver they are melted down into gold and silver bars and shipped to Asia never to return. The demand for gold and silver in Asia never stops.

The Fear Market and the Love Market

Properly understood the gold market can be split into two components. The fear market and the love market. In the west the fear market dominates.

The general consensus of opinion is that the only reason to buy gold is fear and when the fear has been erased you emerge from your bomb shelter and sell your gold. In short gold is only a temporary asset.

In Asia the love trade dominates. Gold and silver are adored and are forever. If you can afford it, you buy gold. If you are too poor to buy gold you buy silver. Which has rightly been called the poor man's gold. Gold and silver are both your savings account and your life insurance account. They are not a short term trade. Centuries of history have convinced Asians that governments cannot be trusted. Only gold and silver can be trusted.

Real estate is an inferior asset. If you doubt this go talk to the Jews. When Hitler appeared, those Jews who placed their faith in real estate were trapped. They knew if they fled, their real estate would be expropriated so they stayed and were wiped out. Those Jews who placed their faith in gold and silver survived and prospered. The wonderful thing about gold and silver is that you can bury it and come back for it later or you can carry a fortune in gold on your person as you are fleeing to safety. Try doing that with real estate. Since the end of the Second World War countless millions of refugees have been driven from their homes. Their legal title to the real estate that they own are worthless scrapes of paper. Their future prosperity and often their very existence is often dependent on their ownership of gold and silver and not on the value of their real estate which cannot be taken with you when are fleeing for your life and can be expropriated at will. According to the latest news reports there are 65 million refugees in the world today who have been forced to flee their homes. This is probably a world record.

As these words are being written a protracted war is being waged between the fear trade of the west and the love trade of the east.

Bear market speculators in New York, Chicago, London and Zurich, by employing the use of futures and sophisticated financial contracts, have been able to smash the price of gold from the record $1,920 an ounce level to the $1,200s level, where it has been oscillating since 2014, and smash the price of silver from the $40s to the $14.00 - $16.00 an ounce level. The Asians are grateful to these speculators for lowering the price of these precious metals. For them a price decline of this magnitude is a wonderful buying opportunity and not the end of the world. You see they know that gold and silver are forever. In the west bear market speculators through the use of futures and other paper derivatives have managed to hammer the price of gold and silver. Every time they earn a 10% profit, they will be happy to tell you that they are masters of the universe. Meanwhile if I am right the status of the dollar, the world's reserve currency may be entering its final days and slowly but inexorably gold and silver departs the bullion vaults of the west for a one way trip to Asia. The day will come when there will not be enough gold and silver remaining in the bullion vaults of the west to support the futures driven bear market raids of the speculators. When that day comes the price of gold and silver will rise to levels that will astonish the world.

The state anointed contender for gold and silver as a store of value is of course paper money. Paper money always ends, and it always ends badly. The first paper money was invented in China in the 13th century. Marco Polo reported on it in amazement. It was only accepted because the refusal to accept it was punished by death. Since that time every paper currency that has been created has ended up with a zero value. There aren't any exceptions to this rule. None!

The only question is, how many generations will it take you to get to zero? It is hard to credit what absolute garbage most of the world's currencies are. The three soundest paper currencies the world has ever known are the British pound, the U.S. dollar and the Swiss franc. Aside from these three currencies there are amazingly few currencies in the world that a prudent investor would regard as being even remotely sound over the long run.

By the way the alleged mighty German mark does not qualify. Twice in the 20th century the German mark became worthless. Check your history books. The first time the mark became worthless was after Germany lost the First World War and the second time it became worthless was after it lost the Second World War.

The British pound when it was created in 1694 was worth a pound of silver. That's why it is called the pound. By the way, a pound of silver today at $16 an ounce is worth about $256. Do you think there might have been some inflation along the way? The U.S. dollar, at birth was fixed at $20 for an ounce of gold. The Swiss franc was created in 1799.

According to a recent report from Dollardaze.org, which keeps track of such things there are currently 177 currencies in circulation. Fourteen of these currencies are ten years old or less. The median age of a currency from creation to extinction is 37 years. Of the 786 paper currencies known to history, only 23% are still in existence. The rest were abandoned after they became worthless. After the world's super active printing presses have destroyed a currency, they either create a currency with a new name to replace the old currency or they do a reverse split of the old currency of say 10:1 or 20:1 or 100:1.

The classic example of the 100:1 reverse split is when France, under the leadership of Charles De Gaulle ,converted the then existing franc that was trading at 360 francs to the dollar, if I remember correctly, into a new strong franc at 3.6 francs to the dollar.

Is the Bull Market in Gold Finished?

As these words are being written gold is consolidating at the $1,300 an ounce level after peaking at $1,920 in August 2011. The consensus opinion has always been that gold is a barbarous relic and therefore a bad investment. After all that is what Keynes said and how could Keynes, be wrong.

However, the real story is far different. In August of 1971 President Nixon took the United States off the gold standard. At that time gold was selling for $35.00 an ounce. In the 48 years since 1971, the price of gold has risen 54 times to an all-time high of $1,920 and 37 times at its current price. When you look at the gold market what hits you in the head is how little gold the speculators own. The following is the recent World Gold Council estimates.

What do the speculators own?

Jewelry - 52%

Central banks - 19%

Investment -16%

Industrial - 11%

Other - 2%

Jewelry at 52% dominates the gold market. What do you think the chances are that if the price of gold falls another 25% or 50% hysterical husbands are going to rip off their wives wedding rings and rush off to the pawnshop to sell it?

Central banks are now second largest holders of gold at 19% and are no longer dumping gold. They are now net buyers of gold. In 2018 they bought 651 metric tons of gold. This was the greatest amount of purchases by central banks since 1967. It is now estimated that central banks now hold nearly 34,000 tons of gold. They no longer trust the currencies of other nations. It is about time that they snapped out of their stupidity. Most of the buyers as usual come from Asian countries with whom we don't have the friendliest relations. Increasingly it has dawned on these nations that keeping their foreign reserves in dollars is not too swift. In addition to the ever present threat of currency depreciation which exist for all currencies. An unfriendly US could place sanctions on the dollars which are all in the form of US debt instruments making it impossible to convert their US bonds into dollars to finance their international activities. Gold ownership faces none of these problems.

The Debt Mountain and
the Coming Explosion in Gold

As these words are being written gold is selling around $1,300 an ounce and has been dead in the water for several years. The major reason for this is not hard to find. In the industrial economies of the west for the first time since the Second World War inflation has ground to a halt. Even more amazing this phenomenon has been occurring during a period when for the first time in history almost every central bank on earth has announced that 2% inflation was its goal, something that would have been unthinkable at any time in the past. In addition, they have been making frantic efforts to achieve this goal. Interest rates in the advanced economies have fallen to levels not seen in generations and in many cases have fallen to the lowest level in recorded history.

Even negative interest rates once unthinkable are now common. Yet inflation has not been ignited and the question is, why not? China and the growing export prowess of Asia have been the major factor in the inability to ignite inflation. The tidal wave of their cheap exports has had a profound deflationary effect on the advanced world, making it extraordinarily difficult to raise domestic prices. But there is another villain hiding in the weeds, the crushing burden of the debt mountain which is now endemic throughout the world. Never has there been this much debt. The Keynesian solution for recessions or slow growth was to increase "aggregate demand" the holy of holies for Keynesians. Their not-so-secret sauce was to lower interest rates so that you could borrow more to spend more, thus firing up the economy. In the short term this works but in the long term the newly acquired debt crushes future demand. Indeed, the best definition of debt I have ever heard is that debt is future consumption denied. The Keynesian solution to this was to inflate the debt away so that you could perpetually borrow more and more. From the end of the Second World War until the great recession of 2007-2009 it worked like a charm and then it stopped working. Basically, what happened is that central bankers hit what is called the "zero bound." In other words, you can't lower interest rates below zero. Then the central bankers amazed themselves and everyone else by pushing interest rates into negative territory for the first time in history and it still didn't work very well. The combined impact of the debt mountain and the deflationary impact of China and the rest of the Asian gang on domestic pricing was too much. Inflation could not be ignited. In such a scenario debt becomes deflationary. Aggregate demand cannot be increased because the debt burden has become so crushing that after servicing the debt there is not enough left over to increase aggregate demand. There is only one solution: Inflation must be ignited again and the level of indebtedness is so horrific that a mere 2% inflation rate isn't going to get the job done. I have great faith in the ability of the central bankers to get inflation rolling again. After all, when you have a printing press in the basement nothing is impossible. Recently noted bond expert Bill Gross of Janus Capital stated that global bond yields are at the lowest level in 500 years of recorded history and that there is a staggering $10 trillion of negative interest rate bonds sloshing around the global economy. It should surprise no one that Global Debt to Global GDP peaked in 2009 at 303% and is probably the true cause of the Great Recession that circled the globe. Today Global Debt has slowly creeped back to an alarming 298% of Global GDP. Debt at this level is simply unsustainable. When the central bankers crack the code to igniting inflation again there is going to be massive inflation because the debt mountain has to be eradicated because it cannot possibly be paid off. When this wave of inflation hits gold and silver are going to the moon. Millions of investors who would never have considered gold as an investment as long as they could earn a decent interest rate on their investment will be driven to gold and silver. But before we get to the stocks themselves it is time to go into more detail about how I analyze penny mining stocks.

How I Analyze Penny Stocks

Penny stocks that are in production are analyzed the way any other stock is analyzed. But most penny stocks are not in production and a different form of analysis is required. I call this process Termination Analysis because I am trying to estimate what the corporation would be worth if they terminated the company and sold off the assets. If you stop and think about it a mining stock that is not in production is in reality a real estate company in drag. It has one asset. Its mining claims which are real estate and if it is an ex-producer its plant and infrastructure. What I needed was a quick and dirty figure that I could apply to all mining companies. I decided that as a broad and general principal I would assume that mining acreage that was not in production would be apt to have a value equivalent to agricultural crop land. I then did a search and found the following data. The national average for crop land was $4,100/acre. California had the highest average value for crop land at $12,000/acre. I finally decided to settle on Iowa which is in the top half of the list with crop land selling at $8,000/acre as my indicator of value.

There are two types of mining claims in the United States, patented mining claims and unpatented mining claims. Patented mining claims are the most valuable because you own the complete bundle of rights to the land. Unpatented mining claims are less valuable because you don't own the complete bundle of rights to the land. You don't own the surface rights to the land, you only own the mineral rights. Therefore, when I am doing a termination analysis I assign a value of $8,000 for each patented acre and $4,000 for each unpatented acre. I never cease to be amazed at how much pushback I get when I tell people how much value I am assigning to each acre of land. The standard response is that the value is too high. Folks, it is probably a good assumption that 80-90% of all the acreage sales in this country sell for $10,000 an acre and up. If you are assuming a value much below $10,000 an acre, I hope that you have comparable sales to back it up. Now $8,000 an acre only works in the United States which is the third most populous nation on earth. It certainly would not work in Canada with its vast northern tundras.

The first thing I do is to figure out the capitalization of the company. In this process you multiply the stock float, which is the total number of issued shares outstanding, by the current stock price, and the resulting figure is the capitalization of the company. This is the price that the company is selling for, lock stock and barrel. I then divide the capitalization by the total number of acres that the company owns. The resulting figure is how much value the market is placing on each acre of land the corporation owns. I then assign a value of $8,000 for every patented acre land that the corporation owns and $4,000 an acre for every unpatented acre the corporation owns and compare the values.

The Revolution in Royalties

I am a big fan of royalty companies and I have already mentioned them. Historically, royalties in the mining world were a one-off event. They were typically given to a prospector or a small miner when they sold out to a major outfit, usually as a sweetener. It had never occurred to anyone that you could build a profitable business around buying, selling and creating royalties until Franco Nevada (FNV) the unchallenged king of the royalty companies appeared on the scene in 2007. It has been a big winner for me. I bought the stock right after the IPO (initial public offering) at $18 a share. It is currently selling at around $85 a share.

To fully understand the attraction of mining royalty companies you have to understand the disastrous career of major blue chip mining companies if they exist at all. I have touched on this problem earlier. Big mining companies all suffer from the same curse, the depleting giant ore bodies that made them what they are. Giant ore bodies are few and far between. With a few exceptions the majors have a disastrous record when it comes to replacing their giant ore bodies at a price that enables them to earn a decent profit.

The star performer in the mining world has always been the up and coming junior producer that is exploiting new ore bodies with a long future ahead of them. In the corporate world buying out the juniors has never been a necessity. In the mining world however it is an absolute necessity unless you are willing to bet the ranch on new, giant, unproven high risk deposits that will cost you the world to develop. The smart money play for the majors is to buy out the juniors after they have de-risked their properties. Of course, the juniors are only too willing to be bought out if the price is right. In fact, there are quite a few shrewd junior mining entrepreneurs who are serial players in this game. Why take on the high cost, high risk gamble of going into production when you can sell out to a major and let them take the risk. But I am digressing. Let's get back to the subject at hand, the royalty company.

The beauty of the new model royalty company invented by Franco Nevada is that it did an end run around the depletion problem. It didn't end the depletion problem. But it shifted the burden of dealing with the consequences of depleting ore bodies onto the shoulders of others. The royalty company makes one big upfront payment when it purchases the royalty and after that it is never on the hook for another dime for as long as the ore body is in production. In addition, if the royalty is written properly it has a claim that is superior to that of the mining company that has granted the royalty. Because the royalty is attached to the ore body and not to the miner that is producing it. If the miner goes broke and a new producer goes into production the royalty must still be paid. There is one other new royalty type that must be discussed that has become wildly popular in the last five or ten years; it is called the Streaming Royalty. A Steaming Royalty is a royalty contract between the royalty company and the miner in which in return for a substantial upfront payment the miner agrees to grant the royalty company a discounted, fixed price for the metal produced that is substantially below the current spot price of the metal when the contract was signed. The streaming royalty can also be a percentage discount from the current spot price rather than a fixed discount.

Now before we go on to natural resources and my gold and silver plays a word of warning. If you are not shocked yet about the low, low prices of the stocks that I am willing to own, stick around. You are going to be shocked! Shocked!

"You cannot be serious? Buying Ely Royalties at 12 cents share? I don't think so."

Before you write off these penny mining plays consider this. Penny mining stocks are the most highly leveraged, hard asset plays on earth. They are perpetual call options on the metal. If the price of the metal that they own is declining or stagnant then they will not do well. That is simply a given that must be accepted. Most of the non-producers in a stagnant or declining market are trapped. The suits will not give them the money they need to go into production as long as gold is selling in the $1,200s. Most of them need gold in the $1,500 range. If the price of gold goes back to $1,500 an ounce, forget about going back to $1,900 an ounce; these plays will go to the moon! To the moon!

Remember my maximum investment in a penny stock is 1% of my investment capital. My typical investment in a penny stock is 1/10 of 1% to 1/4 of 1%. Contemplate this; at 12 cents a share you can buy 10,000 shares for $1,200. Let me make this more concrete. Every week the Northern Miner reports on the stocks of the Toronto TSX and the junior TSXV with the greatest percentage change. Below is the result of the greatest percentage gainers for one week on the junior exchange which as you might guess has the most explosive numbers.

Fusion Gold closed @ 30 cents up 160%
Adex Mining closed @ 2 cents up 100%
Northern Uranium closed @ 2 cents up 100%
92 Resources closed @ 8 cents up 66 %
Solstice Gold closed @ 26 cents up 53%
Pure Nickel closed @ 2 cents up 50%
Jayden Resources closed @ 2 cents up 50%
Arizona Mining closed @ $2.15 up 43%
Gespeg Copper Resources closed @ 4 cents up 40%
Awale Resources closed @ 11 cents up 38%

Welcome to my world. It is not at all unusual for the top four or five percentage gainers on the Venture Exchange to show increases in value of 100% and more. Where else do you see returns like this in a single week? You diversify broadly. Your maximum investment is 1% of your investment capital. If you lose you write it off on your taxes and you will have losers. Get over it! Grow up! If you have $60,000 in capital gains in year and $30,000 in capital losses your $30,000 in capital losses will be subtracted from your $60,000 in profits and you will only be taxed on $30,000 in capital gains. This is not the end of the world. The government is subsidizing your risk taking. How cool is that? The hysterics that the typical investor exhibits when he has Mickey Mouse losses never ceases to amaze me. You will observe that only one stock closed at more than a dollar a share. For chump change you can buy thousands of shares in each position and still have massive diversification. What's not to like?

Natural Resources and the
Law of Supply and Demand

Correctly understood the law of supply and demand works like a pair of scissors. Each blade of the scissors is interrelated and must work together for the law to work. Wall Street does not regard the law of supply and demand as being a pair of scissors. It thinks of demand as a faucet and water as the supply that flows through the faucet. In this model, supply is the always obedient slave of demand. It is only necessary to turn the faucet handle and supply the ever-obedient slave of demand flows through it in the required amounts.

It must be admitted that this model works quite well in the world of manufacturing and services. What Wall Street doesn't understand is that this model may be in the early stages of breaking down in the world of natural resources and that this breakdown is not a temporary phenomenon. To the extent that it is even considered at all, the last bull market in natural resources and commodities is thought of on "the street" as a one-off event that will not soon be repeated.

Everyone will of course admit that in theory the supply of natural resources is ultimately fixed. But that unhappy day is always assumed to be centuries in the future. This fact is always assumed. No serious attempt is ever made to prove it.

We are now more than two hundred years into the industrial revolution with its ravenous demand for natural resources and with the greatest population the world has ever known. At the vanguard of this revolution is the industrializing BRIC nations of Brazil, Russia, India and China. With a gigantic combined population of 2.5 billion people. The sheer size of this demand on the existing natural resource base is without historical precedent. The populations of Western Europe and North America when they were industrializing were minuscule in comparison.

The cheapest and the most easily accessible mineral fields are always put into production first. As these fields are slowly depleted away, they are replaced with ever poorer and less accessible fields. One of the favorite ploys of the natural-resources-in-abundance crowd is to confuse potential-pie-in-the sky assumed reserves in remote and far distant locations as proven reserves. And then to assume or more accurately to insist that these assumed reserves can be developed at the same costs that current producers enjoy. It should be obvious that for the most part, they cannot possibly be developed at anything like the costs being enjoyed by current producers.

A good example of this is the now notorious Kashagan oil field in Kazakhstan on the Caspian Sea. This estimated ten billion barrel super giant field, one of only three such super giants discovered since 1970 was found in the year 2000. It has had political and geological problems galore. What I am trying to say is that the mere fact that natural resources exist does not mean that they will flow out of the faucet on demand.

But the real game changer is the greens. Who are convinced that it is their destiny to stop every new discovery from coming on-stream? Their success rate has been astonishing. And not just in the developed world as so many believe but in the third world as well.

The Northern Miner, which is the Wall Street Journal of the mining industry, has been reporting for years on the truly remarkable ability of a handful of green zealots to mobilize peasants all over the third world. Green field projects from the Andes to Outer Mongolia have been stopped again and again.

There will be consequences! The most important consequence of course is that in the new emerging world order natural resources that can actually be brought into production will produce unusually high profits when compared to historical returns. Wealth in the ground will make you rich.

The Gold Regions

Canada has two major producing gold plays or camps as they are referred to in Canada. The Red Lake gold play and the Kirkland Lake gold play. Traditionally all Canadian mining camps are named after the nearest significant lake.

I know what you are thinking. You are thinking what if there is no lake in the vicinity. The chance of this happening is zero. Canada has tens of thousands of lakes and I do mean tens of thousands. It would not surprise me if Canada had 100,000 lakes. I have owned two mines that were located on an island in the middle of a lake.

Red Lake Gold Camp - is located in northwest Ontario near the Manitoba border. Gold was first discovered in Red Lake in 1926. Historically it has had the richest gold ore body in Canada and one of the highest grade ore bodies anywhere in the world. It has produced ore grades in the unrivaled 1 ounce a ton range. Over 26 million ounces of gold have been extracted from 29 hard rock, underground mines since gold was discovered there in 1926.

Kirkland Lake Gold Camp - is second only to Red Lake in both gold production and ore grade. It is located in southeastern Ontario. It too is a high grade gold camp. Ore grades in the .45 troy ounce a ton range are not considered unusual. Its mines have produced 24 million ounces since the 1920s from hard rock underground mines.

Nevada is called the Silver State but every year it produces about 80% of all the gold that is produced in the U.S. The remaining 20% is for the most part a byproduct of base metal mining, usually copper mines. In a typical year it produces about 175 tons of gold. Since they started keeping records in 1835 the state has produced a most impressive 4,700 tons. Almost all the gold in Nevada is produced from low grade, open pit mines using the cyanide heap leach recovery method.

The Carlin Trend - the vast majority of the gold produced in Nevada comes from the famous Carlin Trend. The Carlin Trend is five miles wide and forty miles long and runs in a northwest to southeast direction. There is a huge amount of gold in the Carlin Trend, but it is of very low grade. It was discovered in 1961 but as a result of its low grade it was not until 1965 that Newmont Mining began mining the low grade but abundant ore. The Carlin Trend has produced more than 1,600 tons of gold, more than any other mining district in the U.S. The Carlin Trend includes the world's third largest gold mine, Barrick's Gold's Goldstrike Mine.

Mexico has to be mentioned but as a silver producer that produces gold as a byproduct. Mexico and Peru have been leading silver producers for 500 years since the Spanish Conquistadors conquered the Aztecs in Mexico and the Incas in Peru.

In the last 500 years the Mexican Silver Belt has produced one-third of the world's silver. Its silver belt is located in the Sierra Madre Mountains in the area around Zacatecas. Mexico is the world's largest silver producer. Silver is produced both as primary silver and as a by-product of gold and base metal operations. The major production states are Zacatecas, Durango, Chihuahua, Guanajuato and Querétaro. The Fresnillo mine in Zacatecas is ranked as the world's largest primary silver mine. The main silver producing companies are Fresnillo Plc, which is the world's largest primary silver producer. Mexico's second largest silver producer is Industrials Peñoles and Grupo Mexico is ranked third. One trend in the Mexican Silver industry is the growth of smaller silver producers. The activities of this new breed of junior developers and producers may be more modest than Fresnillo, but nonetheless they are becoming significant players in the silver market and represent an interesting asset class for investors wanting to invest in pure silver companies. I will mention a few of these that I own later on.

The Legendary Comstock Lode

In 1849 the great California gold rush was in full cry. On their trek west to the California goldfields some of the would-be prospectors who were taking the northern Nevada route stopped at what was to become known as Gold Canyon. The southern entrance to this seven mile Canyon was located a few miles west of what today is Dayton, Nevada. Many of the would-be prospectors made a habit of test sampling the terrain as they moved west for what they called "color" or specks of gold dust and hopefully small nuggets. During this initial surge west, they did indeed find modest amounts of gold in what they rather laughingly named Gold Canyon. But the modest amounts of gold that they were retrieving from Gold Canyon seemed to them to be small potatoes compared to the legendary goldfields that awaited them in California.

By the late 1850s the glory days of the California goldfields was ending. The now experienced, hard-bitten prospectors fanned out from their California base throughout the western United States and some of them remembered and returned to Gold Canyon. In 1859 the returning miners made their first big strike at Gold Hill halfway up the canyon. As they slowly continued to follow their placer deposits, they moved up the canyon until they reached what is now Virginia City. Here they discovered their greatest bonanza. It would be the greatest silver discovery made in the United States up to that time. It would be called the Comstock Lode. It would become the most important mining strike since gold was discovered in California in 1849 ten years earlier.

My connection with the Comstock both as a tourist and as an investor is described below. The Comstock Lode was discovered below the eastern slope of Mount Davidson in northwestern Nevada in what is now Virginia City and Gold Hill both of which are located in Storey County, Nevada.

The Curious Case of Comstock Mining

Comstock Mining (LODE) is a most curious case. If I ever had a pet stock, then this is it. My two favorite subjects in American history are the steamboat era on the Mississippi River and the mining boomtowns of the old west. The greatest boomtown of them all was Virginia City on the Comstock which is located about 25 miles from Reno, Nevada. I first visited Virginia City around the year 2000 as a tourist and I found the place fascinating. Like Wallace, Idaho, another mining boom town that I am connected with, it seemed frozen in time with its Victorian 19th century architecture.

In its 19th century heyday it was called the richest place on earth which wasn't far wrong. Gold and silver gushed from its mines in torrents. It was claimed that its mines financed the Civil War for the union and that almost all of the mansions built in nearby San Francisco in the 19th century were built from profits made in the Comstock. Its golden age was from 1859 when the first big strike was made until around 1880. High tech diamond drilling was introduced in the Comstock in the 1870s. During the bonanza days there were 150 listed mining stocks with mining claims in the Comstock. During the bonanza period 16 large profitable ore bodies were discovered. Most were within 600 feet of the surface. In 1876 just three of the mines paid dividends. From 1886-1894 a small revival occurred mining low grade ore. The Consolidated Virginia and its sister the California paid more than 60% of all Comstock dividends.

Mark Twain was a reporter for the Territorial Enterprise during the bonanza days. The Territorial Enterprise building still exists and is located in Virginia City. Mark Twain had a suitcase full of stock certificates most of which he claimed were worthless. Boy could I have operated out of setup like that. After 1880 its mines slowly went into decline. By the 1920s the remaining mines went bust. At its peak Virginia City had a population of about 28,000 by the 1930s its population had fallen to around 500 and it was nearly a ghost town.

I always enter Virginia City from the north on Highway 341. This is the Section of 341 that starts at Virginia City and heads south until it reaches the intersection with Route 50 and it is aptly named Gold Canyon Road. The road takes you down through the heart of Virginia City and then down past the near ghost towns of Gold Hill and Silver City. These three cities constituted the Comstock. Everywhere you see remnants of the boom days. What is shocking is how few structures remain anywhere in the area. The winters are brutal in the Comstock which has an elevation of almost 7,000 feet. As the population declined and homes and commercial buildings were abandoned the remaining citizens simply tore down the abandoned structures and burned them in their fireplaces.

Gold Hill during the bonanza days had a population of 8,000 people and its own newspaper; in the last census its population was 191 people. I doubt if there are 30 buildings left in Gold Hill.

I will never forget the first time I slowly traveled down Gold Canyon Road soaking up the view. I could almost smell the gold and silver. I just knew there was more gold and silver to be found and I wasn't the only one who could smell the gold and silver but that would come latter in 2012.

Salvation first came to Virginia City from Hollywood. In 1940 one of Hollywood's biggest hits was the Western "Virginia City" which ignited the tourist trade. It starred Errol Flynn, Randolph Scott and Humphrey Bogart. Hollywood struck again with the long running TV series Bonanza which was set in Virginia City. It ran for 14 years from 1959-1973. The only western series that had a longer run was Gunsmoke. Virginia City today remains a very popular tourist destination.

In 2012 the resurrection finally came. In that year Comstock Mining was incorporated. I couldn't buy the stock fast enough. I didn't think that there was more gold and silver in the Comstock. I knew that there was more gold and silver in the Comstock.

I am such a sicko that one of the high points of my year is attending Comstock's annual meeting. I wouldn't miss it for the world. Since I knew that I was going to attend the annual meeting every year and I intended to own the stock for years I talked myself into buying a vacation home in nearby Reno. After all I told myself you are going to need a place to count all the money you will be making off of your Comstock investment and you will need a place to stay for the annual meetings and it will be the perfect place to write your next book, away from the distractions of Fort Lauderdale. Plus, the high desert with its dry climate will be the perfect summer vacation away from the sweltering humidity of South Florida in the summertime.

Boy, can I lie to myself. Strangely enough, most of my reasoning came true. The annual meeting until recently was held in the last week in May in Virginia City; I spend most of the summer in the Reno co-op that I purchased, and this book is being written in my Reno vacation home.

Whoever said that variety is the spice of life knew what they were talking about. I love the high desert in the summer. It is the perfect escape from Florida's humid summers. You wouldn't catch me dead, however, in Reno in the winter. Florida boy does not do winters.

I lucked out and picked the perfect time to buy Nevada real estate at the bottom of the real estate crash in 2012. Nevada was one of the states that was the hardest hit by the real estate crash. I stole a two bedroom, one bath 950 square feet co-op with a garage for $25,000 cash. If you don't know what a cooperative is it is sort of a condo that is a corporation. The heartland of cooperatives is in New York City. The reason why cooperatives are so popular in New York City is that co-op owners do not pay real estate taxes. The cooperative not the owners pays a corporate tax which is almost always lower than it would be if they were condo owners. When you buy a co-op, you are not buying real estate. You are buying stock in a corporation and you are issued a stock certificate that entitles you to occupy the unit that you purchased. All co-op purchases are for cash. You can't get a mortgage because you don't own title to real estate.

On a percentage basis my co-op purchase is one of the best real estate purchases I have ever made. My co-op has almost quadrupled in price since I purchased it.

But I digress. Up to now everyone who has owned the sock has gotten shellacked. No one who has owned the stock has been happy with its performance. When Comstock Mining went into production gold was selling near its peak at about $1,900 an ounce. At that price Comstock would have been very profitable. Break-even was about $1,500 an ounce. Regrettably as soon as it went into production the price started falling and the price has remained under $1,500 an ounce ever since.

Comstock has never been a pink sheet stock. It is listed on the NYSE American Market and has always been honestly run. Let's take a look at the assets.

The stock is currently selling for 15 cents a share. There are 80,790,000 shares of stock issued. Therefore, the current capitalization of the stock is $12,100,000 rounded. You will recall that this is the total value, lock, stock and barrel that the corporation is selling for at its current price. The most interesting asset that the company owns is the Gold Hill Hotel. The hotel was established in 1859 and also includes a restaurant and a bar and is listed in the historical register as the oldest existing hotel in the state of Nevada. Mark Twain used to hang out at the bar. The hotel is only about three miles from the Territorial Enterprise Building where Mark Twain worked as a reporter. The annual meetings are held at the hotel. The shareholders are treated to a free breakfast and dinner and you can see the snowcapped mountains through the restaurant windows while the outside temperature is about 70 degrees.

The company also owns a modern mill and heap processing facility for gold and silver at its office complex at American Flat. It was in production from 2012-2015 but it continued to receive some residual income from the heap leaching pads until 2016. During this period the mine produced 735,252 ounces of silver and 59,515 ounces of gold. Or about 12 ounces of silver for each ounce of gold.

As I have stated the company probably needs about $1,500 an ounce gold to be profitable but there is a good likelihood that it would also be profitable if silver could sustain a price of about $25.00 an ounce. Silver is currently selling at around $16 an ounce and has historically sold as high as $50.00 an ounce.

While management has definitely made mistakes the one thing that it deserves credit for is its relentless acquisition of real estate. In the last year alone, it has acquired an additional 472 acres of mining claims. It now owns 9,272 acres or more than 14 square miles of land and is the largest private landowner in Storey County. Let's do the Termination Analysis. We divide Comstock's current capitalization of $12,100,000 by 9,272 acres and discover that the market in its wisdom is valuing every acre that Comstock owns at a princely $1,305 an acre. Folks can you see why I have a problem with the Efficient Market Hypothesis?

Comstock has 2,347 acres of patented land and I assign this land a value of $8,000 an acre for a total value of $18,776,000 and an additional 6,925 acres of unpatented land which has a lower value and which I assign a value of $4,000 an acre to for an additional value of $27,700,000 or a total estimated Termination Value of $46,476,000 if the corporation was terminated and the land sold at auction. We divide this amount by the 80,790,000 issued shares and we arrive at a value of 57 cents a share and this figure of course assigns a zero value to all of Comstock's other assets. In other words, Comstock is another case in which a mining company is worth more as a real estate company than as a mining company and is also worth more dead than alive. I am holding on to the stock. At a price of $1,500 an ounce for gold this stock will explode. Until then little can be expected of it. Every time I drive down Gold Canyon Road, I can smell the gold. It still has real potential less; than 10% of its mining claims have undergone modern exploratory drilling.

My Gold and Silver Plays

Argonaut Gold (ARNGF)- This stock is currently selling for $1.40 a share. Its 52 week range is from 88 cents - $1.41 a share. It has two producing mines in the Durango region in Mexico and three more solid prospects in Mexico and Canada. In 2018 they produced around 170,000 GEO ounces. It is not currently profitable. The term GEO is a standard term in the industry. It stands for gold equivalent ounces. It is common in the industry for mines to produce both gold and silver. Say a mine produces 20,000 ounces of gold and 83,000 ounces of silver in a year and 83 ounces of silver is selling for the same price as one ounce of gold in that year. It will divide the 83,000 ounces of silver by 83 which will result in a sum of 1,000 GEO ounces. It will then add the 1,000 ounces to the 20,000 ounces of gold it produced that year for a GEO of 21,000 ounces. They have $21 million in cash and $8 million in debt.

Avino Silver & Gold (ASM) is currently selling at 60 cents a share with a 52 week price range of 50 cents -$1.55, it is currently profitable with a PE ratio of 22. It operates two silver mines in Mexico and has a gold prospect under development in British Columbia.

Comstock Mining (LODE) is currently selling for 21 cents a share. its 52 week range is from 12 cents - 40 cents a share. It is not currently profitable and is not in production.

Dolly Varden Silver (DOLLF) is currently selling for 30 cents a share. Its 52 week range is from 21 cents - 54 cents a share. It is not in production. The Dolly Varden Mine encompasses 8,800 hectares (2.47 acres) and was a historic silver producer in British Columbia. The acreage encompasses 4 historic silver mines. The Dolly Varden being the most important. It was in production from1910-1959 and at its peak produced astonishing high ore grades. The mines have produced 20 million ounces of silver.

Dynacor Gold (DNGDF) is currently selling for a $1.22 a share. Its 52 week range is from $1.05 - $1.47 a share. It is earning a profit and has a low PE Ratio of 9. Its mining operations are in Peru. In 2018 it milled 81,300 ounces of gold and it is debt free. It is similar to New Jersey Mining in that its primary profit generator is processing ore in its two mills from independent producers. In Dynacor's case from more than 500 government registered Peruvian artisanal gold miners.

Ely Royalties (ELYGF) is currently selling for 12 cents a share. Its 52 week range is from 6 cents -15 cents a share. It is not currently profitable, but it is receiving income from some of its royalties. Its royalty portfolio is concentrated in Nevada and consists of 27 deeded royalties, which means it has sold the properties and will receive a royalty stream when the property goes into production, and 24 optioned properties in these cases the optionee has paid for an option on the property with the possible intent of exercising the option if they like what they discover in the future about the property.

Endeavour Silver (EXK) is currently selling for $2.50 a share. Its 52 week range is from $1.76 - $ 3.35 a share. It is not currently profitable. It owns 4 high-grade underground silver-gold mines in Mexico, three of which are in production and the fourth is expected to go into production in 2019.

Fortuna Silver Mines (FSM) is currently selling for $ 3.35 a share. Its 52 week range is from $3.16 - $ 6.08 a share. It is currently profitable and has a PE Ratio of 15. It currently has two underground mines in operation, one in Mexico and the other in Peru, and is currently developing a fully permitted gold project in Argentina.

Franco Nevada (FNV) is the king of the royalty companies. It is currently selling at $78 a share. Its 52 week range is from $58.26 - $80.00 a share. It is profitable and has a PE Ratio of 100 which sounds outrageous until you realize the assets that are backing up its price and it pays a modest dividend which is constantly being raised. It is the leading precious metal royalty and royalty streaming company. It has 210 precious metal properties, 84 other mining assets and 83 oil & gas properties. As I have previously stated this stock has been a big winner for me.

Gamco Global Gold (GGN) - This stock is currently selling at $4.34 a share. Its 52 week range is from $3.50 - $ 5.21 a share. This is not strictly speaking a gold play. I hold this stock in my income portfolio but because it deals in gold, I decided to include it here. This is a closed end mutual find that earns its income by investing 80 % of its assets in gold companies and natural resources. It earns its income through an options writing strategy by selling covered calls on the equities in its portfolio. It is currently paying a dividend of 13.89%. In a stock like this you must be automatically reinvesting your dividends, or you are just wasting your time.

Gold Standard Ventures (GSV) is currently selling for $1.02 a share. Its 52 week range is from .97 - $1.86 a share. It is not in production. This is location play with a location to die for in Nevada's fabulous Carlin Trend and Battle Mountain Trends. It owns the second largest contiguous land package on the Carlin Trend, a stunning 208 square kilometers in one of the richest gold mining regions on earth.

Golden Minerals (AUMN) is currently selling for 27 cents a share. Its 52 week range is from 19 cents - 46 cents a share. It is not in production, but it is receiving revenue by leasing one of its mills to Hecla Mining. It owns a silver prospect in Argentina and an ex-producer in Mexico plus a portfolio of 10 silver properties in Mexico.

Globex Mining Enterprises (GLBXF) - This stock is currently selling at 24 cents a share. Its 52 week range is from 18 cents - 36 cents a share. It is not currently profitable. They were incorporated in 1949 and have never had a stock roll back. It is a prospect or project generator with a portfolio of 166 mining properties. They refer to themselves as a mineral property bank. Their earnings come from royalties, property sales and optioning their properties.

Golden Valley Mines (GLVMF) - This stock is currently selling for 25 cents a share. Its 52 week range is from 16 cents - 29 cents a share. It is not in production. It holds royalties and minority positions in 15 plays. Its most valuable minority position is a 49% ownership in Abitibi Royalties currently selling at $10.03 a share.

Harte Gold Corporation (HRTFF) - This stock is currently selling for 27 cents a share. its 52 week range is from 21 cents - 41 cents a share. It has just started production in its Sugar Zone property in Ontario, Canada's Greenstone Gold Belt. The property encompasses 83,850 hectares (2.47 acres).

Ishares Silver Trust ETF (SLV) - This stock is currently selling for $14.22 a share Its 52 week range is from $13.11 - $ 16.35 a share. This is a commodity ETF that invests in silver bullion. Its price therefore will track the price of silver bullion.

Kirkland Lake Gold (KL) - This stock has been a huge winner for me. I bought it for $4.97 and it recently hit $36.74 a share. Its current price is $35.40 cents a share. Its 52 week range is from $14.86 - $36.74 a share. It is solidly profitable, has a PE ratio of 24 and pays a dividend which is being raised almost every quarter. This stock is hands down my favorite non-royalty mining play. It owns two of the richest gold mines on earth. The Macassa Mine located in Ontario, Canada and the Fosterville Mine in Australia. It is on track to produce between 920,000-1,000,000 ounces of gold in 2019. Its highest production ever. It owns three mines in Canada and two mines in Australia.

Maverix Metals (MACIF) - This stock is currently selling for $1.98 a share. Its 52 week range is from .99 - $2.14 a share. It has just become profitable and in 2018 reported record revenue of $34.1 million. It is a new emerging precious metals royalty company. It only went public in 2016. It has acquired a portfolio of 79 royalties, 12 of which are currently generating a revenue stream.

Monetta Porcupine Mines (MPUCF) - This stock is currently selling for 7 cents a share. Its 52 week range is from 5 cents - 12 cents a share. the company holds a 100% interest in 5 historic gold mines in the Timmins Gold Camp which produced over 85 million ounces gold in the past. It is also in a 50% joint venture with Kirkland Lake Gold. The company has been listed since 1910 on the Toronto Stock Exchange and is a former gold producer. It has a total land package of 250 square kilometers.

Nevada Sunrise Gold (NVSGF) - This is another stock that is almost too risky even for me and which I almost decided not to include in this book. This stock is currently selling for 6 cents a share. It has a 52 week range of 4 cents - 13 cents a share. As the name implies it is focused in Nevada. It has a gold property, a cobalt property, a copper property and most important of all 5 lithium properties in Nevada's Clayton Valley. The Clayton Valley plays hold enormous potential if they can just hold on to them. Their situation is very similar to their Clayton Valley neighbor Pure Energy Minerals. Like Pure Energy they acquired their valuable lithium properties through the use of options and are now struggling to hold on to them. The value of the company is largely dependent on the result. If they can hold on to their Clayton Valley assets the value of the stock will explode.

Northern Vertex Mining (NHVCF) - This stock is currently selling for 15 cents a share. It has a 52 week range of between 14 cents - 37 cents a share. It is not currently profitable. Its 100% owned Moss Mine is located in northwest Arizona and went into production in September 2018. It is a heap-leach operation. The mine encompasses 4,030 hectares (2.47 acres). If they can achieve profitability this stock can be a very profitable investment.

Premier Gold Mines (PIRGF) - This stock is currently selling for $1.17 a share. It has a 52 week range between $1.04 - $2.30 share. It has a portfolio of 8 properties. It has interests in two operating mines. It holds a 40% interest in the South Arturo Gold Mine in Nevada which is jointly owned with Barrick Gold and the 100% owned Mercedes Mine in Mexico. It is estimating a production of between 75,000-85,000 ounces in 2019.

Pure Gold Mining (LRTNF) - This stock is currently selling for 38 cents a share. It has a 52-week range from 37 cents - 60 cents a share. Its flagship property is the Madsen Gold property located in Canada's premier gold producing region, the Red Lake District. Since 1925, 28 mines have operated in this district and they have produced 29 million ounces of gold. Over 85% of this gold was produced from just two mines, Gold Corp's Red Lake Mine and Pure Gold's Madsen Mine. The mine operated from 1938-1976 and produced 2.5 million ounces of gold at an average grade of 9.9 grams a ton. The global average today for a producing gold mine is a shockingly low 1 gram a ton. There are 27 levels of underground workings and there is a 550 ton per day mill on site ready to roll. It owns 47 square kilometers of land.

Royal Gold (RGLD) - This stock is currently selling at $91.78 a share. It has a 52 week range from $70.16 - $98.53 a share. It is profitable, pays a dividend and has a PE ratio of 54. This royalty company has been a handsome winner for me. It has a world class portfolio of almost 200 properties, 41of which are now in production. An additional 17 are currently in development.

Rubicon Minerals (RBYCF) - This stock is currently selling for 87 cents a share. Its 52 week range is from 71 cents - $1.29 a share. Its flagship property is the Phoenix Gold Mine. The mine encompasses over 100 square miles in Canada's Red Lake Gold district. The mine includes a modern 1,250 ton per day mill. It is not in production. It also owns 350 square miles of mineral property interests in Nevada's Long Canyon Gold district.

Skeena Resources (SKREF) - This stock is currently selling for 30 cents a share. Its 52 week range is from 19 cents - 52 cents a share. Its properties are located in British Columbia's Golden Triangle. It owns the ex-producer Snip Mine which was in production from1991-1999 and produced 1.1 million ounces of gold and is attempting to bring it back into production. It has also optioned the Eskay Creek Mine another ex-producer in the Golden Triangle with potential. The Eskay Creek Mine produced 3.3 million ounces of gold and 160 million ounces of silver from 1994-2008.

Silver Range Resources (SLRRF) - This stock is currently selling for 6 cents a share. Its 52 week trading range is from 5 cents - 12 cents a share. It is not currently profitable. This prospect or project generator has 42 properties in Nevada and in northern Canada,16 of which are currently optioned. It is seeking joint venture partners for the remaining properties. Its policy is not to drill but to let its partners drill. I like the management it knows what it is doing. This is a high risk speculation. For these penny speculations to do well the price of gold and silver must go up. At a price of $1,500 an ounce these stocks will go to the moon.

Wheaton Precious Metals (WPM) - This stock is currently selling at $23.47 a share. Its 52 week range is from $15.08 - $25.24 a share. It is profitable, pays a divided and has a PE Ratio of 24. This royalty company is currently streaming royalties from 19 operating mines and an additional 9 projects are nearing production status. In 2018 its royalty streams produced 373,239 ounces of gold, 24,474 ounces of silver and 14,686 ounces of palladium.

My Base Metal Plays

There are four precious metals, gold, silver, platinum and palladium. All other metals are referred to as base metals My favorite base metal is copper. If the solar revolution happens it will result in a huge increase in the need for copper wiring both for electric vehicles and to connect the solar panels.

Capstone Mining (CSFFF) - This stock is currently selling for 47 cents a share. Its 52 week range is from 35 cents - 95 cents a share. It is profitable with a PE Ratio of 6.93. I hope that you recall that the average PE Ratio for the S&P 500 is now at 22. It has two producing copper mines. The Pinto Valley Mine in the US and the Cozamin Mine in Mexico. It also has a 70% owned copper play under development in Chile and the Minto Copper Mine in the Yukon currently on a care and maintenance basis.

Copper Mountain Mining (CPPMF) - This stock is currently selling for 75 cents a share. Its 52 week range is from 48 cents a share - $1.08 a share. It is in production and producing 90 million pounds of copper a year but is currently losing money. Its flagship property is the Copper Mountain Mine located in British Columbia. The mine site encompasses 70 square kilometers. It also owns the Eva Copper project in Australia which is currently under development.

Teck Resources (TECK) - This stock is currently selling for $25.12 a share. Its 52 week range is from $18.10 - $30.00 a share. It is profitable and selling for an absurdly low PE Ratio of 6.27. This is the only blue chip mining stock that I like and have a position in. It is Canada's largest diversified natural resource company. In their energy sector their premier property is their 20.89 % interest in the Fort Hills oil sands mining operation. Their copper sector has 4 operating copper mines. They are the world's third largest zinc producer. Most people don't realize this, but coal is broken down into two categories lower grade steam coal which is burned to produce energy and higher grade metallurgical coal that is an essential component in the production of steel. You can't make steel without it. Teck is the world's second largest seaborne exporter of metallurgical coal that is produced in 6 of its mining operations in western Canada.

Trevali Mining Corp (TREVF) - This stock is currently selling for 32 cents a share. Its 52 week range is from 23 cents - 98 cents a share. This zinc producer owns four operational mines but is not currently profitable: The Santander Mine in Peru, the Caribou Mine in Canada and two additional mines in Africa. In 2019 it expects to produce about 401 million pounds of zinc and substantial amounts of lead and silver as a byproduct of their zinc production.

Western Copper & Gold (WRN) - This stock is currently selling for 56 cents a share. Its 52 week range is from 35 cents - $1.01 a share. It is not in production. Its flagship project is the Casino Copper project located in Canada's Yukon. In size this is a giant; it is the largest copper prospect in North America. Its reserves are estimated to have an incredible 4.5 billion pounds of copper and 8.9 million ounces of gold. It has been held up for years going through regulation hell and green hell and is attempting to get permitted. The best strategy for a play like this is to hold a token position and if it ever gets approved pile on.

The Case for Oil

It is now time to start our analysis of the unchallenged king of the resource world, the oil and gas industry. Oil and gas as well are nothing more than ancient sunlight that has been entombed in the fossilized bodies of ancient plants and plant algae that slowly mutated into oil and gas over a period of eons. In the case of oil there were two great generating periods in which all of the world's oil deposits were formed. The first period occurred about 150 million years ago, and the second period occurred about 90 million years ago. In both these periods vast blooms of microscopic plants formed in certain favorable ancient seas. As they died, entombed within them was the energy that they had captured from the sun. They created a submarine rain of dead organic matter that slowly fell onto the sea floors so thick that they formed in layers, which under ideal conditions blocked out oxygen. If the layers were heavy enough, they would sink to the depth of what is called the oil window. For oil to form, these fossilized plants must be trapped into an oxygen deprived sedimentary rock at a depth of between 7,500 feet and 15,000 feet below the earth's surface, the so called oil window, for vast periods of geologic time where they are transformed by heat and pressure into petroleum. When these conditions are present, the result is called "source rock." Above 7,500 feet, there isn't enough heat and pressure to form petroleum, and below 15,000 feet the heat and pressure is too great, and the oil is destroyed and converted into natural gas.

Now oil can only be born at this depth but once formed it doesn't have to remain at this depth. It is common for oil to seep to the surface. It is also common for the forces of erosion and uplift to result in oil fields being found at or near the surface. Unfortunately for us there are additional severe requirements that must be met for petroleum to be extracted. Embedded within the source rock must be a rock that is called " reservoir rock." This is a porous rock in which oil can collect and when drilled will release its oil to the surface. The third requirement is a "cap rock," which stops the oil from escaping from the reservoir rock. Fourth, there must be a "trap" in the structure, or a structure in the rocks usually a giant fold into which oil flows to be trapped under the cap rock. And fifth, the structure must be leak proof; fractures in the rock, which are called "faults," will result in the oil seeping out and being lost forever. The ultimate prize for oil geologists which they spend their lives looking for are the big dome shaped entrapments which are called "anticlines" which meet all the above requirements except for the important fifth one, that the anticlines be leak proof. Here and here alone can oil be discovered.

These are the brutal and exacting requirements that must be met for oil to be present. Only a terrifyingly small percentage of the earth' surface can meet the above requirements. Consider the most basic requirement, sediments with a depth of at least 7,500 feet before you hit bedrock. Most of the world flunks this test big time. Most of the world's mountains are less than 7,500 feet in height. An example of a typical area that comes to mind is New York City. If you swing a pick you will strike bedrock. That is why it is such a wonderful place to build skyscrapers.

The vast deep-water ocean basins, which occupy 60% of the earth's surface, are also losers that can be written off. The reason why they can be written off is that nowhere in these deep-water basins do the sediments exceed a depth of 3,000 feet and thus they fail the all-important sedimentary depth requirement of at least 7,500 feet. However, there is an additional 11% of the earth's ocean surface which covers the shallow water continental shelves of the earth and does meet the sedimentary requirements, and these regions encompass some of the world's richest oil deposits. The Gulf of Mexico, the North Sea and the Persian Gulf are outstanding examples of this.

The general public have no concept of how diligent and how thorough the oil geologists have been in their relentless quest for new oil discoveries and how little has escaped them. By the 1920s they knew that oil existed on Alaska's north slope. And by the 1950s they had invented and were installing the world's first drilling platforms in the Gulf of Mexico. Just ask yourself why any oil company would risk drilling in the hurricane plagued Gulf of Mexico in the 1950s. There is only one answer they were already scraping the bottom of the barrel. Of course, the early offshore rigs were in shallow waters.

By 1945 the first aerial geologic maps had become available and by 1950 all the anticlines that were visible from the surface in the United States had been mapped and drilled. By the 1960s the entire land surface of the earth had been mapped by satellites and every visible surface anticline located.

The Peak Oil Controversy Resolved

M. King Hubert was the visionary who invented the concept of peak oil. In 1956 this geophysicist made the then astounding prediction that the United States would reach its peak oil production sometime between 1966 and 1972 and would then go into an irreversible decline. At that time drillers were hitting gushers everywhere they looked, and the concept of peak oil seemed absurd. Critics were lined up three times around the block to attack him. The actual peak of US oil production however occurred in 1970 with an oil production of 9.64 million barrels a day. From that year onward US oil production declined relentlessly for decades.

Then suddenly two revolutionary inventions hit the US oil industry with tremendous impact. Horizontal drilling arrived first to be followed by hydraulic fracturing or fracking as it is commonly called. Both horizontal drilling and fracking had been around in primitive form for several decades. They had both enjoyed some limited success but were nothing to write home about. The first real success started in the late 1980s in the Austin Chalk fields of Texas when first dozens and then hundreds and later thousands of horizontal wells were drilled that employed the dynamic team of hydraulic fracking and horizontal drilling. It was the combination of the two that delivered revolutionary results.

It took constant experimentation throughout the 1980s and 1990s with various fracking methods plus the falling costs and growing accuracy of horizontal drilling to get the right formula. The Barnett Shale region of Texas in the 1990s piggybacked on what had been learned in the Austin Chalk. Most observers credit Mitchell Energy in 1997 for the game changing breakthrough that ignited the present boom by discovering the right combination of chemicals and sand in the fracking process to deliver eye-opening results. Perhaps the most intriguing thing about the horizontal drilling-fracking boom is not only that it was made in America, but it has stayed in America. There is amazingly little fracking production anywhere in the world outside of the U.S. Europe has two problems with fracking. The first problem is that on average Europe's oil shale and gas deposits are at depths about 1.5 times as deep as in the U.S., which therefore will require greater costs to develop. But a far greater problem is that Europe's powerful Green Movement goes berserk every time the subject of fracking is even brought up.

In 2008 when the fracking boom was just getting started, U.S. oil production had fallen to only 5.1 million barrels a day. The increase in US oil production since 2008 has been stunning. In 2019 it is estimated that US oil production will hit an astonishing 12.4 million barrels a day. Even more astonishing is that the US is now number one. It has overtaken what were the top two oil producing nations, Saudi Arabia and Russia. A feat that would have been regarded as impossible in 2008.

China's efforts to develop fracking has been stymied due to a serious water shortage. Most of China's oil and gas shale deposits are located in the arid and desert regions of western China. Fracking requires huge amounts of water. On average a fracking well will consume 3 million to 8 million gallons of water over its lifetime.

The Oil Regions

My analysis of natural resource oil plays will be confined to the North American continent with a side excursion to Mexico for obvious reasons. First in North America there is no political risk and secondly there are a multitude of junior stocks to invest in that are selling below $5.00 a share. Since Mexico joined NAFTA (the North American Free Trade Agreement) there has been a sea change in the attitude and behavior of Mexico toward foreign investments. It is now reasonably safe to invest in Mexico.

Alaska's North Slope is the one major oil play on the continent that will be ignored. For two reasons. First the major oil companies have total control over the North Slope and second oil production on the slope has been falling like a rock for years.

Companies with claims located in Canada's Athabasca oil sands, the giant of giants, should always be given careful consideration. It is also referred to more accurately as the tar sands or bitumen, since the oil is trapped in a gooey, tar-like substance. The oil sands are located in northeastern Alberta, Canada, and are roughly centered around the oil boom town of Fort McMurray. The Athabasca deposit is the largest known reservoir of oil sands in the world and the largest of three major oil sands deposits in Alberta, along with the nearby Peace River and Cold Lake deposits. Together, these oil sand deposits lie under 141,000 square kilometers or 54,000 square miles of land. The surface terrain consists largely of boreal forest and muskeg or peat bogs. The IEA (International Energy Agency) lists Canada's reserves as being a staggering 178 billion barrels.

With modern unconventional oil production technology, at least 10% of these deposits, or about 170 billion barrels were considered to be recoverable making Canada's total proven reserves the second largest in the world, after Saudi Arabia.

The two extraction methods used are first the "in situ" (Latin, meaning "in place") extraction, when the bitumen (oil or tar sands) occurs deeper within the earth and which is expected to account for 80 percent of oil sands development in the future. The second method is the common surface or open-pit mining, when the bitumen is closer to the surface. Only 20 percent of bitumen can be extracted using open pit mining methods, which involves large scale excavation of the land with huge hydraulic power shovels and 400-ton heavy hauler trucks. Surface mining leaves toxic tailings ponds. In contrast, in situ uses more specialized techniques such as Steam Assisted Gravity Drainage (SAGD). "Eighty per cent of the oil sands will be developed in situ which accounts for 97.5 per cent of the total surface area of the oil sands region in Alberta.

Our largest source of foreign oil comes from Canada and 47% of Canada's oil production comes from the oil sands. The other important North American oil plays are listed below.

Marcellus Shale encompasses 104,000 square miles and stretches across southern New York state, Pennsylvania, West Virginia and southeast Ohio. It is the largest producer of shale natural gas in the U.S.

Utica Shale - named after Utica, N.Y., not too far from my Cortland home. The shale body encompasses western New York state, eastern Ohio and southern Quebec. Shale production began in 2006. This ore body is located directly to the east of the Marcellus shale body. New York placed a moratorium on fracking in 2008 and was followed by Quebec in March 2012. The major producer is eastern Ohio because of richer natural gas liquids that occur with the natural gas and a more enlightened government policy. In certain areas the shale body reaches a thickness of 1,000 feet.

Haynesville Shale encompasses about 9,000 square miles of southwest Arkansas and the adjacent areas of Louisiana and Texas. The shale lies between 10,500 to 13,000 feet below the surface and is about 200 to 300 feet thick. It is regarded as the second largest natural gas shale play in the U.S. after the Marcellus Shale. It exploded into prominence as a major producer in 2008. Production appears to have peaked in November 2011 and has been declining.

Austin Chalk is located in the Gulf coast area around the city of Austin, Texas.

Barnett Shale is centered around Fort Worth, Texas, and is estimated to cover 5,000 square miles. Production started in 1999. From 2002 to 2010 the Barnett was the most productive shale natural gas field in the U.S. It is now ranked third behind the Marcellus and the Haynesville shales. The shale body lies about 8,000 feet below the surface and varies in thickness from 100 to 1,000 feet. The field now has about 16,000 producing wells.

Eagle Ford is an oil and gas producer that extends in a belt that is 50 miles wide and 400 miles long that cuts through 15 counties in southern Texas. The ore body is located 7,500 to 14,000 feet below the surface in bands 100 to 400 feet thick with an average thickness of 250 feet.

Permian Basin- is located in western Texas and southeastern New Mexico.

The basin is about 250 miles wide and 300 miles long. It is both an oil and gas producer. Since the fracking revolution the oil production in the basin has exploded and the Permian is now America's top oil producing region.

San Juan Basin is a natural gas producer located in the four corners region and covers 4,600 square miles of Arizona, New Mexico, Colorado and Utah. In addition to natural gas it also has large deposits of coal and uranium. It is the largest natural gas producing basin in the U.S. Since the 1980s the Fruitland Formation has been one of the major U.S. producers of coal-bed methane gas. Historically it has been a non-shale producer.

Niobrara Shale Formation is located largely in eastern Colorado. It is of some minor interest. My biggest problem with the Niobrara is that the Greens have simply become too powerful in Colorado and that there is little chance of any new mining or energy play going into production.

Bakken Shale Formation is the shale deposit that underlies in the Williston Basin. The Williston basin encompasses 200,000 square miles in North Dakota, eastern Montana and southern Saskatchewan and Manitoba. The U.S. segment of the Williston Basin has an area of 143,000 square miles. Oil was first discovered in the basin in 1951 but production was very modest because like all shale deposits the classic vertical drill well is ineffectual in accessing oil in shale deposits. What is required in shale deposits is horizontal drilling and fracking. With modern production techniques the U.S. Geological Survey estimates that the Bakken holds up to a staggering 7.4 billion barrels of accessible oil. The Bakken Shale formation is located in a band 9,000 to 10,500 feet below the surface. Below the Bakken lies the Three Forks shale formation which is relatively unexplored.

Continental Oil, the largest producer in the Bakken, is estimating an outlandish 24 billion barrels of oil. There are now more than 6,000 wells in the Bakken. In 2019 North Dakota was by far the leading oil producer in the Bakken. Its production has skyrocketed from nowhere 10 years ago to the number two oil producer in the U.S., second only to mighty Texas. Alaska, California and New Mexico are all tied in a dead heat for third place each with about 5% of the nation's oil production.

One final point needs to be made. The top two oil shale producing giants are first, the Permian, and second, the Eagle Ford. The Bakken has slipped badly in the last few years. In America and America alone do we see skyrocketing production in oil and gas. In the rest of the world we see a very worrisome picture of either stagnation or decline in the world's oil and gas fields.

My Oil Plays

Earthstone Energy (ESTE) - This stock is currently selling for $6.83 a share. Its 52 week range is between $4.21 - $11.00 a share. It is currently profitable and has a shockingly low PE Ratio of 4.63. This is a Texas play. It has various assets. Its two major assets are in the Midland Basin of west Texas where it has an 87% working interest in 20,700 net acres. It also has an additional 5,883 net acres of non-operated assets in the basin. In the Eagle Ford region of Texas, it has a working interest of from 17% - 50% in 16,500 net acres.

Jericho Oil (JROOF) - This stock is currently selling for 30 cents a share. Its 52 week range is from 28 cents - 73 cents a share. It is not currently earning a profit, but it is debt free. Its assets are located in the Anadarko Basin's Stack Play in Oklahoma. It has assembled 55,000 net acres in Oklahoma including 16,000 net acres in the Stack play.

Laredo Petroleum (LPI) - This stock is currently selling at $2.94 a share. Its 52 week range is from $2.80 - $11.17 a share. It is solidly profitable, and its PE Ratio is an insanely low 2.03. Its operations are concentrated in the Permian Basin where it owns 120,617 net acres. They hedge about 90% of their oil production. In 2018 they produced an average of 68,168 barrels daily.

Northern Oil & Gas (NOG) this stock is currently selling for $2.68. Its 52 week range is from $1.47 - $4.49 a share. It is profitable and is selling at a PE Ratio 14.37. NOG has an interesting non-operator strategy. It has chosen not to take on the burden of being an oil operator. It is the leading non-operating franchise in the Bakken. They acquire non-operating positions in high quality acreage and partner with leading Bakken operators. They own 165,000 net acres in the Bakken and interests in 5,000 wells. It reported record results in 2018.

Sabine Royalty Trust (SBR) - This stock is currently selling for $47.68 a share. Its 52 week range is from $30.27- $49.95. This stock in my opinion is the king of the old style fixed royalty companies. Its assets were fixed forever at the time the stock was issued and it is 100% passive. It was created in 1982 with a reserve life expectancy of 10 years and it is still going strong. It is incredible to me how so many alleged experts believe that estimated reserves mean anything. The rule that works is that the more you drill the more you discover. The almost universal assumption is that the only reason that a mine or oil field closes down is that it has run out of ore or oil.

However, it is often the case that the operation shut down not because it ran out of ore or oil but because the commodity it was producing crashed, rendering the operation uneconomic, and it was closed down. What I have repeatedly tried to make clear in this work is that given a choice between investing in an ex-producer and investing in green field new discovery I will choose the ex-producer. The smart money bet is to assume that there is more ore or oil waiting to be discovered. The old timers knew what they were talking about when they said that the best place to discover gold is where it has already been discovered.

Most of Sabine's vast acreage hasn't even been looked at let alone drilled. Unlike many royalty companies it has what is called an absolute royalty. It has no obligation whatsoever to bear any of the investment or operating costs of the producers. In other words, its royalties cannot be reduced by producers subtracting a percentage of their costs when computing the royalties that are owed to Sabine. This is not true of many royalty companies which are referred to as bottom line cash payers. In other words, the producers can subtract a percentage of their costs from the royalties that they are required to pay.

Sabine's royalties are located primarily in Texas, New Mexico, Oklahoma and Louisiana with a strong position in the Permian. It holds royalties on a staggering 2,092,292 gross acres. I have held it for years and through the magic of compounding my position in this stock has risen over 600%. The stock is currently paying a dividend of 7.45% which is low for this stock. It has been considerably higher in the past. If you own this stock, you must reinvest the dividends and let Einstein and Godzilla (compounding & dollar cost averaging) work for you. This stock was created so that people who understand dollar cost averaging could make a killing.

If you ask most people what dollar cost averaging is, they just sit there and drool stupidly at you. The ideal setup is high monthly dividends coupled with violent price fluctuations. As the dividends are being reinvested you are purchasing more shares when the price is low and less shares when the price is high. So that over a period of time the average price paid per share keeps dropping. Sabine was made for this strategy. It pays a high monthly dividend and the dividend can rise or fall sharply in a matter of months. It is important to understand that the price of oil is highly volatile and due to the mechanics of royalty payments deviate greatly as wells go in and out of production. It is not unusual for this beauty to pay dividends in the 10%-12% range and a few months later see the dividend cut in half.

Here is an example of what I mean. In August 2018 it paid a dividend of 24 cents a share. By November 2018 it had risen to 40 cents a share. Almost a double. It is hysterical to watch the stupids stampede into this stock when it is paying dividends in the 10%-12% range and then hysterically stampede out of the stock when the dividend drops to 6%-7%. Talk about stupid. They haven't a clue as to what they are doing but they are convinced that the world is coming to an end. May their stupidity endure forever.

Sandridge Permian Trust (PER) - This stock is currently selling for $2.40 a share. Its 52 week range is from $1.70 - $3.00. This is an old style passive royalty with fixed assets on 15,900 net acres in the Permian. It has a termination date in March 2031. At that time the remaining assets will be sold off and the unit holders will receive 50% of the remains assets. What could possibly induce me to buy something this dubious? How about the 20% dividend? That's right I said 20%. Remember the rule of 72. At 20% compounded money doubles in 3.6 years and as this is being written oil is in powerful bull market uptrend which should result in the royalties rising strongly. When I conclude that the bull market in oil is over, I will sell the stock immediately. Obviously, this stock is a short term play and has to be carefully watched. My maximum holding period will probably be about two years.

San Juan Basin Royalty (SJT) - This stock is currently selling for $4.22 a share. Its 52 week trading range is from $ 3.84 - $7.32 a share. It is currently paying a dividend of 8.7%. This royalty company is a marginal play. There are two things I like about it. The first thing I like about it is that it owns royalties on 119,000 net acres in the San Juan Basin in northern New Mexico, the richest natural gas basin in the US. The second thing I like about it is that it is almost a pure play on natural gas. An amazing 96% of its royalties are from natural gas and not oil. This is very rare; most natural gas plays have a much higher component of oil, in the 30-50% range would not be unusual. Natural gas has been hammered in the last year. It has fallen in price from $4.65 to a current price of $2.72. As a result, the dividends paid by San Juan fell from 83 cents share in 2017 to 38 cents a share in 2018. San Juan is an excellent way to play a comeback in natural gas. You just keep reinvesting the dividends and wait for the price to recover. What I don't like about it is the royalty setup. They have this weirdo construct that they call a 75% net overriding royalty interest. This is very similar to an NPI (net profit interest). Which I detest. The wise guys will tell you that what NPI really stands for is "no profit intended" and they aren't far wrong. In 2018 San Juan should have received $25,906,000 in royalties. This is what it would have received if it had the absolute royalty set up that Sabine has but it doesn't. Instead it received only $19,429,000 because its royalty setup allows the producers to subtract a percentage of their costs from their royalty payments. I am a confirmed "Buy them when they are in the gutter" guy. I don't stampede behind Tom, Dick and Harry and I don't buy their crackpot ideology. I know it is insane to buy XYZ because it is up 150% this year but not to worry. I have no doubt that I will be able to dump this stock on a greater fool when it is up 300% for the year." Count me out!

San Juan could be a classic gutter stock. Because of its less than desirable royalty set up I regard this as a short term speculation based on the premise of a bull market rise in the price of natural gas.

Smart Sand (SND) - This stock is currently selling for $4.08 a share. Its 52 week range is from $1.92 - $8.14 a share. It is profitable with modest PE Ratio of only 8.86. This is not an oil company: it is a producer of Northern White Fracking Sand which is regarded as being superior to brown fracking sand and is a proppant used to enhance recovery rates in hydraulic fracking in oil and gas wells. It has a reserve life of 101 years. Its Oakdale facility is superbly located on Wisconsin's largest private rail loop. The fracking sand is dropped into unit train railcars and then shipped by the train load to its clients. The bear argument against this stock is that there are fracking sand deposits called brown fracking sand which are of inferior grade located much closer to the all-important Texas, Oklahoma and New Mexico oil fields. This is true but they are grossly exaggerating the transportation advantage that these closer producers who will all be shipping by truck will have over Smart Sand's highly efficient unit trains.

When you are shipping a bulk product that is cheap enough to be priced by the ton unit trains have an enormous economic advantage over truck transportation. A fact which is seldom realized.

Analyzing Penny Stocks - Part Two

Let's do a deeper dive in how to analyze a penny stock. I have just finished reading the latest annual report of Western Uranium & Vanadium Corporation (WSTRF). This long time penny stock is currently selling at $1.05 a share. Its 52 week range is from 49 cents - $2.69 a share. It is not in production. Reading the annual report is critical for every company that you own. Now most of the annual report is boilerplate and can be safely ignored. What can't be ignored are the financial numbers and management's analysis of what the corporation has achieved over the past year and what its future intentions are.

Since I have just finished reading the annual report let's analyze this report. The first thing I want know is if the stock is selling above or below its Termination Value or fair value. The float is 26,000,000 shares issued when rounded. We multiply the 26,000,000 shares issued times $1.05 a share and we discover that the market is valuing the corporation at $27,300,000. Western Uranium has five plays located in Utah and Colorado. Its Sunday Mines play is its flagship property with 3,800 unpatented acres. The Sunday Mines complex has six past producing mines which is always a big plus for me. I love past producers. It is important to understand that when you acquire an ex-producer not only do you know that it was a viable operation in the past but also a lot of the heavy lifting has been done. Roads and power lines may have been built; there is usually an office, a mill and other infrastructure that doesn't need to be built even though repairs are to be expected. Of course, the stock market with its typical stupidity assigns a zero value to any infrastructure asset that is not currently producing revenue or profits. This could not please me more. I love cashing in on the market's stupidity. Let me repeat it again. I want to stress that reported reserves are meaningless. Contrary to popular opinion a mine is not like a bottle of milk. When the bottle is empty you are out of milk. The reported reserves of any mining play are the minimum expectation and not the maximum expectation. It is appallingly expensive to conduct a meaningful exploratory drilling program which is the only way to establish the size and richness of an ore body over much more than 100 acres. So, what companies will do is prove up two or three years of reserves and then go into production which will then hopefully provide them with the capital to continue exploration. It is common for companies to be in production for 30 years or more and to have never reported more than two or three years of reserves.

Western Uranium's second play is the San Rafael play which has 2,900 acres of unpatented mining claims. Its third play is the Sage play, another ex-producer with 1,900 unpatented acres. Its fourth play is the Dunn play with 220 unpatented acres. Its fifth property is the Van play which is also an ex-producer with 1,900 acres of unpatented acres. To sum up, Western Uranium owns 10,720 acres of unpatented mining claims. You then divide Western Uranium's $27,300,000 market value by 10,720 acres and the resulting figure is $2,546 an acre well below the termination value of $4,000 an acre for unpatented mining claims. Not too shabby. An additional positive factor is that the Northern Miner recently did a modestly positive article on the corporation which is always a big plus.

But let's dig deeper into the annual report. The company lost only 1 cent a share in the last year. Losing only 1 cent a share is really quite good for a non-producer. I was pleasantly surprised that it lost so little. Trust me I have seen non-producers lose considerably more than 1 cent a share. Their most intriguing acquisition is that they have acquired A 25-year 100% license in a mining technology patent from Ablation Technologies LLC which is supposed to be a low cost physical method for uranium and vanadium ore extraction. They are very keen about this I am not. In their opinion it could reduce the cost of production by 33% to 44%. I place a zero value on this. What does impress me is that they have only two full time employees. This means they have their priorities straight. They know what they are. They are a real estate company that happens to own mining claims, and at some future date, if the price of uranium ever crawls out of the gutter where it has been residing since the Fukushima disaster, they can exercise the option of becoming a mining company.

Management states that its flagship property the Sunday Mines complex is fully permitted and nearly ready to go. The only problem is the $23.00 a pound price of uranium. Almost nobody can earn a profit at $23.00 a pound. In June of 2007 uranium reached a high of $136.00 a pound and remained high until the Fukushima disaster in 2011 crushed the price of uranium. It has never recovered. Never have I seen a commodity crushed for such a long period of time. There are currently 450 reactors operating globally which are producing about 11% of the world's electricity and 60 new reactors are under construction. So, there is reason to be hopeful. The last interesting matter that management discusses is that the Sunday Mines complex contains a considerable amount of vanadium ore as a byproduct. Vanadium ore is currently in a bull market; 90% of all vanadium is used as an alloy to produce various high quality steels. New uses for vanadium are being developed the most intriguing of which is the Vanadium Redux Flow Batteries which management believes could have a bright future. Indeed, they are more excited about the vanadium prospects than they are about uranium. I concur and that covers the important matters that the annual report discussed.

My Uranium Plays

Denison Mines (DNN) - This stock is currently selling at 53 cents a share. Its 52 week range is 44 - 69 cents a share. It is not currently profitable. They have a 90% interest in the Wheeler River Mine, which is their flagship project and which is located in Canada's Athabasca Basin. They also have a 22.5% interest in the McClean Lake uranium mill. Their total acreage holdings in the uranium rich Athabasca Basin is 320,000 hectares.

It is also the manager of the Uranium Participation Corporation which I also own. The strategy of this stock is similar to that of Cobalt 27. It was created to own the physical metal, in this case uranium which is stored in its warehouses, with the goal of achieving profits through the price appreciation of its physical uranium holdings.

Energy Fuels (UUUU) - This stock is currently selling for $3.64 a share. Its 52 week range is from $1.74 - $4.09 a share. It is currently producing both uranium and vanadium, but it is not profitable. In 2018 Energy Fuels was the largest producer of uranium in the US and it produced 917,000 pounds of uranium from its Nichols Ranch ISR (in-situ recovery) holdings in Wyoming. It too is shifting its emphasis from uranium to vanadium. Its 100% owned White Mesa mill in Utah is the only conventional uranium/vanadium processing mill operating in the US. It also owns the Alta Mesa ISR project in Texas.

Fission Uranium Corp (FCUUF) - This stock is currently selling for 42 cents a share. Its 52 week range is from 34 cents - 59 cents a share. It is not currently profitable. Its flagship property is the 31,000 hectare Patterson Lake South property located in Canada's Athabasca Basin. This property has some of the highest grade uranium ore ever discovered in the basin.

UEX Corp (UEXCF) - This stock is currently selling for 12 cents a share. Its 52 week range is from 10 cents - 26 cents a share. UEX is not currently in production. Its four projects are also located in Canada's Athabasca Basin. Its current primary interest is in its West Bear cobalt-nickel which is located in the basin.

Uranium Energy Corp (UEC) this stock is currently selling for $1.49 a share. Its 52 week range is from $1.12 - $1.89 a share. It is not currently in production. In south Texas the company has the fully licensed Hobson Processing Facility and in-situ recovery (ISR) mine. In Wyoming it controls the Reno Creek project, which is the largest permitted, pre-construction

ISR project in the US. It also has an interesting portfolio of uranium projects located in the US.

Uranium Participation (URPTF) - This stock is currently selling for $ 3.31 a share. Its 52 week range is from $2.80 - $3.83 a share. This stock is profitable and has a PE Ratio 3.56. As has already been stated this company is managed by Denison Mines. Its investment strategy is to earn profits through price appreciation in its 14,159,354 pounds of warehoused physical uranium holdings.

Western Uranium & Vanadium (WSTRF) - This stock is currently selling at $1.03 a share. Its 52 week range is from 49 cents - $2.69 a share. I have already commented extensively on this stock.

The Secret World of High Dividend Stocks

Now you are probably wondering why high-dividend stocks could possibly be a secret. The answer is simple. With rare exceptions, you will never find a high-dividend-paying stock in the S&P 500. The average S&P 500 stock is currently paying a dividend of 2%. I spit on dividends of 2%. In my world the lowest acceptable dividend is 6%. This is your lucky day. I am going to introduce you to my world a world in which dividends as high as 15% exist. It is truly astonishing how narrow the focus of Wall Street is. I have already commented earlier on this phenomenon. Wall Street at its most generous recognizes only the 500 stocks in the S&P as worthy of any consideration whatsoever and this is a gross exaggeration. For all practical purposes Wall Street seldom even acknowledges that stocks outside of the "nifty fifty" even exist. Have you ever noticed that when you turn on the financial news channels you hear the same 50 names repeated again and again? How often do you hear a stock outside the S&P 500 mentioned? The answer is rarely.

There is a practical reason for this; the street serves the institutional investor. Institutional investors require big cap stocks that they can stampede into and out of in a moment's notice on enormous volume without unduly influencing the price. This is only possible in the big cap universe. For the institutional investor my world, the world of small-cap and micro caps, will always be forbidden territory. The retail investor is also very reluctant to enter this world. Retail investors are very suspicious of stocks that they have never heard of and only a small minority of them are willing to take the time and effort to research these stocks. This suits me just fine. I like being the only fox in the hen house. Let me give you an indication of just how small their world is and how big my world is. The true number of stocks is amazingly high If you count all the stocks in the US both listed and unlisted there are about 16,000 publicly traded stocks in the US. In other words, the S&P 500 is about 3% of the total number of publicly traded stocks.

We will start our analysis with the unchallenged kings of high dividend stocks which come under the Regulated Investment Company Act or RIC. The RIC was created by the Investment Company Act of 1940. Its key components are as follows. It must be registered as an RIC with the SEC and it must be an investment company that derives at least 90% of its income from capital gains, dividends or interest. Further, an RIC must distribute at least 90% of its annual income to its shareholders in the form of dividends. By conforming to these rules, the RIC is granted an enormous privilege, the right to avoid double taxation. All other corporations are essentially taxed twice. They are taxed at the corporate level and then their shareholders are taxed again on the same income even though the taxes on that income has already been paid on the corporate level. Broadly speaking there are three types of RICs in today's world. The first and most popular type is the REIT or Real Estate Investment Trust. The second most popular type is the Mortgage REIT and the third most popular type is the BDC or Business Development Corporation.

First let's take a look at the REITS. They were created in 1960 when President Eisenhower signed them into law. Since then they have proven to be wildly popular; more than 30 nations have signed them into law. According to the latest report from National Association of REITS (NA-REIT), REITS in total own a stunning 511,000 properties with a total real estate value of $3 trillion. There are 226 REITS that own $2 trillion in real estate and that are large enough to be listed on an exchange in the US. Unlisted REITS that are too small to be listed on an exchange own an additional $1 trillion in real estate. This is an economic revolution of historic importance and everyone seems blind to the fact that it has even occurred. To put this in perspective in 2018 the Gross Domestic Product (GDP) of the US was $20.8 trillion. I will have more to say about this unseen and uncommented on revolution later on. Australia is widely regarded as having the world's second largest REIT market with more than 70 REITS listed on the Australian Stock Exchange. You will find regrettably that a few of my positions are paying dividends in the 5% range. A fact that I am not happy about. My excuse is that they were paying at least 6% when I bought them and that they are still too attractive to sell. Little needs to be said of Mortgage REITS because it is obvious what they are. Business Development Companies (BDC) are another matter. They were created by an act of Congress in 1980. Their function is to help small businesses to grow and to meet their capital needs. Primarily by lending to them on terms that are more attractive than those that are available from banks. They also will often lend to private companies. Most BDC loans are senior secured debt and therefore must be paid before bonds. Many of their loans are floating rate loans which reset every quarter. Their typical customer is too small to tap the bond market. Many of their investments are illiquid debts issued by private companies which therefore have no quoted market prices and are therefore very difficult for outsiders to accurately value. The typical BDC is usually leveraged, sometimes too highly leveraged.

My REITS

City Office REIT (CIO) - This stock is currently selling for $11.80 a share. Its 52 week range is from $ 9.73 - $13.20 a share. it is profitable and pays a dividend of 8.01%. It currently owns 64 office buildings with a total size of 5.7 million square feet. It is focused on acquiring high quality office properties located primarily in the southern and western US.

CoreEnergy (CORR) - This stock is currently selling for $37.53 a share. Its 52 week range is from $32.52 - $39.46 a share. It is profitable and is currently paying a dividend of 7.91% This is an unusual REIT in that its properties are energy related. It claims to be the first REIT to be focused on the energy infrastructure. It primarily owns pipelines and oil storage terminals and specializes in long term triple net leases.

Medical Properties (MPW) is currently selling for $18.82 a share. Its 52 week price range is from $12.25 - $18.92 a share. It is profitable and is currently paying a dividend of 5.37%. The company focuses on owning and investing in net-leased healthcare facilities in the US and in carefully selected foreign jurisdictions. Since its founding in 2003 it has grown to encompass 276 properties with 32,000 hospital beds and is now second largest owner of non-governmental hospital beds in the world. This stock has been a huge winner for me, and it illustrates the awesome power of compounding and dollar cost averaging. I made my usual modest investment in MPW. I bought 3,000 shares at an average cost of $4.51 for a total investment of $13,530. I now own 4,276 shares worth $80,490. I have never purchased another share. All the additional shares were purchased solely through reinvesting the dividends. This is the magic of compounding and dollar cost averaging over a multi-year holding period.

Physicians Realty Trust (DOC) is currently selling for $18.30 a share. Its 52 week price range is from $14.34 - $19.16 a share. It is profitable and pays a 5% dividend. It goes without saying that I am not too happy with a 5% dividend. But it is a new corporation; its IPO was in 2018. I was one of the original buyers. It has exploded out of the gate and is one of my favorites. It currently owns a portfolio of 252 medical office buildings in 30 states. The average size of its medical offices is between 50,000-54,000 square feet and DOC has an enviable 96% occupancy rate.

My Mortgage REITS

Blackstone Mortgage REIT (BXMT) this stock has a current market price of $34.47. Its 52 week trading range is from $ 30.14 - $ 35.70. This stock is profitable and is paying a dividend of 7.16%. The company originates and purchases senior loans collateralized by properties in North America and Europe. The company is focused on originating or acquiring senior, floating rate mortgages that are secured by a first mortgage on commercial real estate assets. There is an important point to be made here. The vast majority of residential mortgages are fixed rate mortgages. This is not true of commercial mortgages where it is quite common to have floating rate mortgages. In a rising interest rate environment this can be dynamite. This is a potentially enormous advantage that commercial mortgage REITS enjoy over their residential mortgage REITS cousins. Blackstone Mortgage is definitely a big cap. It has $15.8 billion of mortgages in its portfolio but I don't require all my plays to be small-caps. Just a heavy majority.

Cherry Hill Mortgage Investment (CHMI) - This stock has a current market price of $17.33. Its 52 week trading range is from $16.30 - $ 19.18 a share. The company is profitable and is paying a dividend of 11.26%. This is a residential mortgage company. Its focus is in acquiring residential mortgages in the US. It is also a mortgage servicing rights operation. Mortgage servicing rights or (MSR) can be quite profitable. An MSR provides the servicer with the right to service a pool of mortgages in exchange for a fee. About 74% of the $10 trillion dollar MSR market in the US are owned by banks. There is an important point to be brought up here. This is a small company. It only has 16 million shares issued. Its PE ratio is only 6.33 and for the S&P 500 the PE Ratio is 22. If this company were two or three times larger than it is there is no way in this world that you would be receiving a dividend of 11.26% for owning this stock. This is the small-cap advantage that I keep talking about. Wall Street doesn't even know this stock exists.

Ladder Capital REIT (LADR) - This stock is currently selling for $17.13 a share. Its 52 week range is from $13.70 - $18.82 a share. It is profitable and has a modest PE Ratio of 9.68 and a dividend of 7.93%. Its focus is on fixed rate and floating rate commercial mortgages. It currently has $6 billion dollars of mortgages in its portfolio.

New Residential Investment (NRZ) - This stock is currently selling for $16.64 a share. Its 52 week trading range is from $ 13.86 - $18.74 a share.

It is profitable and is selling for an absurdly low PE Ratio of 5.79 and it pays a dividend of 12.03%. A very important profit center for this stock is MSR (mortgage serving rights). It is also a big player in what is called excess MSR. This is an amount that the servicer receives that is in excess of the stated MSR for that mortgage pool. As its name implies its major source of income is from its portfolio of residential mortgages. It is now the largest non-bank processor of MSRs and the 5th largest MSR processor in the nation and the street doesn't even know that this stock exists.

New York Mortgage REIT (NYMT) - This stock is currently selling for $6.09 a share. Its 52 week range is from $5.58 - $6.54 a share. It is profitable with a well below average PE Ratio of 9.66 and pays a whopping dividend of 13.09 %. This is probably because it invests in some of the riskier mortgage pools. In addition to residential first mortgages it also invests in residential second mortgages, multifamily mortgages and distressed residential mortgage pools.

Pennymac Mortgage Investment (PMT) this stock is currently selling for $ 21.33 a share. Its 52 week trading range is from $16.97 - $21.41 a share. It is profitable with a modest PE Ratio of 10.74 and a dividend of 8.82%. It invests primarily in residential mortgages. To the extent feasible its primary focus is on distressed residential mortgages which are declining in numbers. In the next section I will list my BDC investments below but before I do, I am going to introduce you to a BDC investment that was mistake which I should never have purchased and how I handled it. As I have already stated it would be easy to just give you a list of my triumphs and ignore the losers. No one is in this racket for 57 years without making mistakes. An important part of my success is how you deal with your mistakes because you are going to have them.

My Prospect Capital Fiasco

In 2007 I bought 1,105 shares of Prospect Capital (PSEC) at an average cost of $12.63 a share for a total cost of $13,956. If I knew then what I know now I never would have bought it. Prospect was a high paying monthly dividend play so from day one I was reinvesting the dividends. The play was performing well until February 2015 when it cut its monthly dividend from 11 cents a share to .083 cents a share monthly or a dividend cut of 25%. Naturally the stock took a nasty hit. I reviewed my position and incorrectly decided that the reduced divided was secure. Since even the reduced dividend was very, very attractive I decided to stick with it. Let's take a look at what I mean. After the dividend was cut the stock crashed to $5.21 a share; at that price it was then paying a whopping 19% dividend. At 19% compounded you double your money in less than four years. It turned out that I was wrong again. In September 2017 it cut the dividend again from .083 cents a month to 6 cents a month, a 28% dividend cut. I was not happy the stock crashed to a low of $5.51 before it stopped falling. Once again, I analyzed the stock. At $5.51 a share it was paying a dividend of 13% and once again because of the dividend I decided to stick with the stock. You will notice something very peculiar here; after the second dividend cut the stock bottomed at a higher price than after the first divided cut. What is going on here? The answer is the increasing desperation of investors who are trapped in a low interest world and who cannot survive on the miserable returns that they can earn on safe investments. When they see a double-digit dividend return on a stock that has just cut its dividend, they feel that the new dividend is safe and they pounce.

After bottoming at $5.51 a share Prospect continued to rise. It is currently selling at $6.73 a share and is paying a dividend of 10.94% a share. The $64,000 question is, how much did I lose on this stock? It must be horrific. After all I bought the stock at $12.63 a share and it is now selling at $6.73 a share. I think you may have figured out the correct answer. I didn't lose anything; I have made a profit on my investment. Because of the awesome compounding power of double digit dividend rates and dollar cost averaging my original purchase of 1,105 shares has exploded to 3,063 shares. At today's price my position in Prospect is worth $20,614. A profit greater than $6,000. One last thing: Don't underestimate the power of dollar-cost-averaging in this. The more violent the price swings, the greater the profit. I regard Prospect as a marginal holding and will probably sell it in the next six months.

My BDC Investments

Ares Capital Corp (ARCC) - This stock is currently selling for $17.39. Its 52 week range is from $14.50 - $ 17.63 a share. It is profitable and sells at a low PE ratio of only 8.60 and pays a dividend of 9.23%. It invests primarily in first lien senior secured loans and a modest amount of second lien senior secured loans and mezzanine debt which is lower quality debt but pays a higher interest. It is the largest BDC in both market capitalization and total assets with $12.9 billion in total assets.

Monroe Capital Corp (MRCC) - This stock is currently selling for $12.28 a share. Its 52 week range is from $9.10 - $14.65. It is profitable and sells at a PE Ratio of 8 and pays a dividend of 11.50%. It is focused on providing financing primarily to lower middle market companies in the US and Canada. The company focuses on a combination of senior secured and junior secured debt by providing customized financing solutions for its clients.

Oxford Lane Capital (OXLC) - This stock is currently selling for $10.40 a share. Its 52 week trading range is from $7.35 - $11.73 a share. It is profitable and is selling for a PE Ratio of only 7.23. It pays a shockingly high 15.61% dividend. It is one of only three BDCs that invest strictly in Collateralized Loan Obligations (CLO) which are pools primarily of senior corporate debt securities. This is another case of the small-cap advantage. Oxford has only 36 million shares issued. There is no way in this world that a stock of this quality would be paying a 15.61% dividend if it were two or three larger than it is. But there is more to it than this. CLOs are a rather recent invention. In the old days, banks warehoused all the loans they made until they were paid off. Then some financial genius decided that it would be much more profitable for the banks if they securitized thousands of these loans into investment pools called collateralized loan obligations and then sold them off at a profit. Which is what the banks did.

In its latest annual report Oxford states that it currently owns 70 CLOs. Each of which consists of thousands of individual loans. The net asset value of each individual CLO will shift every month depending upon whether the delinquency rate rises or falls and how many loans have been paid off. To further confuse things CLOs are highly illiquid assets which rarely trade and are typically bought and sold by appointment only and are extraordinarily difficult value. Banks never concerned themselves with what their loan portfolio would sell for today. They only concerned themselves with how well their loans were performing. Most CLOs terminate in 12 years. They are much more profitable than is generally assumed 90% of them are profitable by termination.

I am assuming that by this time you are probably shocked by the dividends that RICs pay. They are a far cry from the miserable 2% that the average S&P 500 pays. I have repeatedly told you that this was the result of the small-cap advantage. But there is more to it than just the small-cap advantage. RICs are extraordinarily difficult to evaluate. For instance, god only knows how vast the army is of investors who are intrigued by the high dividend rates that REITS pay and check out their dividends. The first thing they do is to check out the EPS (earnings per share) and what they almost always discover is that the EPS does not cover the dividends. Therefore, they conclude that the dividend will be cut and they walk away. May they always be this stupid. What determines a REIT's ability to pay dividends is not EPS but FFO (Funds From Operations). In other words, the dividend is covered but they are too stupid to know it.

Much the same phenomenon is operating in BDCs. In Oxford's case the typical investor sees that the company has an EPS of $1.43 a share and is paying out a dividend of $1.62. They conclude that the dividend cannot be sustained, and they walk away. May they always be this stupid. That is why I am earning a dividend of 15.61%. In their latest annual report, the company discusses this matter. Oxford is required to follow GAAP (Generally Accepted Accounting Principles) which weren't designed with CLOs in mind. Under GAAP principles they could only report $71.7 million in income, but their true income was $108.6 million in distributions received from their CLO investments. Oxford has been paying dividends that are higher than their reported EPS income for the last five years. Welcome to my world.

The Enigma of Closed End Mutual Funds

Broadly speaking there are three types of mutual funds today, open end mutual funds, closed end mutual funds and the new kid on the block, ETFs, or exchange traded funds. The first mutual funds were introduced in the US in the 1890s; these mutual funds were all closed end mutual funds. A closed end mutual fund is a fund that issues a fixed number of shares. Because the number of shares is fixed the fund can sell at above or below its net asset value depending on the market demand for its shares. The first open end mutual fund did not even come into existence until 1924. By 1929 only 5% of mutual funds were open end. After the Wall Street crash Congress and the SEC passed a number of laws and regulations that favored the open end mutual fund. Today about 86% of all mutual funds are open end. Open end mutual funds do not have a fixed number of shares. The number of shares issued fluctuates daily depending on the market demand for the stock. When you buy or sell shares in an open end fund you do not buy and sell the shares from other investors; you buy and sell the shares directly from the mutual fund. Every day at the close of trading the open end mutual fund purchases every share that was sold that day at the closing net asset price and sells every share that was bought that day at the closing net asset value. If you stop and think about it this is an appallingly costly and inefficient way to operate a mutual fund.

ETFs were created in 1993. They are open end mutual funds but unlike their open end cousins they trade throughout the day at various prices based on market demand. The daily transactions are cleared not through the mutual fund but through various large broker-dealers with whom the ETFs have contracted. ETFs own their popularity because they offer greater tax efficiency and lower transaction and management costs.

I have owned both types of mutual funds. Currently I only own closed end mutual funds. Like I said you don't have to think very hard about it to realize that closed end mutual funds possess serious advantages because of their fixed structure. Closed end funds typically are leveraged usually in the 20% to 30% range to increase their return. I also like the fact that they can be purchased at a discount from their net asset value. Most of the closed end mutual funds that I now own are income funds rather than growth funds. If you haven't figured it out yet the enigma is why only a tiny minority of mutual funds are closed end funds given the considerable advantage of their fixed share structure. Consider this. Every time an open ended fund has more sellers than buyers it is forced to sell some of its stock holdings even if it doesn't want to. It is forced to accommodate its sellers. When it has more buyers than sellers it is forced to buy more shares on the market even if it thinks the market is overpriced. This is a serious and costly disadvantage that the closed end funds are never forced to deal with and finally you can't purchase their shares at a discount.

My Closed End Mutual Funds

Aberdeen Income Credit Strategy (ACP) - This stock currently sells for $12.41 a share. Its 52 week trading range is from $10.07 - $14.48 a share. It sells for a 6.19% discount from its net asset value and pays a dividend of 11.64%. The fund invests 80% of its assets in high yield bonds better known as junk bonds and other high yielding securities and it uses 31% leverage to boost its income.

John Hancock Preferred (HPS) - This stock is currently selling for $18.56 a share. Its 52 week range is from $14.53 - $19.21 a share. It has risen to a 3.08% premium and pays a dividend of 7.84%. I have recently cut my position in half because it is selling at a premium and will probably buy it back when the stock is selling at discount to net asset value again. This fund invests in preferred stocks and boosts its income through the use of 35.4% leverage.

Neuberger Berman Real Estate (NRO) - This stock is currently selling for $4.97 a share. Its 52 week trading range is from $3.85 - $5.27 a share. It is profitable and is paying a 9.66% dividend. It is currently priced at a 10.93% discount from its net asset value. It is leveraged 29.4%. This closed end fund as the name suggests is focused on investing in REITs.

Pimco Income Strategy (PFN) - This stock is currently selling for $10.46 a share. Its 52 week range is from $8.88 - $10.79 a share. It is selling for a 6.19% premium and pays a dividend of 9.21%. I have recently cut my position in this stock in half because I think the premium is too high but this stock typically sells at a premium. When it drops below net asset value again, I will probably increase my position. It is employing leverage of 22.7%. The company invests 80% of its assets in floating rate debt instruments. No more than 20% of its portfolio can be invested in junk rated debt.

Virtus Total Return (ZF) - This stock is currently selling for $9.87 a share. Its 52 week range is from $8.11- $ 11.31 a share. It is selling for a 9.21% discount to net asset value and it is paying a dividend of 14.65%. It employs 26.9% leverage. This fund is invested 60% in equities and 40% in bonds. This fund is for speculators only. It is very much like Gamco Global GOLD (GGN) in that it is substantially reliant on successful options trading to generate its profits. Here is something that I find intriguing and which you will see repeatedly on high income plays like Virtus. Three years ago, Virtus sold for $13.26 a share and paid an annual dividend of $1.42 a share.

Today it is selling for $9.87 a share and the dividend has not been cut, indeed, it has been raised slightly to $1.44 a share. Efficient market theoreticians, explain this one to me.

REITS and Real Estate - a Deeper Dive

I have commented extensively in this work on REITS and real estate. But more needs to be said about this important subject. Historically the divide between real estate investments and the stock market was as wide and as deep as the Grand Canyon. Historically a substantial segment of the real estate investor community has regarded the stock market with fear and loathing. They have been adamant in their assertions that real estate is superior to real estate as an investment. They have often insisted in the face of colossal evidence to the contrary that you cannot lose money in real estate. While the stock market is of course a dangerous gambling casino.

The rise of the REITS has had a crushing impact on their assertions. A phenomenon of colossal importance has been occurring in plain sight in the real estate world and almost no one appears to have recognized or commented on it. The phenomenon is that REITS are conquering the commanding heights of the real estate market and making real estate subservient to the stock market in a manner that is nothing short of revolutionary. REITS currently own over $3 trillion in real estate and more REITS are being created every year because the REIT form of ownership is dramatically superior to the traditional form of property ownership. It is eradicating the historic divide between the stock market and real estate in the commanding heights of the real estate economy. When I use the term "commanding heights," I am referring to all privately owned commercial real estate with a market value of at least $20 million. It is obvious that condos, single family homes, duplexes, quadplexes and small apartment buildings will always be the domain of the private investor. Traditionally commercial properties in this price range were owned by wealthy individuals in various types of partnerships such as TICs (tenancy in common) or LLCs. TICs allows up to 35 partners to purchase real estate. These partnerships used to be the most common form of ownership in this price range.

It is highly probable that ten years from now at least 80% of all privately owned commercial real estate with a market value above $20 million will be REIT owned. Let's imagine that a private partnership of wealthy owners is attempting to purchase a $20 million office building. The probability is overwhelming that it will have to get a mortgage from a bank. Typically, it will have to make a down payment of around 20% and borrow the rest.

This is the bank's bread and butter. Rest assured that the mortgage terms will be the most severe the bank feels it can get away with. The partnership has only one option. Borrow from the bank. The REIT has three options. It can borrow from the bank. It can issue a bond on terms that are much more favorable than any bank would ever agree to or it can issue stock XYZ.

REIT decides to issue stock. The stock is selling for $20 a share and it has 20 million shares issued. The only thing it has to do is issue an additional one million shares and it can pay cash for the office building. Granted some stock dilution has occurred but it has acquired for all practical purposes a debt free and nearly cost free $20 million office building. Are you kidding me? They issue a million shares and get a $20 million dollar office building! Compare this with what the partnership is facing. What are the partnerships doing? Whenever possible these partnerships are converting to unlisted REIT status because most of them are too small to apply for a stock market listing.

Another place the dispute between the real estate partisans and the stock market is currently occurring is on the Seeking Alpha website. I can highly recommend this free website. In Wall Street lingo alpha is performance that is superior to beta which is the market index or benchmark. It offers free crowd sourced financial articles from professional commentators and knowledgeable amateurs about the stock market. Currently there is a dispute on the website between one of the commentators, Jussi Askola, and his critics about the superiority of REITS over the traditional private ownership of real estate. I basically agree with Jussi. The traditionalists are having a hissy fit. They extol the benefits of leverage and the ability to depreciate and manage your property. Leverage is a two-edged sword as anyone who has been foreclosed on can tell you and of course the old canard that real estate is safer than REITS because REITS are a stock and we all know how risky that is. As you are now aware of this is my pet peeve. It is time to look at the data. It is easy to lose 10-20% of your investment in the stock market but losing 100% of your investment in a single stock is a real trick. It is amazingly hard to do. Just ask any short seller. When you strike out in real estate, they foreclose on you. You don't lose 10% or 20% of your investment but 100% of your investment. You are wiped out. Below are the national foreclosure rates from 2007-2018. If you will recall 2007 is when the real estate crash began. The below data is from ATTOM Data Solutions, a real estate data provider.

The numbers are even worse than I thought they would be.

2007 - 1,285,000
2008 - 2,330,000
2009 - 2,824,000
2010 - 2,871,000
2011 - 1,887,000
2012 - 1,836,000
2013 - 1,361,000
2014 - 1,117,000
2015 - 1,083,000
2016 - 933,000
2017 - 676,000
2018 - 624,000

The total number of foreclosures comes to a stunning 18,827,000 fore-closures since 2007. You will observe that the numbers peak in the real es-tate crash years 2008, 2009 and 2010 and have been declining steadily ever since. If my Uncle Paul were still alive, he would keel over and drop dead if he saw these numbers. So much for the vaunted safety of traditional real estate investing. The stock market triumph over the commanding heights of real estate in the form of REITS is guaranteed.

The traditional form of individual and partnership owned real estate simply cannot compete. There is one last study that we need to analyze put out by J.P Morgan.

J.P Morgan 20 Year Annualized Returns
By Asset Class (1998-2017)

REITS	9.1%
GOLD	7.8%
S&P 500	7.2%
60/40%	6.4%
OIL&GAS	6.4 %
40 /60%	6.1%
BONDS	5%
HOMES -	3.4%
INVESTOR	2.6% (avg. retail)

A few explanations are needed about the above figures. The 60/40% return refers to the popular strategy of being 60% invested in stocks and

40% invested in bonds. The 40/60% refers to a popular variation of that strategy being 40% invested in stocks and 60% in bonds. It is interesting to note that the two highest performers are REITS at 9.1% and gold at 7.8%. Both of which outperformed the popular S&P 500 at 7.2%.

The next interesting return is homes at a substandard average return of 3.4%. Let me hit this issue on the head one last time. When Joe Birdbrain is talking about the alleged fantastic returns to be made by investing in real estate he is talking about condos and homes. What Joe Birdbrain and the boys will never, ever, understand is that national wages determine how fast national condo and home prices can rise and historically national wages have risen about 4% - 5% a year. Since 2012 it has oscillated at around 4.8% a year. You cannot have condos and home prices rising at a rate much faster than the national wages over a sustained period of time because would be purchasers will not be able to qualify for a mortgage and will be priced out of the market.

The last interesting figure is the return that the average retail investor earns in the stock market. It is a shockingly low 2.6%. It is obvious that the returns of the average investor should track the 7.2% return of the S&P 500 and yet it is far worse. This deviation is startling because the average investor will only buy familiar blue chip stocks. I have commented extensively about this problem. Joe Birdbrain does not buy low and sell high. Joe Birdbrain does the reverse. He buys high and sells low. Joe Birdbrain and the boys want to stampede with the herd. They only feel comfortable when they are running behind Tom, Dick and Harry. After all, how can Tom, Dick and Harry possibly be wrong? They are above all else trend chasers. They are convinced that all rising stocks will go up forever and that all declining stocks will go down forever. Show them a stock that is up 150% for the year and they will jump all over it. Just try to get the boys to buy a stock that is down 40% to 60% and is a screaming bargain. They will look at you as if you have lost your mind. They will not touch it with a 10 foot pole. They are forever chasing after stocks that have had an unsustainable rise and hysterically selling stocks when they fall 10% in value. They operate on a see loss, take loss quickly strategy. They are constantly locking in their loses. For them investing is simply a game of locking in one loss after another until they are dragged out of the blood stained arena floor feet first.

Cashing In On 10% Dividends - A Deeper Dive

Now I know that many of the readers of this work have been horrified, horrified at the high yielding dividend plays that I own. Come on be honest. There is no way in this world that you are going to buy a stock that pays a dividend above 6%.

" What? What? Buy a stock that pays dividends of 10%, 12%, 14%, 16%, you must be out of your mind."

You are far too clever for that. You know exactly what is going to happen. The dividend is going to be cut and the stock will crash. You come from the world of big cap, blue chip stocks where the standard dividend is from 2-4%. In this world any dividend above 5% is highly suspect because the only reason that they would be paying a dividend this high is that the dividend is in trouble and about to be cut.

In this section I am going to reiterate and expand upon points that I have made earlier in this work. The typical blue chip, dividend paying stock pays out about 50% of its earnings in dividends. When these blue chips cut their dividend that means they are in serious trouble and the stock collapses. In the world of the RIC things are radically different. Remember these stocks must pay out 90% of their earnings in dividends. In any given year it is normal for any business to report a rise or fall in their income in the 10% range. Therefore, in the world of the RICs a dividend reduction in the 10-15% range is not unusual and does not have the catastrophic impact that they have in the world of the blue chips. Except that is in the fear crazed minds of investors who are hysterically bolting out of the stock because they are convinced that the world is coming to an end.

Let's take a look at the strategy I employ in my 10% plus dividend payers. Any time I purchase a stock paying 10% or more I always assume that there is a 50-50 chance that the dividend will be cut. As long as I believe that the maximum dividend cut will not be greater than 10-15% I will not be concerned. When I research these stocks, I ask myself two questions. First do I like the stock? I have to believe that it offers good value at its current price or I will not buy it. Second, if there is a cut, do I think that the maximum cut will be 15% or less? If the answer is yes to both questions I frankly don't care if there is a dividend cut because I have a strategy that I am ready to employ as soon as the dividend cut is announced.

Let's take a look at my strategy. After the stock market closes for the day XYZ, which is selling at $20 a share, announces that it is cutting its 12% dividend from $2.40 a share to $2.16 a share. A cut of 10%. It's freak-out time. Let's all panic and run around in hysterics as we bounce off the walls and bounce on our heads three times as we head to the computer to hit the sell button before XYZ goes to zero. There is a vast army of XYZ investors out there who believe that god will strike them dead with a lightning bolt if they don't sell the stock. But XYZ isn't going to zero. It never even dawns on these people that maybe they should not sell the stock. Since they are all frantic to sell the stock, they all put in orders to sell at the market. When the market opens the next morning there is a vast number of sell at the market orders and almost no buy orders. Except for me and a few other players who know how this game is played. That night I will review my analysis of XYZ. If I decided that I was wrong about the stock I will wait two or three weeks before I sell it. By that time the post panic recovery will be well underway, and the stock could have easily recovered 50-75% of its losses. If I decide that I still like the stock, I will put in a limit order to buy the stock at a price of $15.42 or better. If the stock does not fall to a price of $15.42 or less my order will not be executed. Typically, if it is not executed in a day or two I will cancel the order. Why $15.42? Because at that price I will be earning a 14% return based on the new dividend. If I really like the stock, I will put in a second limit order to buy the stock at an even lower price that will earn me say a 16% or 18% return based on the new dividend if the stock really crashes. Remember that these orders will only be executed if the stock falls to my limit price. Let's assume that the stock falls to $15.42 and my buy order is executed. Both my original stock purchase and my new purchase will now be earning a dividend of 14% in future dividends. Has the world come to an end? Before the dividend cut my 12% compounded return would double my money in six years. At the new 14% compounded return my money will double in five years. This is not exactly the end of the world now is it?

Now here is where it gets really interesting. Within a few weeks XYZ will start a relentless rise. This is totally contrary to what happens with a blue chip stock that has cut the dividend it was paying from say a crummy 3% to a pathetic 2%. No one will have the slightest interest in buying this wounded blue chip. What inducement is there? It certainly isn't going to be because of that big, big 2% return.

Things are radically different in the small-cap world of XYZ. It is rising relentlessly. Why is this rise occurring? When during the same period the unloved blue chip is lying dead in the water. It is because of the desperadoes who are hiding in the weeds. They are desperate, desperate for high income plays. They cannot survive on a pathetic 3% return. Because XYZ has cut its dividend the safety of the current dividend has been greatly enhanced and it is now paying an irresistible 14%. As soon as the stock stops falling the desperadoes strike like sharks in a feeding frenzy and here it gets very interesting. Before the dividend cut the stock was selling at $20 share. Now that the dividend is considered to be safer because it has been cut the stock could easily rise above its old $20 share price in six months or so as the desperadoes attack the stock. This is not what happens to a blue chip stock when it cuts its dividend. There are no desperadoes out there desperate to buy the blue chip stock after the dividend has been cut so that they can receive that big, big 2% return.

Summing It All Up

The greatest wealth destroyer is betting the ranch on a sure thing. Nothing else even comes close. It has destroyed millions over the generations, and it will continue to destroy millions in the future. There are no sure things, just risk-reward ratios.

The second greatest wealth destroyer is selling stocks because they have fallen 10% or putting stop-loss orders 10% below the selling price of your positions. Price declines of 10% are far, far more common than is generally realized. This 10% price decline also holds true for both "nifty-fifty" blue chips and high flying wonder stocks. The reason why it is not realized how amazingly common these 10% declines are is that most of these 10% declines occur over a period of two or three months and are then reversed before the end of the year. As a result, most people fail to realize just how common they are. That also includes the victims who can't figure out why they keep getting blown out of their positions by their stop-loss orders even though they only invest in blue chip stocks and high flying wonder stocks. The formula for success is amazingly simple. Research your stocks before and not after you buy them. Diversify broadly, no more than 5% in any position, and the riskier the play the less of your money should be in it. Lastly, stick to your guns. Listen to Warren Buffet as he has often stated his favorite holding period is forever. Tap dancing in and out of your positions every six months will destroy you. When you buy a stock, you are the owner of a business. Think of it that way. You haven't bought a lottery ticket. If you follow these rules, that 15% loss that you are obsessing over will vanish in six to twelve months. If you threw 20 darts at a stock market page and held the positions for five years at least 50% of the plays would be profitable and every one of them would have fallen 10% or more on multiple occasions.

Think about it.